In Search of Gandhi

Essays and Reflections

B.R. Nanda

OXFORD
UNIVERSITY PRESS

OXFORD

UNIVERSITY PRESS

YMCA Library Building, Jai Singh Road, New Delhi 110 001

Oxford University Press is a department of the University of Oxford. It furthers the
University's objective of excellence in research, scholarship, and education
by publishing worldwide in

Oxford   New York

Auckland   Cape Town   Dar es Salaam   Hong Kong   Karachi   Kuala Lumpur
Madrid   Melbourne   Mexico City   Nairobi   New Delhi   Shanghai   Taipei   Toronto

With offices in

Argentina   Austria   Brazil   Chile   Czech Republic   France   Greece Guatemala
Hungary   Italy   Japan   Poland   Portugal   Singapore   South Korea   Switzerland
Thailand   Turkey   Ukraine   Vietnam

Oxford is a registered trademark of Oxford University Press
in the UK and in certain other countries

Published in India
by Oxford University Press, New Delhi

First published 2002
Reprinted 2002
Oxford India Paperbacks 2004
Second impression 2007

ISBN-13: 978-0-19-567203-9
ISBN-10: 0-19-567203-8

Printed in India by Rajshri Photolithographers, Delhi 110 032
Published by Oxford University Press
YMCA Library Building, Jai Singh Road, New Delhi 110 001

To Baba

Preface

The twenty-nine essays in this book encompass my reflections on various facets of Gandhi's life and thought. Written over the years, on different occasions, and with varied themes, length, and depth, they were designed to respond to the interest of the particular audience for which they were written. Some of them have not been published before, others have appeared in books, journals and newspapers not easily accessible now; a few are amplified versions of talks given by me at seminars. Friends, whose judgement I value, believe that these essays provide a composite picture of Gandhi's personality and thought, his public life, and his relations with colleagues, disciples, and opponents. A few essays deal with overlapping themes, thus there may be a degree of repetition in some of the pieces. However, I hope this helps provide a more seamless and whole perspective of Gandhi's life and thought.

I am deeply grateful to Professor T.N. Madan, Professor Ralph Buultjens, Professor S.R. Mehrotra, and my son, Naren Nanda, for finding the time to read these essays and to make valuable suggestions. I alone, however, am responsible for the views expressed in the book. Finally, I must express my thanks to my wife for her constant support when these essays were being written.

B.R.N.

Acknowledgements

C hapters 2, 17, 18 and 23 first appeared in *Gandhi Marg*; chapters
8, 9, 10, 19, 20 and 27 in *The Times of India*; chapters 14, 24 and
25 in *The Hindustan Times*; chapter 21 in *The Book Review*; chapter
7 in Antony Copley and George Paxton (ed.) *Gandhi and the Contemporary
World*; chapter 26 in B.R. Nanda and V.C. Joshi (ed.) *Studies in Modern
Indian History*; and chapter 16 in Amrik Singh (ed.) *The Partition in
Retrospect*. I thank all these, and where necessary, also for permission to
republish.

B.R.N.

Contents

PART III: TOWARDS UNDERSTANDING GANDHI

PART I

The Making of the Mahatma

ONE

In Search of Gandhi

O n the evening of 30 January 1948 I was at Ferozepore, a deserted town situated on the recently created border between India and Pakistan. I had just entered the English Book Depot, the only bookshop in the town, and begun to browse through the new books when good old Narain Das, the owner of the bookshop, came up to me and told me that he had heard over the radio that Mahatma Gandhi had been shot dead. I immediately left the bookshop and started walking towards my house. It was a bleak winter evening, there were no street lights, and not a soul on the road. I noticed that I was crying. I was desolate, inconsolable, unable to hold back my tears. As a student at Lahore I had never been an uncritical admirer of Gandhi, and was therefore astonished at my highly emotional reaction to his death. As a budding historian, already working on a history of India, I took a secret pride in my objectivity. I asked myself how Gandhi had entered into my bloodstream without my realizing it and was determined to find out. The following day I returned to the bookshop and bought everything that had anything to do with Gandhi and the history of the national movement.

My first priority now was to understand Gandhi. I had no idea how long it would take. Fortunately for me, after a few months I was transferred to Delhi where I could have access to libraries and archives. The Central Secretariat Library had a good collection of books. The government records in the National Archives, such as had survived, had scarcely been tapped. An enormous amount of unpublished material was being collected by the Gandhi Smarak Nidhi which was later to fill the hundred volumes of *The Collected Works of Mahatma Gandhi* (henceforth *C.W.M.G.*). I found the exploration of the source materials, both published and unpublished, rewarding. One of my limitations was that I had a full-time job and could work on my Gandhi project only in the early hours of the morning and on Sundays and holidays. My work was proceeding rather slowly so I feared I would be overtaken by professional writers and perhaps my book would become redundant. In 1950 Louis Fischer's *The Life of Mahatma Gandhi* was published and soon after, the eight volumes of Tendulkar's *Mahatma*, both to great acclaim. Louis Fischer's very readable book was a journalist's chronicle, based on his personal encounters with Gandhi and his observation of the Indian political scene in the 1940s. He did not have access to Gandhi's correspondence and government records. Tendulkar's eight volumes were useful compendia of Gandhi's activities and speeches, culled mostly from newspapers and arranged chronologically, but they made very little use of Gandhi's correspondence and unpublished records. After these well-known authors had published their books, I felt that there was still scope for a book seeking to explore Gandhi's personal and public life in a historical perspective.

I found Gandhi's autobiography fascinating, but I felt that his self-image could be only one of the inputs to the biography. I had to place him in the social and political milieu, to see the options he had at every stage in his life, and the choices he made. I was also conscious of my possible bias as an Indian historian writing about the nationalist struggle against the British Raj, and felt I must hold the scales even between the antagonists. In this effort I was buttressed by Gandhi's own approach: the ultimate aim of satyagraha was not victory over the enemy, but a reconciliation and meeting of minds.

By the beginning of 1957, I was reaching the end of my book. The manuscript was likely to be over five hundred printed pages. I looked around for a publisher. Indian publishing was in its infancy. I made enquiries about the possibilities of publishing abroad. One of the major publishers in the United States, without seeing the manuscript, wrote to me that if my book was suitable for an American audience it would fall flat in Britain and India. I sought the advice of Nirad C. Chaudhuri, whose *The Autobiography of an Unknown Indian* had recently made him a celebrity. He suggested that I should select a publisher in England who published books on India and send him a one-page note on my manuscript. I wrote a letter to Sir Stanley Unwin, chairman of George Allen & Unwin. Sir Stanley's first reaction was that there was already a glut of books on Gandhi in the market and he wondered whether there was scope for another one. He nonetheless asked me to send the manuscript. Within three weeks he wrote back to say that he would be glad to publish the book, but it was long and might 'be priced out of the market at 42 shillings', and therefore he needed the collaboration of an American publisher to make the project viable. Eventually, he was able to sign an agreement with Beacon Press, Boston and the book was published simultaneously in the UK and the USA in 1958. The reception of the book surprised and delighted me. There was scarcely a prominent newspaper or journal in the UK, the USA, and India which did not review the book. *The Times* (London) wrote that the book 'rescues Gandhi both from the sentimentalists and the debunkers'. The *New York Times* wrote that the book made 'the Father of Indian Independence a personality from the opening paragraphs'. Lord Attlee, who had presided over the winding up of the British Raj in India in 1947, wrote a laudatory review in *The Spectator* in which he made a special mention of its impartiality. The book elicited favourable reviews even from newspapers and journals which had not been noted for their sympathy with the Indian freedom movement. Insofar as this warm reception indicated the contribution of my book to a better understanding of Gandhi, his aims and methods, and the ethos of his nonviolent struggle, I felt amply rewarded.

My biography of the Mahatma was reprinted in England within three months and publishers were pleased with it. I thought then that my affair with Gandhi and the national movement was over, but the book had an unexpected sequel. Prime Minister Jawaharlal Nehru liked it and invited me to write a biography of his father. He said he would give me access to his private papers, something which he had not yet given to anybody else. He told me, however, that there had been police searches of his house in Allahabad during the freedom struggle and very few letters of the early period had survived. The project appealed to me because a biography of Motilal Nehru required an in-depth study of Indian politics in the 1920s when Motilal's position was second only to that of Gandhi. It was also a period during which Jawaharlal Nehru's political stature was rising. Fortunately for me, in one of my visits to Anand Bhawan in Allahabad, I discovered a mass of unpublished correspondence relating to these years which made it possible for me to explore not only the fascinating father–son relationship but also the complex story of a critical decade in the history of the nationalist movement. *The Nehrus, Motilal and Jawaharlal*, was published in 1962; it covered Motilal Nehru's entire life and the first forty years of Jawaharlal's.

After the publication of *The Nehrus* it occurred to me that as Gandhi had hailed Gokhale as his 'political guru', it should be worthwhile exploring the relationship between them. Also, a study of the first thirty years of the Indian National Congress, before Gandhi burst upon the Indian political scene, could help in unravelling continuities and contrasts between the pre-Gandhian and Gandhian phases of the movement. The Gokhale project proved to be more laborious, and rewarding, than I had anticipated. I found that very little scholarly work had been done on the period, and I had to reconstruct the historical background in order to place Gokhale in the social and political context of the late nineteenth and early twentieth centuries. The book was published simultaneously in India, the UK, and the US by a triangular collaboration between Princeton University Press in the US, and Oxford University Press in the UK and India.

In 1964, while I was collecting material in London from the India Office Library and other British repositories for my book on Gokhale, the Government of India decided that on my return I should be asked to head the national memorial to Nehru which was to be housed in Teen Murti house in which Nehru had stayed as Prime Minister for sixteen years. The memorial was to take the form of a museum of the Indian freedom movement and a library and research centre of modern India. Mr M.C. Chagla, the Education Minister in the Shastri Cabinet, told me: 'I did not know you, but I had read your books.' He was very enthusiastic about the project and asked me for a broad outline of the structure and functions of the institution to be set up, and had it approved by the Cabinet. I agreed to accept the job for three years, but stayed on for fifteen. Building a new institution from scratch was not an easy task, but the discovery, retrieval, and preservation of source materials on a period of Indian history in which I myself was personally interested was a reward in itself.

My long stint as Director of the Nehru Memorial Museum and Library gave me an opportunity not only of acquainting myself with a vast amount of source material on the history of modern India, but also of interaction with scholars working in the same field. I was able to complete my book on Gokhale and write occasional articles, but I looked forward to freedom from administrative responsibilities and to more time to read and write.

In July 1979 when I retired from the Nehru Memorial Museum and Library, I was offered a national fellowship by the Indian Council of Social Science Research. I planned a book on Gandhi's encounter with the British Raj, covering the three decades from 1915 to 1947. When I was writing the first chapter, I was invited to attend a seminar on Maulana Mohamed Ali at Jamia Millia Islamia University in Delhi. I recognized that Gandhi's attitude to the Khilafat movement, and indeed to the whole Hindu–Muslim problem, was grossly misunderstood, and I could perhaps take six months off from the work in hand to write a long article or a short treatise to set the record straight. The projected article grew into a book, *Gandhi: Pan-Islamism, Imperialism and Nationalism in India*, taking not six months to complete but six years. It became a threefold study of Gandhi's first ten years (1915–25) after his return from South Africa, his dramatic emergence on the Indian stage, his confrontation with British imperialism and Muslim separatism, and his heroic efforts to apply his non-violent techniques to the complicated and fast-changing situation in India. It was, and still remains, my hope to complete a sequel to the book in an account that will bring the story up to 1947.

Political history has been my passion. It is one of the principal themes of the Gandhi biography and the other books I have written. As is well-known, Gandhi's public life in South Africa and in India, extending over half a century, was dominated by his struggle against racialism and imperialism. It was in the course of this struggle that he discovered satyagraha, his unique method of non-violent resistance to injustice and oppression. He, however, employed it only as a last resort and after great deliberation. In the course of thirty years, there were only three major satyagraha campaigns in India: the non-cooperation movement (1920–2), the civil disobedience movement (1930–3), and the Quit India movement (1942–4). Gandhi's critics, the communists, the socialists, and even the radicals in the Congress party, did not appreciate the long intervals between the satyagraha campaigns, and chafed under Gandhi's emphasis on truth and non-violence, and his precondition that the atmosphere in the country had to be peaceful and conducive to a non-violent struggle. They were continually clamouring for an 'aggressive strategy' and were furious when Gandhi halted a campaign in 1922 because of a violent incident. They failed to understand the dynamics of Gandhi's method. The Mahatma wanted to mobilize the people of India for struggle against foreign rule, but it had to be a non-violent mobilization: no easy task in a subcontinent. He wanted a disciplined following and did not set much store by numbers. He knew that no non-violent struggle could be kept up at a high pitch indefinitely: the number of people who were prepared to directly pit themselves against the imperial power and risk their liberties, livelihood, and property was limited. In each campaign a stage was bound to be reached when the torrent of satyagrahis, the civil resisters, became a trickle. Gandhi was not unduly embarrassed or worried by such a situation, even though some of his followers were disheartened and the British authorities gleefully boasted that they had 'crushed' Gandhi and the Congress. They could not see that Gandhi's non-violent battles were waged on premises different from those of violent conflicts.

No one had ever conceived a non-violent struggle on a continental scale, and therefore it was natural for Gandhi's critics to judge his non-violent campaigns by yardsticks pertaining to armed conflicts. However, satyagraha was designed not to seize any particular objective or to crush the opponent, but to set in motion forces that could lead to his ultimate conversion. In such a strategy it was perfectly possible for Gandhi to lose all the battles and still win the war. This is indeed what happened. Every satyagraha campaign that Gandhi led against the Raj, such as the agitation against the Rowlatt Bills, the non-cooperation movement, the Salt Satyagraha, the Second Civil Disobedience movement of 1932–4, the Individual Civil Disobedience of 1940–1, and the Quit India struggle of 1942, reached its peak and then either petered out or was suspended by Gandhi. The British authorities were elated by their triumph, writing off Gandhi as a 'spent bullet', but before long, they discovered their miscalculation. The repression of the non-violent struggles had the effect of eroding the moral authority of the British authorities and their Indian collaborators, the zamindars, the titled gentry, the princely rulers. This was proved by the elections to the provincial and central legislatures in 1923, 1934, 1937, and 1946. Far from being wiped out, the Congress grew into the most popular and important political party in the country. As the British historian Judith Brown says in her biography of Gandhi, his non-violent struggle alienated from the imperial regime moderate men and women in India, who may not have been otherwise interested in politics; it also cast the British in the role of 'a moral villain' in the eyes of the United States and other countries. At the end of the Second World War, the British saw that crushing a large-scale movement was too costly in moral and material terms for what it could achieve.

Gandhi's political struggles formed the greatest part of my work on him. His role as the head of a non-violent rebellion against the Raj had etched itself on the minds of his contemporaries. There were, however, long intervals between his satyagraha campaigns, during which he announced his retirement from politics and divided his time between his ashram and tours across the subcontinent to propagate his 'constructive programme'. In this programme he included such activities as his crusade against untouchability, the promotion of hand-spinning and village industries, basic education, and harmony between the religious communities. The British authorities heaved a sigh of relief when he engaged himself in such apparently innocuous activities, but it hurt Gandhi when some of his close colleagues missed the significance of the constructive programme and grumbled that it was a distraction from active politics. They could not see the connection between the spinning wheel and Swaraj. Gandhi's attempt at a moral, social, and economic uplift 'from bottom up' was not an easy task; it did not hit headlines in the press but Gandhi insisted that this work, however modest, could not wait until independence was won. It occurred to me to explore Gandhi's involvement in the constructive programme through a biography of one of his closest disciples, Jamnalal Bajaj. Jamnalal was in the highest echelons of the Congress party and was one of the few Congress leaders who fully identified with Gandhi in this programme. While writing this book, I had to shift the focus to Gandhi's apparently apolitical activities, yet it was obvious that they helped to bring him close to the masses, thus indirectly making a tremendous contribution to political awakening. In 1932, when a delegation of the India League, which included members of the British Labour Party, visited India, they noted that every villager they met had great reverence for Gandhi. In delineating the relationship between Gandhi and the Bajaj family I was struck by Gandhi's flair for human relationships. The apolitical Gandhi was no less fascinating than the political Gandhi.

In 1983, while I was working on my book on Pan-Islamism, my work was interrupted by a curious incident. The spectacular success of Richard Attenborough's film on Gandhi had an unexpected sequel. The film had run for weeks in theatres packed to capacity from one end of the world to the other. Its release coincided with one of those periodical spurts of the peace movement which the looming threat of a nuclear holocaust used to trigger during the cold war. This coincidence seems to have provoked a sharp reaction from those who feared that the Gandhi film would (to use the idiom of the period) 'weaken the will of the free world' to fight a war, should the need arise. For these conservative lobbies in the West, Attenborough's film was a red rag. They reacted by assailing the film and its hero. Suddenly there was a spate of articles ridiculing and belittling Gandhi. It was an orchestrated campaign of distortion of Gandhi's life and thought, and of the history of India's freedom movement. An astringent mixture of pique, prejudice and ignorance was readily lapped up by scores of newspapers and journals, some of which were supposed to be highly 'responsible', in the United States, UK, Canada, Australia, the Middle East, and the Far East. I decided to refute the calumnies in these articles. Gandhi had not lacked critics during his lifetime. Even within his own party there were radicals who chafed under his moral straitjacket and grumbled against his patient and peaceful methods. However, the smear campaign against Gandhi that followed the screening of Attenborough's film was in an altogether different category. I decided that rejoinders in the press would not do, and that it was better to discuss the issues raised and to set the record straight. The result was the 150 page book *Gandhi and His Critics* which the Oxford University Press published in 1985. It was well received and has since been reprinted several times.

The Gandhi I studied and sought to portray in my books was the man who had laboured for the solution of social and political problems in his own country. He had no doubt that his non-violent method was meant for all countries and all times, but he felt that he could not recommend it to other countries until he proved its efficacy in India. He did not avail himself of the invitations which came to him from foreign countries; indeed, between 1915 when he returned from South Africa and 1948 when he died, he went abroad only once, in 1931, to attend the Round Table Conference in London. He died five months after India became independent, before he had any opportunity of presenting his method to foreign countries. However, during the fifty-odd years since his death there has been a growing interest in his life and thought all over the world. This came home to me when I edited a commemorative volume *Gandhi 125 Years* on his 125th birth anniversary in 1994; it carried sixty-four articles from forty-three countries. The contributors included eminent political and religious leaders, diplomats, scientists, ecologists, scholars, and statesmen. Many of the contributors did not content themselves with paying homage to the memory of Gandhi; they sought insights and inspiration to cope with the formidable problems facing mankind at the turn of the century, such as violence within and between countries, religious fundamentalism, ethnic conflicts, terrorism and ecological degradation.

The twenty-nine essays in this book contain my reflections on various aspects of Gandhi's life and thought. As I have mentioned in the preface, they vary in theme, length and depth to respond to the needs of the particular audience I had in view. They were by-products of my research, but as I look back, they seem to me small milestones on the odyssey on which I had dared to embark on that fateful winter evening of 30 January 1948.

TWO

Gandhi and Religion

I t is a curious paradox that though Gandhi's attitude to religion holds
the key to the understanding of his life and thought, its nuances and
significance have often been missed by his admirers as well as his critics.
That he should have been misunderstood or deliberately misrepresented
by his political opponents was only natural. Few British critics would have
gone so far as Archbishop Cosmo Lang, who in a letter to Lord Irwin,
described Gandhi as 'a mystic, fanatic and an anarchist',[1] but most of
them would have agreed with Lord Reading, the Viceroy of India, who
wrote after his first meeting with the Mahatma: 'Mr Gandhi's religious
and moral views are, I believe, admirable, but I confess that I find it difficult
to understand the practice of them in politics.'[2] The leaders of the Muslim
League, the protagonists of the two-nation theory, could not but malign
the man who insisted that the function of religion was to unite rather
than divide people, and religion was an unsatisfactory basis for nationality.
As for Gandhi's left-wing critics, from M.N. Roy to R.P. Dutt and E.M.S.
Namboodiripad, they have accused Gandhi of exploiting religion to rouse
the masses, and then deliberately curbing their political consciousness
in the interests of the Indian bourgeoisie. Among Gandhi's own adherents,
there were not a few radicals who chafed under the moral constraints he
imposed on the struggle with the British. Then there were the 'modernists'
who equated all religion with irrationalism and obscurantism, and
resented Gandhi's saintly idiom. Finally, some latter-day historians have
advanced the thesis that by using Hindu symbols, Gandhi contributed
to the communal polarization that culminated in the division of India.

This is a formidable indictment, but in my opinion, it rests on a
misreading of Gandhi's ideas and actions as well as of the history of the
period. I propose, therefore, to examine it by briefly sketching the evolution
of Gandhi's religious thought, disentangling its basic strands, evaluating

their impact on his personal and public life, and by reassessing their true significance in the historical perspective.

II

Strange as it may seem, even though Gandhi grew up in a devout Hindu household, steeped in Vaishnavism, and was also exposed to strong Jain influences,[3] his acquaintance with religion, even with the religion of his birth, was of the meagrest, when in 1888 at the age of nineteen, he arrived in London to study law. A year later when some English Theosophist friends invited him to read Sir Edwin Arnold's *The Song Celestial*, it was with some embarrassment that he confessed that he had never read the Bhagavad Gita in Sanskrit or even in Gujarati. He also came across another book of Sir Edwin's, *The Light of Asia*, which told the story of the Buddha's life, renunciation, and teachings. It was in England too that a fellow-vegetarian enthusiast introduced young Gandhi to the Bible. The New Testament, particularly the Sermon on the Mount, went straight to his heart. The verses, 'But I say unto you that Ye resist not evil; but whosoever shall smite thee on thy right cheek, turn to him the other also. And if any man will sue thee at the law, and take away thy coat, let him have thy cloak also,' reminded him of the lines of the Gujarati poet Shamal Bhatt, which he used to hum as a child: 'For a bowl of water give a goodly meal, for a kindly greeting bow thou down with zeal'. Gandhi tells us in his autobiography that the idea of returning love for hatred and good for evil captivated him, yet he did not comprehend it fully.

The truth is that though Gandhi's interest in religion was awakened, it was not yet deep, and might have faded were it not for the happy accident which took him to South Africa in 1893. In Pretoria he met some ardent Christian missionaries whose central goal in life (in Gandhi's words) was 'to persuade followers of other faiths to embrace Christianity'. Gandhi's knowledge of Hinduism was yet superficial, but he felt with the religion of his birth a vague bond of sentiment. Michael Coates, one of the missionaries, asked Gandhi to cast off his necklace of Vaishnava beads. 'This superstition does not become you. Come, let me break the necklace', suggested Coates. 'No, you will not', replied Gandhi, 'it is a sacred gift from my mother.' 'But do you believe in it?' asked Coates. 'I do not know its mysterious significance', rejoined Gandhi. 'I do not think I should come to harm if I did not wear it. But I cannot without sufficient reason give up the necklace that she put round my neck out of love.' The necklace was a symbol; Gandhi could no more discard Hinduism than the necklace he was wearing without sufficient reason, both having come down to him from his beloved parents. This sentimental bond with Hinduism was reinforced by correspondence with some of his friends in India to whom he turned when he was under pressure from the Christian missionaries in South Africa. Among these friends was a remarkable man, Rajchandra (or Raychandbhai, as Gandhi called him), a jeweller, a poet, and a saint rolled into one, whom Gandhi had known in Bombay. Gandhi has left a pen-picture of the man who came nearest to being his guru:

During the two years I remained in close contact with him I felt in him every moment the spirit of *vairagya* (renunciation). One rare feature of his writings is that he always set down what he felt in his own experience. There is in them no trace of unreality I never saw him being tempted by objects of pleasure or luxury in this world ... There was a strange power in his eyes; they were extremely bright and free from any sign of impatience or anxiety. They bespoke single-minded attention ... These qualities can exist only in a man of self-control ... Raychandbhai disproved the prevalent idea that a man who is wise in the sphere of *dharma* will not be wise in the affairs of practical life.[4]

Rajchandra, who was only two years older than Gandhi, died at the age of thirty-three in 1900. The qualities which Gandhi admired in Rajchandra were those he was himself to try to imbibe. Gandhi never forgot his debt to him. He described him as one of the three 'moderns' who had influenced him most, the other two being Leo Tolstoy and John Ruskin. Tolstoy's *The Kingdom of God is Within You,* by exposing the contradictions of organized religion, had helped Gandhi to fend off the proselytizing missionaries in South Africa, and Ruskin's *Unto This Last* had brought home to him the value of a life of simplicity and the dignity of manual labour. But it was Rajchandra who had given a sense of direction to Gandhi's religious quest. Of particular importance was Rajchandra's insistence on accord between belief and action; it was the way a man lived, not the recital of a verse or the form of a prayer, which made him a good Hindu, a good Muslim, or a good Christian. Rajchandra was himself a Jain, but he restored Gandhi's faith in Hinduism. He regarded different faiths 'like so many walled enclosures' in which men and women confined themselves. He was always bored by religious controversy and rarely engaged in it. He would study and understand the excellence of each faith and explain it to the followers of that faith.[5]

III

The book which became Gandhi's strongest bond with Hinduism as well as the greatest influence on him, and which he called his 'spiritual dictionary',

was the Bhagavad Gita. He had first read it in London in 1890 in Sir
Edwin Arnold's verse rendering, *The Song Celestial*. In South Africa, he
studied other translations with the original and the book became his daily
reading. He memorized one verse every morning while going through his
morning toilet, until he had the entire poem by heart.

Two words in the Gita, *aparigraha* (non-possession) and *sambhava*
(equability) opened to Gandhi limitless vistas. Non-possession implied
that he had to jettison the material goods which cramped the spirit; to
shake off the bonds of money, property and sex, and to regard himself as
the trustee, not the owner, of what he could not shed. Equability required
that he must remain unruffled by pain or pleasure, victory or defeat, and
work without hope of success or fear of failure, in short, without 'hankering
after the fruit of action'. The Mahabharata, the epic of which the Gita
forms a part, has been a part of Hindu heritage for at least 2,500 years.
Gandhi put forward the view that the epic was an allegorical work and not
a historical work. The real object of the Gita, as he understood it, was to
point to the goal of self-realization and to show that *nishkama karma*
(detached activity) was the way to achieve the goal. He did not accept the
traditional interpretation of the Gita as the poetic presentation of Lord
Krishna's exhortation to Arjuna, the warrior, to go forward and meet his
cousins in combat; the battlefield of Kurukshetra was only a symbol of
the battle between good and evil that rages in every human heart,
Duryodhana and his party being the baser impulses in man, Arjuna and
his party the higher impulses, and Krishna 'the dweller within'. To those
who insisted on taking the story of Mahabharata literally, Gandhi pointed
out that even if the story was taken at its face value, the Mahabharata
had demonstrated the futility of violence: the war had ended in universal
devastation in which the victors had been no better off than the vanquished.

Gandhi's critics had a shrewd suspicion that he deliberately underplayed
the quietistic and esoteric elements in Hinduism because of the harm that
excessive preoccupation with them had done to Hindu society, and that
he sought confirmation in the Gita for his own framework of values: ahimsa
(non-violence), *varnashrama* based on division of labour rather than on
birth, manual work, and *brahmacharya*.[6]

Gandhi did not claim to be a profound scholar, such as B.G. Tilak or
Aurobindo Ghose were. He did not, however, regard the Gita as a book
for the learned; its message was meant to be lived. He had, he said, endeavoured to enforce the teachings of the Gita in his own life, and come
to the conclusion that perfect renunciation was impossible without perfect observance of ahimsa in every shape and form.

Gandhi had a strongly rational and sceptical streak which enabled him to fashion for himself a religious philosophy which, though grounded in Hinduism, acquired a deeply humanist and cosmopolitan complexion. As a student in England, he had been attracted by Theosophy, but had steered clear of its occult aspect. The fervent preaching of Christian missionaries in South Africa not only failed to sweep him off his feet, but also set him off on a critical study of other religions. It is not, therefore, surprising that his interpretation of the Gita was so novel and unorthodox. No book, however sacred, he said, could be limited to a single interpretation, irrespective of time and place; the meanings of great writings were subject to a process of evolution. 'Every living faith', he averred, 'must have within itself the power of rejuvenation.'[7] Every formula of every religion had to be subjected to the acid test of reason; no scriptural sanction was valid if it resulted in unjust or inhuman practices.

Gandhi did not hesitate to apply the acid test to the Hinduism of his own day. He was ruthless in his criticism of evils that had crept into Hindu society. In his autobiography he tells us how he was scandalized by the animal sacrifices and 'rivers of blood' he saw in the Kali temple at Calcutta, and the avarice of the priests at Varanasi. He denounced purdah, the dowry system, child marriage and its concomitant, enforced widowhood. On the position of women, his views were far ahead of his time and in some ways remarkably similar to those of present-day women reformers. 'Woman is the companion of man', he affirmed as early as 1918, 'with equal mental capacities ... and she has the same right of freedom and liberty.' He advocated equal legal status and the right of vote for women. The oft-quoted text, 'for women there can be no freedom', ascribed to Manu, he dismissed as an interpolation, and if it was not an interpolation, he could only say that in Manu's day women did not have the status they deserved. Against the abuses of caste system and untouchability he waged an unrelenting war. When B.S. Moonje, the Hindu Mahasabha leader, tried to prove that untouchability was an integral part of Hinduism, Gandhi retorted: 'Happily for me, my Hinduism does not bind me to every verse because it is written in Sanskrit ... in spite of your literal knowledge of the *shastras*, yours is a distorted kind of Hinduism. I claim in all humility to have lived Hinduism all my life.'[8]

IV

To understand Gandhi's impact on Hinduism, it would be useful at this stage to say something about the predicament of Hindu society during

Gandhi's formative years. Throughout the nineteenth century, Hinduism believed itself to be beleaguered. The problem, as the founders of a new religious society, Tattvabodhini Sabha, expressed it in 1839, was how 'to propagate an ancient, dignified and intellectual form of Hinduism ... to put a bar to the spread of atheism and Christianity'.[9] Four years before Gandhi was born, an Anglo-Indian writer predicted in the *Calcutta Review*[10] the doom of Hinduism: 'We believe the combined influence of Railways and Education will prove to have brought out the long-wished-for result.' In 1872 a high British administrator and scholar, Sir Alfred Lyall, stated in the *Fortnightly Review* that 'the old gods of Hinduism will die in these elements of intellectual light and air as a net full of fish, lifted up out of water'. That same year, Robert Knight, one of the most eminent and liberal-minded British journalists in India, said:[11] 'Our own conviction is profound that India will never possess Home Rule until she has cast away the false systems of religion ... that have been the cause of her degradation and become Christian.' Two years before the First World War, Sir Andrew Fraser, a former Governor of Bengal, commenting on the work of Christian missionaries stated in his book *Among Indian Rajahs and Ryots*[12] that the 'influence of Christianity was growing in a most remarkable manner and there is an opportunity now such as never existed before'.

The Hindu response to this challenge in the last quarter of the nineteenth century took several forms. The Arya Samaj, founded in 1875 by Swami Dayananda, harked back to the pristine purity of the Vedic times, and was assertive, almost belligerent, in its attitude towards Christianity and Islam. M.G. Ranade, the great judge and social reformer of Maharashtra, believed that the genius of Hindu culture lay in its continuity, tolerance, and capacity for assimilation, and called upon Hinduism not only to purify itself, but to emulate the Christians' power of organization, indignation against wrongdoing, and active philanthropy. Swami Vivekananda warned the Hindu intelligentsia that all talk of social reform had little meaning if it was confined to a small social circle of the urban middle class. 'Go down to the basis of the thing, to the very root', he said, 'put the fire there, and let it burn upwards and make an Indian nation ... So long as millions live in hunger and ignorance, I hold every man a traitor, who having been educated at their expense, pays not the least heed to them.'

Gandhi was destined to give the broad base and the urgency to the purification and revitalization of Hinduism, for which Vivekananda had so passionately pleaded. Vivekananda himself died young in 1902. Ranade's Social Reform Conference remained a one-man band, and hardly penetrated beyond the tiny English-educated urban class; Swami Dayanand's success was greater, but the appeal of the Arya Samaj was limited by its belligerence and sectarianism. There were other exponents of enlightened Hinduism, Lajpt Rai, B.C. Pal, N.G. Chandavarkar, and Annie Besant, but none of them possessed the mass appeal and the tenacity that was to enable Gandhi to pit himself against Hindu orthodoxy. G. Subramania Iyer, an eminent Congress leader of Madras, had asked in 1897: 'Cannot reformers instal Swami Vivekananda or some spiritual hero like him into a "Reform Shankarcharya" as there was a second Pope for some time in Europe?' Iyer's hope was to be realized twenty years later after Gandhi's return form South Africa. Gandhi's charisma dispensed with the need for any formal authority as a religious leader. He knew that élitist Hinduism tended to be abstract and mystical, while popular Hinduism tended to be ritualistic and obscurantist. He was tempted neither by the intellectual pleasures of theology nor by the blissful joys of mysticism. He challenged age-old notions and prejudices with impunity. He had a healthy aversion to occult phenomena and never encouraged superstition in any form. When asked about miracles, he said, 'What is the good of overturning nature?' He did not think of God in anthropomorphic terms. 'Truth for me is God', he said, 'and God's Law and God are not different things or facts in the sense that an earthly king and his law are different ... When we say He rules our actions we are simply using human language and we try to limit Him.' Gandhi's Hinduism was thus reduced to a few fundamental beliefs: in the supreme reality of God, the unity of all life, and the value of ahimsa (love) as a means of realizing God.

He did not hesitate to reinterpret traditional beliefs and reject practices that were repugnant to his reason or conscience. He believed that Hinduism possessed the power to rejuvenate itself. He gave the example of the concept of *yajna* (sacrifice):

At one time they sacrificed animals to propitiate angry gods. Their descendants, but our less remote ancestors, read a different meaning with the word 'sacrifice' and they taught that sacrifice was meant to be of our baser self, to please not angry gods, but the one living God within.[13]

It would be safe to say that Gandhi was one of the greatest innovators in the history of Hinduism. He reshaped and redefined time-honoured concepts. I have already mentioned his treatment of the story of Mahabharata as an allegory. He did the same thing with the Gita, in which Krishna became 'the *atman* [soul] and Gopis the many senses of man. They are obedient servants of the self-controlled *atman* and dance before

it as it wills'.[14] *Sadhana*, the pursuit of spirituality, which is commonly
supposed to draw one away from mundane affairs, came to mean that the
aspirant had to make himself an instrument of service to his fellow men.
An ashram was to be not merely a haven from the cares of worldly life, but
a training ground for social and political workers. *Moksha* was liberation
from impure thoughts. *Ahimsa* was not merely a question of what to eat
or not to eat, but the motive force for satyagraha—Gandhi's non-violent
technique of effecting social changes. Fasting was not merely a recipe for
nature-cure or mortification of the flesh, but an ultimate weapon in the
armoury of satyagraha. *Brahmacharya* was not merely sexual restraint,
but a way of life, demanding self-control in thought, word, and deed.
Go-seva (cow-protection) did not consist in building *pinjrapoles* for old or
infirm cows, but called for scientific breeding of cows and well-equipped
dairies for supply of milk to towns and villages.

Gandhi added a new dimension even to the meaning of prayer. 'The
relation between God and myself', he wrote, 'is not only at prayer but at
all times that of master and slave.'[15] Prayer was simply a means of self-
purification; it was to the heart and mind what a daily bath was to the
body.[16] Since divinity pervaded everyone and everything, when he prayed,
he was not begging or demanding something from God, but from himself,
'my Higher Self, real self with which I have not yet achieved complete
identification'.[17]

One cannot but admire Gandhi's revisionist strategy in his encounter
with Hindu orthodoxy. He declined to fight it on its own ground by denying
unqualified allegiance to scriptural authority, and claiming the right to
interpret religious texts in the light of reason, morality, and common sense.
His task was made easier by the fact that he selected one Hindu scripture,
the Gita, and made it a common symbol between himself and the Hindus
of his generation. When his interpretations were called in question, he
disarmed his critics by suggesting that the text on which they relied could
be an interpolation, or simply by asserting that he had all his life 'lived
Hinduism', and knew what he was talking about. He did not, however,
make any claim to infallibility. 'The opinions I have formed', he wrote,
'and the conclusions I have arrived at are not final. I may change them
tomorrow.'

Gandhi could take all these liberties with Hinduism, because he was
an 'insider', and was seen by the people as a devout Hindu, a great Hindu,
a Mahatma. His unique position as a political leader stood him in good
stead as a social reformer. His insistence on the autonomy of human reason
and conscience in the interpretation of religious ideas and practices not

only for himself, but for everyone else, makes him one of the most daring religious reformers in history.

Ramana Maharishi, one of the most venerated Indian saints of the twentieth century, is stated to have remarked that Gandhi 'was a good man who had sacrificed his spiritual development by taking too great burdens upon himself'.[18] Gandhi's signal service to Hinduism lay in his attempt to shift it from its individualistic moorings. He went so far as to say that the only way to find God was to 'see Him in His Creation and be one with it'. He did not know, he said, any religion apart from human activity; the spiritual law did not work in a vacuum but in the ordinary activities of life; religion which took no account of practical problems and did not help to solve them was no religion.[19] God, he once said, 'can only appear to the poorest of the poor in the form of work'. He told N.K. Bose, the anthropologist (who worked as his secretary for a few months in 1946–7 and edited a selection of his writings), that a man was best represented not by the highest flights of thought which he reached at rare moments, but by the actual measure of the ideals of his daily life.[20] C.F. Andrews, who closely studied Gandhi's life, wrote to Romain Rolland that in Gandhi's inner life 'it is the passion for others which is supreme'.[21] Another British friend of Gandhi's, Horace Alexander, also observed how the Mahatma had deviated from the beaten path of Indian saints. 'Gandhi was a mystic', Alexander wrote, 'but he was a very matter-of-fact mystic no dreamer of heavenly dreams, no visionary, who saw things unutterable when in a state of trance. When the inner voice spoke to Gandhi, it was only to tell him, what to do tomorrow—how to act more effectively to bring union of heart between Hindus and Muslims or how to hasten the downfall of untouchability.'[22]

V

Rajchandra, Gandhi's religious mentor, used to say that the real test of spiritual progress was the extent to which one could translate one's beliefs in workaday life. After pondering day after day on the Gita, Gandhi himself came to the conclusion that 'what cannot be followed in day-to-day practice cannot be called religion'. Meditation and worship were 'not exclusive things to be kept like jewels locked up in a strongbox. They must be seen in every act of ours'.[23]

As a lawyer in Durban, and later in Johannesburg, where he came to command a peak practice of £5000 a year, Gandhi did not consider it his professional obligation to defend a client if he was in the wrong. If he was convinced during the progress of a case that his client had withheld material facts from him, he did not hesitate to repudiate him openly in the court. When a client failed to pay his dues, he did not have recourse to law; it was, he said, his own error of judgement which was responsible for the loss.

As he meditated on the Gita, and the ideal of non-possession (*aparigraha*) grew upon him, Gandhi began to reduce his needs, and pay less and less attention to what passed for prestige in the middle class. This trend towards simplicity received a great boost in 1904. One evening that year, as Gandhi was taking a train from Johannesburg to Durban, a friend gave him a book to read. It was Ruskin's *Unto This Last* (1862). Gandhi sat through the night and read it from cover to cover. Before the train reached Durban next morning, he had already resolved to adopt the design of the simple and austere life Ruskin had outlined. Within a few months the Phoenix Ashram had come up; here, away from the heat and dust of towns, and working on a farm among people who shared his ideals, Gandhi could retire from time to time to pose questions about his inner growth. Over the next decade in South Africa the transformation in Gandhi's life, the snapping of the bonds of money, property, and sex, and his conversion into, what Churchill was later to describe, a 'naked faqir', enhanced Gandhi's capacity for single-minded application to public causes. It sustained him in conducting his unequal and long-drawn-out battle with General Smuts, and it certainly contributed both to his unique mass appeal and stamina when he became the dominant figure in Indian politics.

Gandhi's religious quest helped to mould not only his personality, but the political technique with which he confronted racialism in South Africa and colonialism in India. In the evolution of satyagraha as a mode of non-violent struggle, he acknowledged his debt not only to Tolstoy and Thoreau, but to the Gita and the Sermon on the Mount. One can be an atheist or agnostic and still practise satyagraha. It is, however, easier for men of religion than others to accept the basic assumptions of satyagraha: that it is worthwhile fighting, and even dying, for causes that transcend one's personal interests, that the body perishes, but the soul lives, that no oppressor can crush the imperishable spirit of man, that every human being, however wicked he may appear to be, has a hidden nobility, a divine spark, which can be ignited.

VI

'Why I am a Hindu', was the title of an article Gandhi wrote in 1927. Gandhi gave two principal reasons for his attachment to the religion of his birth:

I have found it to be the most tolerant of all religions ... Its freedom from dogma ... gives the votary the largest scope for self-expression. Not being an exclusive religion, it enables the followers of that faith not merely to respect all the other religions, but ... to admire and assimilate whatever may be good in the other faiths. Non-violence is common to all religions, but it has found the highest expression and application in Hinduism ... Hinduism believes in the oneness not of merely all human life but in the oneness of all that lives.[24]

It is significant that he should have highlighted those elements in Hinduism that gave primacy to individual judgement and conscience, on the one hand, and to coexistence and toleration in relations with followers of other religions, on the other.

Ever since he had made a comparative study of religions in his South African days, Gandhi had been impressed by the underlying unity of all religions. In an article in his weekly paper, *Indian Opinion*, in August 1905, Gandhi declared that the time had passed when the followers of one religion could 'stand and say, ours is the only true religion and all others are false'. For the next four decades, Gandhi continued to emphasize the need for coexistence and tolerance between the adherents of different faiths. The various religions were 'as so many leaves of a tree'; they might seem different but 'at the trunk they are one.' God, Allah, Rama, Narayan, Ishwar, Khuda were descriptions of the same Being. Gandhi quoted the saint Narasimha: 'The different shapes into which gold was beaten gave rise to different names and forms; but ultimately it was all gold.'[25] God's grace and revelation were not the monopoly of any race or nation; they descended equally upon all who waited upon God. No religion was 'absolutely perfect. All are equally imperfect or more or less perfect', Gandhi told an American missionary in 1937:[26]

I ... do not take as literally true the text that Jesus is the only begotten Son of God. God cannot be the exclusive father and I cannot ascribe exclusive divinity to Jesus. He is as divine as Krishna or Rama, Mahomed or Zoroaster. Similarly I do not regard every word of the Bible as the inspired word of God even as I do not regard every word of the Vedas or the Koran as inspired. The sum total of each of these books is certainly inspired, but I miss that inspiration in many of the things taken individually. The Bible is as much a book of religion with me as the Gita and the Koran.

Asked what he would do when there were conflicting counsels from different religions, Gandhi replied: 'Truth is superior to everything, and I reject what conflicts with it. Similarly that which is in conflict with non-violence should be rejected. And on matters which can be reasoned out, that which conflicted with Reason must also be rejected.'[27]

The extraordinary catholicity of Gandhi's religious outlook intrigued and sometimes infuriated his contemporaries. Joseph J. Doke, his first biographer in South Africa considered his views 'too closely allied to Christianity to be entirely Hindu and too deeply saturated with Hinduism to be called Christian, while his sympathies are so wide and catholic that one would imagine he has reached a point where the formulae of sects are meaningless'. In his lifetime he was variously labelled a Sanatanist (orthodox) Hindu, a renegade Hindu, a Buddhist, a Theosophist, a Christian and a 'Christian–Mohammedan'. He was all these and more. He chided Christian missionaries for their 'irreligious gamble' for converts. His opposition to conversion from one religion to another was based on principle. While he was in South Africa, he exhorted the Arya Samaj against undertaking any missionary activity in that country. He did not permit proselytization in his ashrams. Contrary to the impression at the time, his English disciple, Miss Slade (Mirabehn), was never converted to Hinduism. As Gandhi was at pains to explain, she was given not a Hindu but an Indian name, and this 'had been done at her instance and for her convenience'. Similarly, Richard Gregg, who wrote extensively on non-violence and stayed in Gandhi's Ashram, was called Govind, but never became a Hindu.

We have in the Ashram today several faiths represented. No proselytizing is practised or permitted. We recognize that all these faiths are true and divinely inspired, and all have suffered through the necessarily imperfect handling of imperfect men.[28]

When some Hindus protested that he was relatively 'tender' when speaking to Christian and Muslim audiences, but unsparing in his criticism of the Hindus, Gandhi pleaded guilty to the charge. For one thing, he said he did not claim to know as much about Christianity and Islam as he knew about Hinduism. For another, he felt that Christians and Muslims were more likely to misunderstand him than Hindus.[29]

Gandhi had studied both Christianity and Islam, and had many Christian and Muslim friends. He tells us in his autobiography how certain aspects of Christianity—the life and death of Jesus, the Sermon on the Mount and the crystalline purity of some Christians—appealed to him. He called Christ the 'Prince of Satyagrahis'. He read a translation of the Koran and the life of the Prophet, and was struck by the courage with which he and his first followers had faced the humiliations and hardships heaped upon them. Many years later when he was in Yeravda jail, Gandhi advised his English disciple, Mirabehn (Miss Slade), who had been reading the Upanishads, to read the Koran, and assured her that she would find many 'gems' in it.[30]

Gandhi's reverence for the Bible and the Koran did not, however, prevent him from exercising the critical faculty which he applied to the study of Hindu scriptures. We learn from Mahadev Desai's diary (4 March 1925) that Gandhi was deeply shocked when told that Maulana Shaukat Ali subscribed to 'the law of an eye for an eye and a head for a head', and had argued that 'if there is a mention of stoning to death in the Koran, the act must be accepted as right and proper'.[31] The place of violence in Islam had been a vexed issue during the Khilafat movement; most Muslim leaders had insisted that they had agreed to adhere to non-violence as a matter of expediency and not as a principle. Gandhi's own view was that in the Koran, 'non-violence is enjoined as duty, violence is permitted as a necessity'.[32] On another occasion when told that Prophet Muhammad had prescribed the use of the sword in certain circumstances, Gandhi replied:

I suppose most Muslims will agree. But I read religion in a different way. Khan Saheb Abdul Ghaffar Khan derives his belief in non-violence from the Koran, and the Bishop of London derives his belief in violence from the Bible. I derive my belief in non-violence from the Gita, whereas there are others who read violence in it. But if the worst came to the worst and if I came to the conclusion that the Koran teaches violence, I would still reject violence, but I would not therefore say that the Bible is superior to the Koran or that Mohammed is inferior to Jesus. It is not my function to judge Mohammed and Jesus. It is enough that my non-violence is independent of the sanction of scriptures.[33]

Gandhi's advocacy of mutual tolerance and respect between different religions originally arose from his study of comparative religion, but it had a practical aspect too. All his adult life he was leading struggles against racial, social, and political injustice, and his adherents in these struggles belonged to all the major religions. Muslim merchants had been the backbone of his movement in Natal and Transvaal. Gandhi was aware of the gulf between the two major communities of India and wanted to bridge it. In 1905, in an article in his weekly journal, he had asked: 'Is it not also a fact that between Mahomedan and Hindu there is a great need for ... toleration? Sometimes one is inclined to think it is even greater than between East and West.'[34] A few months earlier, in a lecture on Hinduism at Johannesburg, he argued that 'when there were no political influences at work, there was no difficulty about the Hindus and the Mahomedans living side by side in perfect peace and amity, each respecting the prejudices of the other, and each following his own faith without let or hindrance'.[35]

This was a remarkably perceptive comment on the shape of things to come when he returned to his homeland ten years later.

VII

Those who blame Gandhi for mixing religion with politics evidently do not know what he meant by religion. There is no excuse for this ignorance, for Gandhi repeatedly made his meaning clear. For example, in reply to criticism in a British journal that he was introducing religion into politics, he wrote in 1920:

> Let me explain what I mean by religion. It is not the Hindu religion, which I certainly prize above all other religions, but the religion which transcends Hinduism, which changes one's very nature, which binds one indissolubly to the truth within and which ever purifies. It is the permanent element in human nature which ... leaves the soul restless until it has found itself.[36]

Four years later, while affirming that for him there was no politics without religion, he explained that this was 'not the religion that hates and fights, but the universal religion of Toleration'.[37] In 1940 he reiterated that 'religion should pervade every one of our actions,' but added, 'here religion does not mean sectarianism. It means a belief in ordered moral government of the universe ... This religion transcends Hinduism, Islam, Christianity, etc. It does not supersede them; it harmonizes them.'[38] Gandhi's concept of religion had little in common with that which generally passes for organized religion: dogmas, rituals, superstition and bigotry. Indeed, shorn of these accretions, Gandhian religion was simply an ethical framework for the conduct of daily life. Unfortunately, most intelligent people who concede the value of an ethical framework in domestic and social spheres, are sceptical about its feasibility in politics. Politics is considered to be a game in which expediency must take precedence over morality. Tilak, Gandhi's great contemporary, told him in 1918, 'Politics is not for *sadhus.*'

Gandhi did not and could not accept the commonly accepted view of politics, because satyagraha, the mode of struggle he had evolved for fighting against social and political oppression, was rooted in morality. It excluded untruth, secrecy, and hatred; it eschewed violence; it invited suffering at the hands of the oppressor rather than inflicting it on him, and it presumed that it was possible to convert the enemy of today into a friend of tomorrow.

Satyagraha could be moral or nothing; it was a form of struggle in which Gandhi could lose all the battles but still win the war. His self-imposed constraints irked some of his followers, but he had good reasons for enforcing them. The non-violent struggles which Gandhi waged in South Africa involved a few thousand Indians in a limited area whom he could personally guide. In India, however, the scale was continental, and the numbers involved directly and indirectly were in millions. Gandhi's constant concern was how to arouse these millions, and yet to prevent his movement from dissolving into disorder and anarchy. He never forgot the terrible sequel in Punjab in April 1919 soon after he had launched satyagraha against the Rowlatt Bills. All his energies were, therefore, directed to keeping a tight rein on the movement. He did not induct the industrial workers into his campaign; he did not permit peasants to withhold rent from the landlords. He deliberately excluded the despotic princely states from his civil disobedience campaigns. All these self-denying ordinances baffled his radical critics, who accused him of curbing the 'revolutionary stirrings' of the masses. What they could not see was that the basic strategy of a non-violent struggle must necessarily be different from that of a violent one. For Gandhi it was not a question of capturing a particular outpost by superior force, or of overwhelming the enemy by sheer numbers. The purpose of satyagraha was to generate those processes of introspection and rethinking that would make it possible to arrive at a readjustment of relationships between the contending parties, and all this had to be done without generating hatred and violence. Non-violence was the central issue; on this the Mahatma would accept no compromise. 'I would welcome', he said, 'even utter failure with non-violence unimpaired, rather than depart from it by a hair's breadth to achieve a doubtful success.' It was because of his supreme anxiety to keep the movement firmly under control that he invariably began his campaigns cautiously, and only gradually extended them in range and intensity. He went on to call them off, as he did after the Chauri Chaura tragedy in 1922, when he sensed that indiscipline and violence were creeping into the movement. It is the absence of this scruple and caution that has made most mass struggles in the post-Independence period a travesty of the Gandhian satyagraha.

Ten years before Gandhi's return to India from South Africa, Gopal Krishna Gokhale, whom Gandhi hailed as his political guru, had talked of 'spiritualizing politics'. Gokhale, whose secular credentials were beyond question, was convinced that India needed men who would devote all their talents and their time to her service. For centuries India had her bands of Sanyasis, who had turned their backs upon worldly ambitions; why could this reserve of self-sacrifice not be tapped for the social and political regeneration of India? This idea of evoking abnegation and self-denial for secular causes which inspired Gokhale to establish the Servants of India Society in 1905, found a wider application not only in Gandhi's ashrams, but in the social and political campaigns he conducted in India. Inevitably, these movements had moral and religious overtones which jarred on the westernized Indian intellectuals, who in Gandhi's time (as in our own), tended to postulate a sharp antithesis between science and religion, and treated all religions as irrational and obscurantist. They did not fully grasp the deep humanism and universality of Gandhi's religious outlook. They failed to see the philosophical implications of the advance of science from the mechanistic and materialistic moorings of the nineteenth century. Albert Einstein, a great scientist, contemporary and admirer of Gandhi, wrote in 1934 that the more profound scientists were not without a religious feeling though it was different from the religiosity of the common man:

But the scientist is possessed by the sense of universal causation. His religious feeling takes the form of a rapturous amazement at the harmony of the natural law which reveals an intelligence of such superiority that compared with it, all the systematic thinking and acting of human beings is an utterly insignificant reflection.

Einstein added that this feeling of the scientist was the guiding principle of his life, and 'in so far as he succeeds in keeping himself from the shackles of selfish desire, it is ... akin to that which possessed the religious geniuses of all ages'.[39] Among these geniuses, Einstein included Gandhi. He believed that the moral qualities of its leading personalities 'are perhaps of even greater significance for a generation and for the course of history than purely intellectual accomplishments'. His tribute to Gandhi paid sixty-two years ago in 1939 can scarcely be improved upon:

A leader of his people unsupported by any outward authority; a politician whose success rests not upon craft nor the mastery of technical devices, but simply on the convincing power of his personality; a victorious fighter who has always scorned the use of force and inflexible consistency, who has devoted all his strength to the uplifting of his people and the betterment of their lot; a man who had confronted the brutality of Europe with the dignity of the simple human being and thus at all times risen superior.

Generations to come, it may be, will scarce believe that such a one as this ever in flesh and blood walked upon this earth.

VIII

The mental barrier between the westernized Indian intelligentsia and Gandhi which existed in his lifetime survives today in a different way: a peculiar lack of will even to study and understand him. This barrier has indeed even contributed to the denigration and distortion of his pivotal role in the struggle for freedom. It has been a fashion in certain circles to foist the responsibility for the partition of India on him, and to arraign him for the communalization of politics which culminated in the division of India.

Gandhi's support to the Khilafat movement has especially come in for much uninformed criticism. This support in 1919–22 stemmed neither from a momentary impulse nor from tactical calculation. Gandhi had his reasons, which have often been missed by his admirers as well as his critics, for intervening in a crisis which was not of his making, but which had brought millions of Indian Muslims on the verge of desperation. The resultant Khilafat–Non-cooperation alliance turned out to be an unprecedented demonstration of Hindu–Muslim unity, the like of which had never been seen before, nor was to be seen again in this subcontinent. The alliance gladdened the hearts of Indian nationalists as much as it bewildered the ruling power. It brought Indian Muslims for the first time in very substantial numbers into the mainstream of Indian nationalism, but the experience was much too brief and, thanks to Kemal Ataturk, had an unhappy ending. To the historian seeking to unravel the history of this period, the important question is not only why Gandhi agreed to support the pleas of Indian Muslims on behalf of the Ottoman Khilafat, but how the fate of Turkey and its Sultan Caliph came so completely to obsess the minds and sway the hearts of a whole generation of Indian Muslims. It was not only the semi-literate village *maulvis*, school-teachers, artisans, and small shopkeepers, who were swept off their feet, but graduates of British universities such as Dr M.A. Ansari, Maulana Mohamed Ali, Dr Syed Mahmud; seasoned barristers such as Jinnah and Mazharul Haq; and confirmed loyalists of the British Raj such as Ameer Ali and the Aga Khan, who were deeply agitated over the misfortunes of Turkey. I shall not, however, enlarge here upon this subject, as I have dealt with it in my book, *Gandhi: Pan-Islamism, Imperialism and Nationalism in India* (Delhi, 1989) as well as in another essay in this book (see Chapter 11).

Gandhi's use of such words as swaraj, *sarvodaya*, ahimsa and satyagraha was exploited by the Muslim League during its campaign for Pakistan to estrange Muslims from the nationalist struggle. The truth is that these expressions, when used by Gandhi, had little religious significance. They were derived from Sanskrit, but as most of the Indian languages are derived from Sanskrit, this made them easily intelligible to the masses. The English translation of these words, or a purely legal or constitutional terminology, may have sounded more modern and secular, but it would have passed over the heads of all but a tiny urbanized English-educated minority. The protagonists of Pakistan made much play with the phrase 'Ram Rajya', which Gandhi occasionally employed to describe the goal of the Indian freedom struggle. 'Ram Rajya' was simply Gandhi's equivalent for the English term 'utopia'. The common people, to whom his writings and speeches were usually addressed, instinctively knew that he was not referring to the monarchical form of government in ancient India but to an ideal polity free from inequality, injustice, and exploitation.

Gandhi's prayer meetings were held not in temples, but under the open sky, and became a symbol of religious harmony by including recitations from Hindu, Muslim, Christian, Sikh, Parsi, and Buddhist texts. When the prayers and hymns had been recited, he spoke on the problems that faced the country. In the last months of his life, at a time of bitter religious tension, his prayer meetings became a defiant symbol of tolerance and his post-prayer talk served the purpose of a daily press conference.

Thus the symbols used by Gandhi had ceased to be exclusively Hindu ones. The saintly idiom remained but its content changed; this is something that often escaped the attention of Gandhi's critics. One of them, M.N. Roy, who, in his Communist as well as Radical Humanist phases, had ridiculed Gandhi's religious approach to politics, confessed later that he had failed to detect the secular approach of the Mahatma beneath the religious terminology, and that essentially Gandhi's message had been 'moral, humanist, cosmopolitan'.[40]

As regards Gandhi's responsibility for the partition of India, all I would say is that no one did more to avert it, or to mitigate its consequences when it came. Gandhi took little part in the final negotiations for 'the transfer of power', but his opposition to Partition was an open secret. 'We are unable to think coherently', he declared, 'whilst the British power is still functioning in India. Its function is not to change the map of India. All it has to do is to withdraw and leave India, carrying out the withdrawal, if possible, in an orderly manner, may be even in chaos, on or before the promised date.' The very violence, which in the opinion of Nehru, Patel, and other Congress leaders, and that of the British Government, provided a compelling motive for Partition, was for him a strong argument against it. To accept Partition because of the fear of civil war was to acknowledge that everything was to be got 'if mad violence was perpetrated in sufficient measure'. Gandhi believed that communal tension, however serious it seemed in 1947, was a temporary phase, and the

British had no right to impose Partition 'on an India temporarily gone mad'. His plea that there should be 'peace before Pakistan' was not acceptable to Jinnah and the Muslim League. On the contrary, their case was that there could be no peace until Pakistan was established.

Few people are aware of Gandhi's great contribution to the concept of secularism in India. Deeply religious as he was, he said that he would have opposed any proposal for a state religion even if the whole population of India had professed the same religion. He looked upon religion as a personal matter. He told a missionary: 'The State would look after your secular welfare, health, communications, foreign relations, currency and so on, but not your or my religion. That is everybody's personal concern.'[41]

The resolution on fundamental rights passed by the Karachi Congress in 1931 with Gandhi's cordial approval, affirmed the principle of religious freedom and declared that 'the State shall observe neutrality in regard to all religions'. This doctrine was embodied in the Constitution of independent India even after the Muslim League waged and won the campaign for the partition of the country on the basis of religion. Louis Fischer, Gandhi's American biographer, noted the strange paradox that Jinnah, who had grown up as a secular nationalist in his younger days and who apparently had little interest in religion, founded a State based on religion, while Gandhi, wholly religious, worked to establish a secular State.[42]

NOTES AND REFERENCES

1. Quoted in Margaret Chatterjee, *Gandhi's Religious Thought* (London, 1983), p. 90.
2. H. Montgomery Hyde, *Lord Reading* (London, 1967), p. 352.
3. Stephan Hay, 'Jain Goals and Disciplines in Gandhi's Pursuit of Swaraj' *in* Peter Robb and David Taylor (eds), *Rule, Protest and Identity: Aspects of Modern South Asia*, (London & Dublin, 1978), pp. 120–32.
4. Raghavan Iyer, *The Moral and Political Writings of Mahatma Gandhi*, vol. I, (London, 1986), pp. 145–6.
5. Ibid., p. 152.
6. Agehananda Bharati, 'Gandhi's Interpretation of the Gita', in Sibnarayan Ray (ed.), *Gandhi, India and the World* (Melbourne, 1970), pp. 61–3.
7. *Harijan*, 28 Sept. 1935.
8. Gandhi to Moonje, 14 May 1927, Gandhi Papers (henceforth G.P.).
9. S.R. Mehrotra, *The Emergence of the Indian National Congress* (Delhi, 1971), p. 35.
10. Ibid., p. 126.

11. *Indian Statesman*, 13 Dec. 1872.
12. Andrew Fraser, *Among Indian Rajahs and Ryots* (London, 1912), p. 280.
13. *Harijan*, 3 Oct. 1936.
14. *Collected Works of Mahatma Gandhi* (henceforth *C.W.M.G.*), vol. xxxiv, p. 34.
15. Gandhi to V.M. Tarkunde, 30 Oct. 1926, G.P.
16. Gandhi to Dhan Gopal Mukerjee, 29 July 1926, G.P.
17. *Harijan*, 19 Aug. 1939.
18. Raghavan Iyer, *Moral and Political Thought of Gandhi* (New York, 1978), p. 380.
19. *Young India*, 7 May 1925.
20. N.K. Bose, *My Days With Gandhi* (Calcutta, 1974), p. 22.
21. Margaret Chatterjee, op. cit., p. 88.
22. Horace Alexander, *Consider India* (London, 1961), p. 75.
23. *Harijan*, 20 April 1935.
24. *Young India*, 21 Oct. 1927.
25. *Young India*, 14 Aug. 1924.
26. *C.W.M.G.*, vol. 64, p. 397.
27. Ibid., p. 398.
28. *Young India*, 20 Feb. 1930.
29. *C.W.M.G.*, vol. xxxiv, p. 537.
30. M. Slade, *The Spirit's Pilgrimage*, p. 171.
31. *Day to Day, the Diary of Mahadev Desai*, vol. 6, p. 48.
32. *Harijan*, 13 July 1940.
33. *C.W.M.G.*, vol. 64, p. 399.
34. *Indian Opinion*, 26 Aug. 1905.
35. *C.W.M.G.*, vol. iv, p. 377.
36. *Young India*, 12 May 1920.
37. *Young India*, 27 Nov. 1924.
38. *Harijan*, 10 Feb. 1940.
39. Albert Einstein, *Ideas and Opinions* (New Delhi, 1988 rpt.), p. 40.
40. Dennis Dalton, 'Gandhi and Roy: The Interaction of Ideologies in India' *in* Sibnarayan Ray (ed.), *Gandhi, India and the World* (Melbourne, 1970), p. 166.
41. *Harijan* 22 Sept. 1946.
42. Louis Fischer, *The Life of Mahatma Gandhi* (London, 1951), p. 430.

THREE

Gandhi in South Africa

'The best part of my life' is how Gandhi described his days in South Africa twenty-five years after he had left it. It was certainly the most formative period of his career. Without the challenges, the trials, and the opportunities that his South African experience brought him, it is unlikely that his personality and politics could have been cast in the unique mould which made him one of the most charismatic and creative leaders of the twentieth century.

Curiously, it was an accident that provided the impulse for Gandhi's visit to South Africa in 1893. Two years earlier, he had returned from England after qualifying as a barrister. He started his legal career in Bombay, but made little headway, and decided to settle at Rajkot in Gujarat to make a modest living. He, however, fell foul of Ollivant, the British Political Agent in Rajkot, in whose court most of his work lay. It was at this time that Dada Abdulla, an Indian merchant in Natal, offered to engage him for a civil suit in that country. The contract was for a year; the remuneration was £105, a first-class return fare, and actual expenses. The fee was modest, and it was not quite clear whether he was being engaged as counsel or a clerk, but Gandhi wanted to get away from Rajkot and accepted the offer with alacrity. Towards the end of May 1893 he landed at Durban. Unpleasant surprises and shocks were in store for him. In a Durban court he was ordered by the European magistrate to take off his turban. He refused and left the courtroom. A week later, when he was on his way to Pretoria, he was unceremoniously thrown out of the first-class carriage at Martizburg station. It was a bitterly cold night as he crept into the unlit waiting-room of the railway station and brooded over what had happened. His client had given him no warning of the humiliating conditions under which Indians lived in South Africa. Should he not call off the contract and return to India? The Indian merchants had learned to pocket these humiliations as they pocketed their earnings. What was new was not Gandhi's experience, but his reaction to it. In retrospect, this incident seemed to him one of the most creative experiences of his life. So far he had not been conspicuous for assertiveness; on the contrary, he had been pathologically shy and retiring. Something, however, happened to him in that bleak, windswept waiting-room of Maritzburg railway station as he smarted under the insult inflicted on him. Iron entered his soul. He resolved not to accept injustice as part of the natural or unnatural order in South Africa. He would reason; he would plead; he would resist, but he would not be a willing victim of racial arrogance. The timidity which had dogged him as a student in England and as a lawyer in India vanished.

While in Pretoria he studied the conditions under which his countrymen lived, and tried to educate them on their rights and duties, but he had no intention of staying on in South Africa. In June 1894, when the year's contract drew to a close, he was back in Durban, ready to sail for India. It was at the farewell party given by his grateful client that he happened to glance through the local newspaper *The Natal Mercury* and learnt that the Natal Legislative Assembly was considering a bill to deprive Indians of the right to vote. 'This is the first nail in our coffin', Gandhi told his hosts. They pleaded with him to stay on to take up cudgels on their behalf. He agreed to defer his return to India for a month. Neither as a student in England nor as a lawyer in India had Gandhi taken much interest in politics. Indeed, there had been occasions when he had been overcome by stage fright when he rose to read a speech at a social gathering or to defend a client in a court. However, in July 1894, when he was barely twenty-five, he blossomed overnight into a proficient political campaigner.

A sound instinct guided young Gandhi in organizing his first political campaign. He drafted petitions to the Natal Legislature and the British government, and had them signed by hundreds of his compatriots. He failed to prevent the passage of the disfranchisement bill, but he succeeded in drawing the attention of the public and the press in Natal, India, and England to the Natal Indians' grievances.

Meanwhile, the month for which Gandhi had postponed his departure for India came to an end. The Indian community begged him to stay on to continue the fight on their behalf. As he would not hear of payment for public work, twenty merchants offered retaining fees to enable him to pay his way in Durban. Gandhi felt that what the Indians urgently needed was a permanent organization to look after their interests. In deference to Dadabhai Naoroji, who had presided over the Indian National Congress in 1893, he named the new organization Natal Indian Congress. He knew little about the constitution and functions of the Indian National Congress. This ignorance proved an asset, as he was able to fashion the Natal Congress in his own way to suit the needs of the Natal Indians; unlike the Indian National Congress of those days it became a live body functioning throughout the year.

An indefatigable secretary though he was, Gandhi enlisted popular interest and enthusiasm at every step. His strategy was twofold. In the first place, a spirit of solidarity had to be infused into the Muslim merchants and their Hindu and Parsi clerks, the semi-slave indentured labourers from Madras and the Natal-born Indian Christians. Secondly, the widest publicity was to be given to the Indians' case to quicken the conscience of the peoples and governments of Natal, India, and Great Britain. It was a measure of his success as a publicist that such important newspapers as *The Times* (London) and *The Statesman* and *Englishman* of Calcutta, editorially commented on the grievances of the Indians of Natal. As for himself, Gandhi refused to accept anything from public funds. In these early years of his political apprenticeship, he formulated his own code of conduct for a politician. He did not accept the popular view that in politics one must fight for one's party, right or wrong. The passion for facts, which he had recently cultivated in his practice of law, he brought to bear on politics; if the facts were on his side, there was no need to embroider on them. He avoided exaggeration and discouraged it in his colleagues. He did not spare his own people; he was not only the stoutest champion of Natal Indians, but also their severest critic.

In 1896 Gandhi went to India to fetch his wife and children and to canvass support for the cause of Indians overseas. Garbled versions of his activities and utterances in India reached Natal and inflamed its European population. On landing at Durban in January 1897, he was assaulted and nearly lynched by a white mob. It was characteristic of him that he refused to prosecute his assailants; it was, he said, a principle with him not to seek redressal of a personal wrong in a court of law. Two years later, he raised an Indian ambulance corps during the Boer War: a fine but vain gesture to the British. The British victory in the Boer War brought little relief to the Indians of South Africa. The new regime grew into a partnership, but only between Boers and Britons for the preservation of white supremacy. 'What we [Indians] want,' Gandhi told the British High Commissioner in South Africa, 'is not political power, but we do wish to live side by side with other British subjects in peace and amity, and with dignity and self-respect.' This is precisely what the Boers and Britons did not want. General Smuts later declared that the South African government had made up its mind to 'make this a white man's country and, however difficult the task before us in this direction, we have put our foot down and would keep it there'.

In 1906 the Transvaal government published a particularly humiliating ordinance for the registration of its Indian citizens. The Indians held a mass protest meeting at Johannesburg, and under Gandhi's leadership took a pledge to defy the ordinance if it became law and to suffer all the penalties resulting from their defiance. Thus was born satyagraha, a new method of redressing wrongs and fighting oppression without hatred and without violence. The principles and the technique of the new movement evolved gradually in the ensuing months and years; its author was a man for whom theory was the handmaid of action.

The satyagraha struggle in South Africa lasted eight years. It had its ups and downs, but under Gandhi's leadership the small Indian minority sustained its resistance against heavy odds. Hundreds of Indians chose to sacrifice their livelihood and liberty rather than submit to laws repugnant to their conscience and self-respect. In the last phase of the struggle in 1913, hundreds of Indians, including women, went to jail, and thousands of Indian labourers, who had struck work in the mines, braved imprisonment, flogging, and even shooting. It was a terrible ordeal for the Indians, but it was also a bad advertisement for the rulers of South Africa. Even Lord Hardinge, the Viceroy of India, committed a calculated indiscretion by publicly condemning the measures adopted by the South African government 'which would not for one moment be tolerated by any country that calls itself civilized'. Under pressure from world opinion and from the Government of India and the British government, the South African government concluded in 1914 what came to be known as the Gandhi–Smuts agreement. Not all the Indian grievances were redressed, but the first dent had been made in the armour of racial discrimination, and Gandhi was able to return to India. Perhaps he had already sensed that the racial problem in South Africa could not be solved so long as European imperialism—rule over Asian and African peoples by European nations—continued. It was Gandhi's head-on clash with British imperialism in India which was to undermine colonial rule in the continents of Asia and Africa, destroy the *raison d'être* of white supremacy, and eventually open the prospects of a multiracial and democratic polity in South Africa.

It was fortunate for Gandhi that he began his legal and political career in South Africa. Dwarfed as he had felt by the great lawyers and leaders of India, it is unlikely that he would have developed much initiative in his homeland. In South Africa he could try out ideals which in an established political organization would have been laughed out of court. For a man who was no doctrinaire, it was a decided advantage that the scene of his early activities should have been one where he was unfettered by political precedents or professionals. He was thus able to lay down his own code of conduct, whether as a lawyer, journalist, or political leader. His ethical and spiritual idiom puzzled not only his opponents, but most of his contemporaries in the Indian political élite. *Hind Swaraj*, Gandhi's compendious political and social manifesto, published in 1909, was proscribed by the Government of India, but equally drew little response from Western-educated Indians.

The Gandhi, who left South Africa in 1914, was a very different person from the callow, diffident youth who had arrived at Durban twenty-one years earlier. South Africa had not treated him kindly; it had drawn him into the vortex of the racial problem created by the European domination of Africa. The unequal struggle he had waged against racial discrimination had matured him, and helped him to evolve an original philosophy and a novel technique of social and political agitation. It was as the author and the sole practitioner of satyagraha that Gandhi was to enter the Indian political stage and dominate it for nearly thirty years.

It was not only Gandhi's politics but his personality that was shaped in South Africa. Indeed, without this inner transformation, he could scarcely have acquired the remarkable qualities of leadership that made him the dominant figure in Indian politics. His interest in moral and religious questions had dated back to his childhood, but it was in South Africa that he had an opportunity of systematically studying them. The Christian missionaries, who had made a dead set at him on his arrival in South Africa, had failed to convert him, but they had whetted his appetite for religious studies. He delved deeply into Christianity as well as other major religions, including the religion of his birth. The study of comparative religion, browsing through theological works, and the conversations and correspondence with the learned brought him to the conclusion that there was an underlying unity in the clash of doctrines and forms, that true religion was more a matter of the heart than of the intellect, and that genuine beliefs were those that were literally lived. The real test of spiritual progress, Gandhi came to believe, was the extent to which one could translate one's beliefs in workaday life.

The book that became Gandhi's bond with Hinduism as well as the greatest influence on him was the Bhagavad Gita. It was from it that he imbibed the ideal of *aparigraha* (non-possession) which set him on the road to voluntary poverty. The ideals of service without self and of 'action without attachment' enlarged his vision and equipped him with an extraordinary stamina for his public life. He learnt to transcend the barriers of race, caste, creed, and class. He simplified his life, sank his savings in public work, and finally gave up his lucrative legal practice. His private life gradually shaded into public life; he snapped the ties of money, property, and family life, which hold back most men and women from fearlessly following the dictates of their conscience. Personal renunciation was an invaluable asset to him in his public life. This can be illustrated by two vignettes of Gandhi, which have come down to us from contemporaries of his South African days. The first is from the pen of Joseph J. Doke, a Baptist Minister of Johannesburg, Gandhi's first biographer, who saw him for the first time in December 1907.

To my surprise, a small, lithe, spare figure stood before me, and a refined earnest face looked into mine. The skin was dark, the eyes dark, but the smile which lighted up the face, and that direct fearless glance, simply took one's heart by storm. I judged him to be some 38-years of age, which proved correct ...

There was a quiet assured strength about him, a greatness of heart, a transparent honesty, that attracted me at once to the Indian leader. We parted friends.

Our Indian friend lives on a higher plane than most men do ... Those, who do not know him, think there is some unworthy motive behind, ... to account for such profound unworldliness. But those who know him well are ashamed of themselves in his presence ...

Money I think has no charm for him. His compatriots are angry. They say, 'He will take nothing. The money we gave him when he went as our deputy to England he brought back to us again. The presents we made him in Natal, he handed over to our public funds. He is poor because he will be poor.'

They wonder at him, grow angry at his strange unselfishness, and love him with the love of pride and trust. He is one of those outstanding characters with whom to walk is a liberal education, whom to know is to love.

Doke also noted that 'to hold in the flesh with a strong hand, to crucify it, to bring the needs of his own life, Thoreau and Tolstoy-like, within the narrowest limits' were positive delights to Gandhi, equalled only by the joy of guiding others along the same path.

The second pen-picture of Gandhi was drawn by a distinguished British academic, Professor Gilbert Murray, who had met Gandhi in England, And in a perceptive, almost prophetic article, entitled 'The

Soul As It Is and How To Deal With It' in *The Hibbert Journal* in 1918, warned persons in power to be 'careful how they deal with a man who cares nothing for sensual pleasure, nothing for riches, nothing for comfort or praise or promotion, but is simply determined to do what he believes to be right. He is a dangerous and uncomfortable enemy because his body, which you can always conquer, gives you so little purchase upon his soul.'

FOUR

Gandhi against Racialism

*T*he South African Gandhi,[1] a massive volume edited by Fatima Meer and sponsored by the Institute for Black Research, University of Natal, provides fascinating glimpses of the twenty-one years from 1893 to 1914 that Gandhi spent in South Africa. Divided into twenty-three parts, each covering a particular phase or facet of Gandhi's life, the book consists of documents compiled from the first twelve volumes of the *Collected Works of Mahatma Gandhi*. The reader thus gets a feel of the period and insights into the evolution of Gandhi's personality, his philosophy of life, and public career. The meticulous documentation, thanks to a combination of chronological and thematic methods, unfolds the process of the transformation of the callow, shy, and diffident lawyer, who landed in Durban in 1893 into a powerful charismatic figure destined to leave a permanent mark on the history of our time. We are provided with cameos of the young lawyer, the resister, the negotiator, the prisoner, the lobbyist, the journalist, the social reformer, the man of God, the educationist, and the family man amongst others.

In some ways the work covers well-trodden ground, not only in the biographies of the Mahatma, but in the monographs by D.S. Chandran Devanesan, Robert A. Huttenback, Maureen Swan, and most recently by J.N. Uppal. The volume, however, has a special merit; it enables the reader, if he has the interest and the patience, to see the unfolding of a remarkable career and of history in the making.

All serious students of Gandhi's life agree that his two formative decades in South Africa had a profound influence on the moulding of his personality and political life. However, in recent years, opinion has changed on Gandhi's impact on the course of events in South Africa. Sceptics have pointed out that Gandhi confined his campaign to the removal of the grievances of Indian immigrants. Did he lack the vision to see the wider issue of racial discrimination? Some critics have even argued that Gandhi himself was not free from racial prejudice, and cited in support of this view his initial shock at the Indian satyagrahi prisoners being classed and lodged with the 'Natives', the black prisoners, in jail. Nelson Mandela's comments in this book are pertinent regarding this. The prejudice was obvious, he says, but Gandhi was reacting not to African 'Natives' in general but to 'criminalized Natives'. Mandela adds that in fairness Gandhi should be judged 'in the context of the time and circumstances', and that here we are looking at the young Gandhi yet to become the Mahatma, when he would be 'without any human prejudice save in favour of truth and justice'.

There is evidence in this volume to indicate that had Gandhi nurtured any prejudice, he was fast outgrowing it. In his speech at the YMCA in June 1908, he stressed the complementary nature of various cultures, and refuted the notion that differing civilizations could not coexist. Through his journal, the *Indian Opinion*, he kept his readers informed of the problems of the Africans. He wanted each racial group to fight its own battle, but to be supportive to one another. He backed the demands of the Africans for franchise in Transvaal and Orange River Colony, and was deeply concerned about the insidious move of the whites threatening Africans' land rights. He denounced the jury system in South Africa because, as he put it, 'inherent to the sense of justice is the requirement that the accused is tried by his equals. It is an insult to man's intelligence to contend that there is any such trial in South Africa'.

It was not racial prejudice, but political realism that seems to have guided Gandhi in limiting his agenda to the eradication of the disabilities of his countrymen in South Africa. It is difficult for us today to imagine the heavy odds against which he was fighting. It was the heyday of European imperialism, when domination over coloured races—brown, black and yellow—was accepted almost as a fact of nature. He had to reckon with the unrelenting hostility of the European population and colonial government. In 1897, when he was twenty-seven years old, he was nearly lynched by a white mob in Durban. The Indians in Natal and Transvaal were a socially and economically heterogeneous community. It was no easy task for Gandhi to infuse a spirit of solidarity into Muslim merchants and their Hindu and Parsi clerks from western India and the semi-slave indentured labourers from Madras and the Indian Christians born in South Africa. Small in number, scattered in several colonies, the Indians lived in constant dread of fresh restrictions and humiliations. They did not have the right to vote and were defenceless against a whole arsenal of discriminatory laws enacted by the colonial legislature. Boers and Britons, whatever their differences, were united in their resolve to preserve the white monopoly of economic and political power. The Government of India, which had permitted emigration to the colonies in South Africa, was not conversant with the true state of affairs, and the Colonial Office in London was reluctant to interfere in what was described as the 'internal affair' of self-governing colonies.

Gandhi had to evolve a strategy to suit the situation facing him in South Africa. He organized the Indian immigrants, presented their case on its merits, opposed the colonial regime, but at the same time sought support of world opinion. He worked for a series of moral pressures, by Indian political leaders and public opinion, on the Viceroy and the Government of India, by the latter on the British government in London, and by the British government on the colonial government in South Africa. He based his case against racial discrimination on (what he claimed to be) the inherent rights of British Indian subjects guaranteed to them in the British Empire by the Proclamation of Queen Victoria in 1858. Incidentally, this was the argument that Dadabhai Naoroji and the founding fathers of the Indian National Congress were using at that time to advocate a greater share for the people of India in the governance of their country.

Gandhi deliberately moderated his demands to elicit the widest sympathy for his cause. He challenged the South African government on specific and limited issues, eschewing extreme postures. His technique of satyagraha permitted continuing dialogue, and appeal to the reason and conscience of the opponent. Even in the last phase of his struggle he did not demand the redressal of all the Indian grievances, confining himself to the few issues on which the position of the colonial administration was demonstrably untenable. All that he was able to achieve by 1914, when he left South Africa, was to make the first dent in the armour of white racialism. The most important demands of the Indians, such as the right to vote and to be represented in the colonial legislatures were not even put forward by Gandhi; they were reserved for a later occasion.

If the black population did not figure in Gandhi's campaign, it was partly because it did not suffer from the disabilities against which the Indians were protesting, such as the £3 tax on indentured labourers, which turned them into semi-slaves, the restrictions on immigration from India, and the discrimination against Indian traders. Indeed, in some ways, such as eligibility for ownership of land, the natives of Africa were better off than the Indians. Moreover, it is doubtful whether, at the turn of the century, the black population in South Africa would have readily accepted a young Indian barrister as its leader. The position which

Gandhi came to acquire in the Indian immigrant community during those two decades owed a great deal to a certain ethos: his personality, his methods, and his cult of non-violence were hardly likely to have the same appeal for other racial groups. In February 1936, Gandhi told a visitor that he had deliberately not invited the blacks to join his movement in South Africa. 'They would not have understood,' he said, 'the technique of our struggle nor could they have seen the purpose and utility of our non-violence.'

A sound instinct seems to have guided the young Gandhi to wage his battle against racialism on a limited front. It was during these years in South Africa that he acquired those remarkable qualities of leadership that later enabled him to play his great role in the Indian struggle for freedom. The rulers of South Africa stubbornly opposed even the very modest demands of the tiny Indian minority because they were worried about its implications for the millions of the natives of Africa. If Gandhi had challenged the Boer–British combine on the all-embracing issue of racial equality, he would have been immediately thrown out of South Africa. In that event, Gandhi's great experiment in satyagraha would have been cut short and the cause of racial equality would have suffered the most in the long run.

There is evidence that by 1909 Gandhi had realized the inherent limitations of the Indians' struggle in South Africa. The satyagraha campaign had its ups and downs, and his trip to England had been a failure. He needed a successful conclusion of the struggle in Transvaal not only for its own sake, but also as a prelude to his return to India, taking satyagraha with him, to challenge British imperialism. He seems to have sensed the basic truth that white racialism was nurtured by white rule over the subject races of Asia and Africa. If European colonialism could be ended, racialism would also go. In 1921, in the course of his first major campaign against the British Raj, Gandhi declared: 'I seek to deliver the so-called weaker races of the earth from the crushing heels of western exploitation in which England is the greatest partner. India's coming into her own will mean every nation doing likewise.' Twenty-six years later, when Indian independence became a reality, it accelerated, as Gandhi had predicted, the process of the liquidation of both colonialism and racialism in Asia and Africa.

It is a curious irony of history that the country in which Gandhi for the first time raised his voice against racialism was the last to free itself from it. The racial problem in South Africa was complicated by the fact that a sizeable segment of the population consisted of immigrants of British and Dutch origin, who had settled in the country and who possessed a monopoly of political and economic power and regarded other races—black, brown and yellow—as inferior. Gandhi left South Africa in 1914, but he blazed a trail which the coming generations were to follow. The South African National Native Congress (later renamed African National Congress) had come into existence in 1912, two years before Gandhi's departure; its constitution endorsed 'passive action', i.e. passive resistance or satyagraha as a means of fighting against injustice and oppression. Repression by the police and aggression by the dominant European community frustrated the use of the Gandhian strategy but in 1946 the Indian Congress in Natal and Transvaal, under a new leadership, embarked upon a passive resistance campaign. Thousands of people joined, including the younger African nationalists such as Nelson Mandela. In 1949, and in the early 1950s, a programme embracing boycott, strikes and civil disobedience was adopted by the African National Congress (ANC). Three years later, there was a 'Defiance Campaign' in which Gandhi's son Manilal participated and 8500 Africans and their allies went to jail. The Zulu chief Luthuli, the President-General of the African National Congress from 1952 to 1967, who was later to receive the Nobel Peace Prize, was profoundly influenced by Gandhi's teachings. He advocated non-violent resistance as a 'non-revolutionary, legitimate and humane means to bring about partnership in the government of the country on the basis of equality'.

For nearly forty years the African National Congress adhered to the principle of non-violence, the legacy of Gandhi's struggle in South Africa. It was not until the late 1950s, after the Sharpeville massacre, that the ANC abandoned non-violence. The same thing happened in the Portguese colonies of Angola and Mozambique and the UN Trust territory of Namibia (which was under the South African government) and the British colony of Rhodesia. The liberation movements in these countries too forsook constitutional and peaceful methods and opted for guerilla warfare.

It is a remarkable fact that even after the adoption of armed struggle by the African National Congress, the liberation movement in South Africa received valuable assistance from students, industrial workers, religious bodies, and women's and youth groups which organized peaceful struggles on specific issues and culminated in the 'United Democratic Front'. All these forms of resistance were not consciously Gandhian. Indeed, many of those who led the resistance believed in violence, but discovered that 'active civil resistance' was more relevant to the conditions in which they had found themselves. As Yash Tandon points out in a recent article,

And this is the point about the resistance against the South African state and system between Sharpeville and the release of Mandela—it was conducted, by and large, by methods which Gandhi would have generally approved, i.e. by methods of active civil resistance ... The true liberators of South Africa ... are the millions—men, women and children—who fought inside South Africa, in factories and farms, in schools and colleges, in shanty towns and street committees. They fought by means which would have made Gandhi proud.[2]

'The saint has left our shores', General Smuts wrote in 1914 to a friend soon after Gandhi's departure, 'I sincerely hope for ever.' What Smuts failed to foresee was that the spirit and example of Gandhi would continue to inspire the oppressed races of Africa for the rest of the century. *The South African Gandhi* provides a fitting answer to those critics of Gandhi who have sought to belittle his contribution to the struggle against apartheid. The best minds of South Africa today have no doubt about his contribution.

Indeed, they are asking themselves whether Gandhi's ideas will continue to inspire them in the coming years in facing the challenges of political and social integration and economic reconstruction. Lewis Skweyiya, the president of the Institute for Black Research, which sponsored *The South African Gandhi*, describes Gandhi as 'a universal man ... as relevant today as he was yesterday, as he will be tomorrow'. Justice Ismail Mahomed harks back to Gandhi's unique 'pulsating restlessness' which had the power to release the spiritual potential of the people. Alec Erwin wonders whether the spirit of Gandhi will 'translate into a new form of participative governance' in the new multiracial South Africa.

One of the finest tributes to Gandhi in this volume comes from an unexpected quarter. In a perceptive commentary, F.W. de Klerk argues that Gandhi highlighted the truth that governments ultimately cannot govern without the consent of the governed. He describes satyagraha or non-violent resistance, as Gandhi's greatest contribution to global politics for bringing about social change. 'We have completed', de Klerk says, 'the task of dismantling the edifice of apartheid. The causes for which Gandhi fought have been won.'

NOTES AND REFERENCES

1. Fatima Meer (ed.), *The South African Gandhi: An Abstract of Speeches and Writings of M.K. Gandhi, 1893–1914* (Madiba Publishers, Durban, 1996).
2. Yash Tandon, 'Gandhi's Relevance in Contemporary Southern Africa', *in* B.R. Nanda (ed.), *Mahatma Gandhi 125 Years* (Delhi, 1995), p. 301.

FIVE

Encounters with Death

On 21 January 1948, the day after a bomb exploded in Birla House, D.W. Mehra, the Chief of the Delhi Police, went to see Mahatma Gandhi and sought his permission to search for any 'suspicious looking characters' who came to his prayer meetings. 'If you do this', the Mahatma said, 'I will leave Delhi and denounce you as the reason for my departure.' Mehra reported the result of his interview to the Home Minister, Sardar Patel. The following day the Sardar met the Mahatma, but found him adamant on this point. He repeated to Patel what he had told Mehra: 'My life is in God's hands and nobody can save me from death if it has to come.'

Such a remark may seem natural when coming from a man of faith who believed that 'not a leaf moves but by His will'. It could, however, also have stemmed from the experience of a lifetime. There were several occasions when Gandhi's life had hung by the slenderest thread. In February 1943, the doctors had at one stage lost all hope of his surviving the 21-day fast, and the government had prepared plans for his funeral; in 1934, a bomb narrowly missed him in the course of his Harijan tour when he was on his way to the Poona Municipal Hall; in 1927 he miraculously escaped an attack of apoplexy; in 1918, an acute attack of dysentery had brought him to the verge of a collapse; in 1908, he had been savagely belaboured by a rugged compatriot in Johannesburg. However, perhaps the most serious threat to his life came very early in his political career when, at the age of twenty-seven, he was nearly lynched in the streets of Durban. That first encounter with death was one of the most dramatic episodes in his life, which revealed, as if in a flash, the nature of the virulent racialism in South Africa a hundred years ago, and the calibre of the man who was to challenge it.

As is well-known, Gandhi had gone to South Africa in 1893 on a year's contract as the legal adviser of Dada Abdulla, an Indian merchant, who was involved in litigation with another merchant. In 1894, when he came to Durban to catch a steamer for India, the news of imminent racial legislation in Natal to disenfranchise Indian immigrants led him to stay back. He founded the Natal Indian Congress and mobilized the Indian community to protest against racial discrimination. When it appeared that public activities and legal work would keep him tied down to Natal, he paid a visit to India in the summer of 1896 to fetch his family, and incidentally to canvass whatever support he could for the Indian cause in South Africa. He visited Bombay, Calcutta, Poona, Madras, and other towns, interviewed eminent leaders such as Ranade, Pherozeshah Mehta, Gokhale and Tilak, and addressed public meetings to educate Indian opinion on the disabilities of Indians in South Africa.

Unfortunately for Gandhi, distorted versions of his utterances and activities in India were published in newspapers in Natal, and inflamed the Europeans of that colony. A four-line cable from Reuter's London Office was prominently featured in the Natal papers:

September 14. A pamphlet published in India declares that Indians in Natal are robbed and assaulted and treated like beasts and are unable to obtain redress. *The Times of India* advocates an enquiry into these allegations.

The reference in this news item was to a pamphlet which Gandhi had published in India. This pamphlet was, if anything, more subdued in tone than what he had written and said in Natal. His speeches in India had been delivered from carefully prepared texts. So reasonable was his stand, and so transparent his sense of fairness, that the editor of Calcutta's *Englishman* let him see the draft of an editorial on the Indian question in South Africa.

Gandhi's trip to India was abruptly interrupted when he received a cable urging him to return immediately. He sailed by SS *Courland* along with his wife and three young sons, Harilal, Manilal, and Ramdas. It so happened that another ship, SS *Naderi* left Bombay for Natal at about the same time. Gandhi's client, Dada Abdulla, was the owner of one ship and the agent of the other. It was just by coincidence that the two ships had sailed almost at the same time at the end of November 1896 and they reached Durban on 18 December. To the Europeans of Natal, already excited by Reuter's report, the coincidence had the appearance of a conspiracy. On the day Reuter's summary appeared in the newspapers, there was a meeting of Europeans at Maritzburg at which it was decided to form a 'European Protection Association' 'to preserve and defend the rights and privileges of European colonists'. Ten weeks later, when Gandhi was about to sail from Bombay, the Mayor of Durban addressed a meeting in the Town Hall; on 4 December, a 'Colonial Patriotic Union' was constituted 'to prevent influx of Asiatics into Natal'. A 'Demonstration Committee' was formed to prevent the landing of Indian passengers in the two ships. All kinds of rumours were rife in the city of Durban. It was said that the two ships had 800 passengers, all bound for Natal, and that Gandhi had organized an immigration agency to land one to two thousand of his countrymen every month.

After the two ships cast anchor in the port, attempts were made to coax, cajole, or coerce the Indians. A free return passage was dangled before those who would agree to go back; and those who declined were threatened that they would be pushed into the sea. The shipowners were left in no doubt that if they did not return their unwelcome cargo to India, they would incur the implacable wrath of the government and the European population of Natal. On 18 December the Governor-in-Council declared Bombay to be a plague-infected port; on the following day it was notified that all vessels arriving from Bombay would be quarantined 'till further notice'. As there had been no sickness aboard and the ships had been at sea for eighteen days, the period of quarantine should not have exceeded five days. However, when the duration of quarantine was prolonged to three weeks, its political implications became obvious.

Meanwhile, feeling was running high in the European community in Durban. On 4 January 1897 two thousand Europeans assembled in the Town Hall and called upon the government to prevent 'the free Indians' from disembarking, and to order their repatriation. There was more than a veiled hint of the use of force against the Indians in the two ships. One of the leaders of the Demonstration Committee, Dr Mackenzie, who was 'Captain of the Naval Carbineers', declared that Gandhi had 'dragged the people of Natal in the gutters' and painted them 'as black and filthy as his own skin'. J.S. Wylie, a solicitor, who was 'Captain of the Durban Light Infantry', delivered an inflammatory speech:

The Indian Ocean was the proper place for these Indians [applause]. Let them have it [laughter]. They were not going to dispute that right to the water there.

The hall resounded with cries of 'Sink the Ship'. When Wylie was granted a two-hour interview by Harry Escombe, the Attorney-General and Defence Minister of Natal, he told Escombe: 'If you do nothing, we will have to act ourselves; and to go in force to the Point [the harbour] and see what could be done.'

These were anxious days for Gandhi. The lives of these passengers, most of whom he did not know, and of his own family were in jeopardy on his account. It was he who was the *bête* noire of the Europeans of Natal. On Christmas Day the Gandhi family were the chief guests at a dinner given by the captain of the ship. Someone asked Gandhi what he would do if the Natal Europeans were as good as their word and used force to obstruct the landing of the Indians. 'I hope', he said, 'God will give me the courage and the sense to forgive them and to refrain from bringing them to the law. I have no anger against them. I am only sorry for their ignorance and their narrowness.'

On 11 January 1897, Dada Abdulla, whom the 'political quarantine' of the ships was costing £150 a day, suggested in a letter to Escombe, the Attorney-General, that the passengers should be allowed to disembark quietly at night. Escombe was evasive. However, Dada Abdulla and his legal adviser F.A. Laughton, decided to force the government's hand. On 12 January they informed the Attorney-General that the ships would land their passengers on the following day, 'relying on the protection which we respectfully submit the government is bound to give us'. The stratagem succeeded. Escombe, who had done much to fan the fanaticism of the Europeans, now tried to check it. Thousands of European demonstrators had assembled in Alexandria Square, and were being addressed by their leaders. Cries of 'Send these Indians back', 'Why don't you bring Gandhi ashore?' rent the air. Escombe commanded them in the name of the Queen (Victoria) to disperse peacefully, and assured them that the Natal government would look into the whole question of Indian immigration.

At 3 p.m. on 13 January the Indian passengers from the two ships disembarked without incident. Gandhi and his family, however, remained aboard the SS *Courland*. Escombe had sent a message to him to wait till the evening, when he would be escorted by the Superintendent of Water Police. At about 4.30 p.m., however, Laughton, the solicitor, who was also a friend of Gandhi, came aboard, announced that all danger was at an end, and that in any case it was undignified for him to slip out into Durban like a thief at night. Laughton had seen innuendoes in the Natal press, suggesting that Gandhi was a coward, that he was hiding himself below decks in the *Courland*, and was afraid to land. 'If you are not afraid', Laughton said, 'I suggest that Mrs Gandhi and the children should drive to Parsi Rustomji's house, whilst you and I follow them on foot.' 'Let us go then', Gandhi replied. With the Captain's permission, he went ashore with Laughton. He was recognized by some European boys who began to shout 'Gandhi', 'Gandhi Boo-oo', 'Thrash him', 'Surround him'.

The sky was overcast; Parsi Rustomji's house was two miles away; the crowd was swelling and becoming more and more menacing. Laughton hailed a rickshaw, but the Zulu boy pulling it, was scared away. Gandhi and Laughton then started walking together, followed by the screaming mob. At the junction of West Street, the principal thoroughfare of Durban, Laughton was torn away. A hailstorm of rotten eggs, mud, stale fish, and stones was raining round Gandhi. 'Are you the man who wrote to the Press?', shouted a European and gave him a brutal kick. Another European hit Gandhi with a riding whip. His turban fell off and he was thrown down. A stone struck him on his head. 'I was about to fall down unconscious,' Gandhi recalled later, 'when I held on to the railings of a house nearby. I took breath for a while and when the fainting was over, proceeded on my way. But it was impossible. They came upon me boxing and battering ... I had almost given up the hope of reaching home alive. But I remember well that even then my heart did not arraign my assailants.' Then (in the words of Joseph Doke, Gandhi's first biographer) 'a beautiful and brave thing happened'. Mrs Alexander, the wife of the Superintendent of Police at Durban, happened to be walking from the opposite direction. Both she and her husband knew Gandhi well. She recognized him and began to walk alongside him and opened her sunshade, even though it was already dark, to stave off the flying missiles. The Europeans had run amuck, but they dared not raise their hand to a white woman. Meanwhile, a few constables arrived and escorted Gandhi to Parsi Rustomji's house.

Hardly had Gandhi's wounds been dressed, when a European mob collected around the house of his host and shouted: 'We want Gandhi.' Superintendent Alexander, who had taken his position at the entrance to the house, vainly tried to persuade the crowd to disperse. He sent for the Deputy Mayor, but the mob did not listen to his appeals either, and threatened to burn the house if Gandhi did not surrender himself. Alexander sent word to Gandhi to agree to being smuggled out of the house if he did not want to have all the inmates, including women and children, to be roasted alive. At first Gandhi strongly objected to the suggestion of the Police Superintendent, but then he realized that this was perhaps the only way of saving several innocent lives. Dressed as an Indian constable, with a metal saucer under his turban, and attended by a detective, he slipped through the crowd and after jumping fences, squeezing between rails and passing through a grocer's store he reached the police station. Superintendent Alexander then allowed two Europeans from the crowd along with a police inspector to search the building to satisfy themselves that Gandhi was no longer there. When the crowd realized that it had been outwitted, it melted away.

Gandhi did not have to remain in the police station for long. The Natal Europeans had been provoked by Reuter's brief and garbled report of Gandhi's activities in India. On the morning of the day on which he was assaulted, he had, in an interview with a press correspondent, explained away the various charges against him. It became clear that he had been the victim of a misunderstanding. For the events of 13 January the Natal Government came in for severe criticism even in the European press in South Africa. As *Cape Argus* put it, 'For a week the Natal Ministry permitted the situation to develop, without pretence at the feeblest intervention, their policy suggesting an unofficial sanction of the whole business.' 'The Natalians', wrote the *Johannesburg Times*, 'appear to have lost their heads.' 'A crime', wrote the *E.P. Herald*, 'is no less a crime because it has been committed by a whole town instead of by one man.'

Harry Escombe, the most powerful member of the Natal Government, who combined great ability, tact, ambition, and lack of scruple, had his own reasons for playing a dubious role in this whole affair. A general election was in the offing; he did not want to lose any votes. His tactics paid off when later in the year he emerged as the Premier of Natal.

It was quite natural that the news of the assault on Gandhi should have shocked those of his compatriots, who took an interest in the problems of Indians living abroad. Gokhale described it as 'a tale which no Indian can read without bitterness, and no right-minded Englishman ought to read without a feeling of deep shame and indignation'.

Gandhi had no illusions about the risks he was running, but he accepted them as part of the responsibility he had undertaken in leading the beleagured Indian community in that part of the world. Of the 400-odd Indians who had landed from the two ships at Durban on 13 January, 190 returned to India when the SS *Courland* and the SS *Naderi* left Durban on their return voyage to India. Ten weeks after the incident Gandhi wrote to F.S. Taleyarkhan, a young barrister who was planning to come to Natal: 'It is a question whether it would be advisable, in the present state of public feeling, for you to land in Natal as a public man. Such a man's life in Natal is at present in danger.' Gandhi's friend, barrister Laughton, who had witnessed Gandhi's ordeal on 13 January, paid a tribute to him in the *Natal Mercury*: 'Throughout the trying procession, his manliness and pluck could not have been surpassed, and I can assure

Natal that he is a man who must be treated as a man. Intimidation is out of the question, because, if he knew, the Town Hall were going to be thrown at him, I believe from what I saw, that he would not quail.'

Among the Europeans who condemned the outrage was A.M. Cameron, special representative of the *Times of India* in Natal. He described the European demonstration as 'a perfect disgrace ... an Englishman must blush at it ... I did not know him [Gandhi] and would never have known him, but for these doings ... I am sure he showed more courage in landing and facing his situation than all the hundreds who mobbed him.'

When questions were asked in the House of Commons, Joseph Chamberlain, the Secretary of State for Colonies in the British Cabinet, cabled the Natal government to take action against Gandhi's assailants. Harry Escombe, the Attorney-General, invited Gandhi to meet him. Gandhi told Escombe that it was a principle with him not to seek redress of a personal wrong in a court of law. 'Prosecuting my assailants is', he told the Attorney-General, 'out of the question. This is a religious question with me.' When the Attorney-General asked him to put this down in writing, Gandhi did so at once. Escombe was glad to get this letter which saved him and his government from embarrassment.

Gandhi did not indulge in self-pity or heroics, but he turned the incident to good account in his political battle against racial discrimination. He sent off a 500-word cable to *The Times* (London), copies of which were sent to Bhownaggree, the Indian member of the British Parliament, and the British Committee of the Indian National Congress. He drafted a memorial on behalf of the Indian community which ran to nearly 50,000 words and detailed the lawless conduct of the Durban Europeans, and the new anti-Indian laws which the Natal government was hurrying through the Natal legislature.

A quarter of a century after the incident, Gandhi wrote that he had 'a most valuable experience and whenever I think of that day, I feel that God was preparing me for the practice of Satyagraha'. In January 1897, Gandhi had been in South Africa for less than four years; his struggle for basic human rights of the Indian immigrants there was to continue for another seventeen years. His discovery of satyagraha was yet nine years away. That voluntary surrender of his right to seek redress against his assailants was a remarkable gesture, but much was to happen to Gandhi and to South Africa before the young barrister and the budding politician of 1897 would grow into a world leader. It is a mind-boggling thought that Gandhi's life might have been snuffed out on the threshold of his career before he had completed his twenty-eighth year, fifty-one years before he fell to Godse's bullets. Mercifully, that night of terror in Durban on 13 January 1897 did not end in tragedy; Gandhi survived it and other ordeals that in subsequent years brought him face to face with death. He was firmly convinced that God would keep him alive on this earth so long as He had some work for him; this belief did not induce fatalism in him but only helped him to take upon himself the sins and sorrows of his countrymen, and to fearlessly face the unending series of crises— some of his own seeking and others forced upon him—which were to be his lot in his long and crowded public life.

SIX

Gandhi's Identity Crisis

He was wearing a high silk top hat burnished bright, a Gladstonian collar, stiff and starched, a rather flashy tie displaying almost all the colours of the rainbow under which there was a fine striped silk shirt. He wore as his outer clothes a morning coat, a double-breasted vest, and dark-striped trousers to match and not only patent leather boots, but spats over them. He carried leather gloves, and a silver mounted stick, but wore no spectacles. He was, to use the contemporary slang, a nut, a masher, a blood—a student more interested in fashion frivolities than in his studies.

This is how the twenty-year old Mohandas Gandhi struck the future liberal leader, Sachidananda Sinha, when he saw him in Piccadilly Circus in February 1890. Gandhi had already been in England for nearly sixteen months, but was still struggling to make the transition from the rural surroundings of Rajkot to the cosmopolitan atmosphere of London. Adaptation to Western food, dress, and etiquette had not been easy. His friends feared that his food fads would ruin his health and make of him socially, a square peg in a round hole. To disprove his critics and to prove that, vegetarianism apart, he was not impervious to the new environment, he decided to assume a thick veneer of 'English culture'. He set out to transform himself into an 'English gentleman', and spared neither time nor expense to do so. He ordered new suits from the most fashionable tailors in London, adorned his watch with a gold chain from India, and took lessons in elocution, dancing, and music. He could not, however, throw himself into this experiment with complete self-abandon. As the habit of introspection had not deserted him, it dawned upon him that drapers and dance halls could turn him into an English gentleman, but only an English gentleman about town. Back home in Rajkot, his brother, Lakshmidas, was straining the slender resources of the family, perhaps incurring debts, to enable him to continue his studies in England. After a brief three months' excursion, the introvert returned to his shell; there was a rebound from extreme extravagance to meticulous economy. He changed his rooms, cooked his own breakfast, and to save his fares walked eight to ten miles a day. He was able to pare down his expenses to £2 a month. Simplicity harmonized his inward and outward life.

We may laugh at young Gandhi's effort to anglicize himself; the chapter dealing with it in his autobiography is entitled 'Playing the English Gentleman'. The fact was that most Indian students, who went to England for higher studies or to compete for the Indian Civil Service, readily put on the Western veneer. Jinnah, the future founder of Pakistan, who came to England four years after Gandhi, lost no time in casting off his traditional Kathiawari coat and turban and switching to smart suits. Jinnah's transformation was not merely sartorial; his anglicism, unlike Gandhi's, was uninhibited and total; till the end of his life he kept up the lifestyle of an upper-class English gentleman. Before leaving England he even modernized his name by changing 'Mohammad Ali Jinnahbhai' to 'M.A. Jinnah'.

Of the fascination of Westernization for the Indian middle class an interesting example is furnished by Aurobindo Ghose, the great patriot and sage of Pondicherry, who was three years younger than Gandhi. His father had packed him off to England at the age of seven, and instructed his English tutor not to let him make acquaintance of an Indian or expose himself to any Indian influence. These instructions were faithfully carried out, and Aurobindo grew up in complete ignorance of India, her people, her religions, and her culture. Indeed, he learnt his mother tongue, Bengali, only when he returned to his country at the age of twenty-one.

Jawaharlal Nehru, who was twenty years younger than Gandhi, belonged to one of the most anglicized families in India at the turn of the century. His father, Motilal Nehru, enjoyed an enormous practice at the Bar of the Allahabad High Court. He had clashed head-on with Hindu orthodoxy, defied the caste taboo on foreign travel, dressed, lived, and even looked like an Englishman. The process of 'modernization' in the Nehru household included Western furnishings and the use of knives and forks at the dining table as well as the employment of European governesses and resident tutors for the children. He sent his son to study in England, and even envisaged for him a career in the Indian Civil Service, the 'steel frame' of the British Raj. In 1922, in his statement to the court, Jawaharlal confessed that when he returned from England after seven years' stay, he had 'imbibed most of the prejudices of Harrow and Cambridge' and in his likes and dislikes 'was perhaps more an Englishman than an Indian'.

Most Indians who completed their education in England, came to consider the two or three years they spent in that country as the most eventful period of their lives. They became aliens to their cultural heritage, and were proud to show off their anglicism. The British writer, Malcolm Muggeridge, who was on the editorial staff of *The Statesman,* (Calcutta) in early 1930s, vividly described one such 'Brown Sahib' in his memoirs:

There was for instance, B, a barrister-at-law, who had been at Harrow and Oxford. His ostensible purpose was to collect a book for review ... His appearance still bore some traces of Inns of Court formality—alpaca jacket, winged collar, watch chain, but with the lost eyes, weak mouth and sometimes tremulous hands of a drunkard. He had legal tales to tell—repartee of a Birkenhead, eloquence of a Patrick Hastings, skill of a Birkett. 'My guru', he said to me once, 'is Hilaire Belloc'. It was almost unbearably poignant; after all he was our creation.

Fortunately for Gandhi, the three years he spent in England did not turn him into a 'Brown Sahib', but nonetheless constituted a strong formative influence. After his return to India in 1891, he began, as indeed was expected of a young barrister, to 'modernize' his mode of living. Oatmeal porridge, cocoa, Western furnishing and attire were some of the 'reforms' he introduced; they added to the mounting expense of his household at a time when he was able to contribute very little to it. When he sailed for Durban in 1893, he was unable to secure a first-class passage, but preferred squeezing himself into the captain's cabin to the indignity of travelling on deck.

Gandhi's pride as an England-educated barrister had been hurt in the brush he had with Charles Ollivant, the British political agent at Rajkot, and this indeed had led him to welcome the not overly attractive offer of a year's assignment in South Africa. Further assaults on his self-esteem came in quick succession soon after he arrived in Natal. He was ordered by a European magistrate at Durban to take off his turban. His journey from Durban to Pretoria proved to be a nightmare. When his train reached Maritzburg station late in the evening, he was ordered to shift to the van compartment and when he refused, he was unceremoniously ejected from the first class carriage.

Hitherto, neither in India nor in England had Gandhi been conspicuous for assertiveness, but something happened to him in that bleak, windswept waiting room of Maritzburg railway station as he smarted under the insult inflicted on him. His humiliation was the more galling because he was conscious of his Western education and status as a barrister of the Inner Temple. In retrospect, this incident struck him as one of the most creative experiences of his life. The iron entered his soul. He resolved that he would not be a willing victim of racial arrogance. It was not merely a question of redeeming his own self-respect but that of his community, his country, even of humanity. The helpless resignation of the mass of Indian immigrants in Natal, the fact that they were mostly illiterate, possessed few rights and did not know how to assert their rights, all had the miraculous effect of dissipating his own diffidence.

II

While Gandhi was still bracing himself to face the challenge of racial discrimination, he was confronted with yet another. In Pretoria, he met some zealous Christian missionaries, who perceived his religious bent and decided to annex him to Christianity. They gave him books on Christian theology and history; they prayed with him and for him. They took him to a Convention of Protestant Christians in the hope that mass emotion would sweep him off his feet. The first impact of Quaker proselytization in a strange country must have been strong on young Gandhi. Even though he had grown up in a devout Hindu household, it was in England that he was first introduced by some Theosophist friends not only to the Bible but to the Bhagavad Gita. There is no doubt that the sojourn in England aroused Gandhi's interest in religion, but it was not yet deep, and might well have faded were it not for the missionaries in Pretoria, especially Michael Coates, who befriended him and sought to convert him. His mind was in a turmoil, but he had a rational and sceptical streak; he was in no greater hurry to become a Christian in Pretoria than he had been to become a Theosophist in London. His knowledge of Hinduism was yet superficial, but he felt a vague bond of sentiment with the religion of his birth.

The sentimental bond with Hinduism was strengthened by Gandhi's correspondence with some of his friends in India. Among them was a remarkable man, Rajchandra (Raychandbhai, as Gandhi called him), whom Gandhi had known in Bombay. Rajchandra deeply influenced Gandhi's religious quest. Rajchandra advised Gandhi to be patient and to seek in Hinduism its unique subtlety and profoundity of thought, its vision of the soul. Rajchandra's scholarly exposition helped to resolve Gandhi's doubts about Hinduism. 'I gained,' Gandhi wrote later, 'peace of mind. I felt reassured that Hinduism could give me what I needed.' Rajchandra was a Jain, but he had studied Hindu scriptures such as the Bhagavad Gita, the Bhagavata and Vedanta. He had read the Koran and Zend-Avesta in translation. He taught Gandhi to seek the underlying unity in the teachings of major religions.

Thanks to Rajchandra and the study of Hindu scriptures, Gandhi had realized his religious and cultural identity, which was to profoundly influence his personal and public life. There is no doubt that Hinduism transformed Gandhi, but he too transformed Hinduism. He gave a new meaning to several other age-old Hindu beliefs and practices such as sadhana, moksha, *brahmacharya*, ahimsa, *go-seva*, etc. Gandhi knew that elitist Hinduism tended to be abstract and mystical, and popular Hinduism, ritualistic, obscurantist and superstitious. He himself was tempted neither by the intellectual pleasures of philosophical disputation nor by the blissful joys of mysticism. 'What cannot be followed in day-to-day practice', he wrote, 'cannot be called religion.' 'The only scientific method', he wrote to a correspondent, 'of studying religious books is to study a little at a time and proceed after due assimilation, never accepting anything that is repugnant to one's moral sense. Each one must find out for himself how much he can read and digest.'

With such views it was inevitable that Gandhi's personal and professional life would take a different path from that of most of his contemporaries. As a lawyer in Durban and later in Johannesburg, he followed his own code of conduct for legal practice and considered it unethical to defend a client if he was in the wrong. His first civil suit in South Africa had convinced him that litigation dragged on because litigants feared the loss of face and the lawyers the loss of fees. To a colleague who protested that clients came even on Sundays, his answer was 'a man in distress cannot have Sunday rest'.

Ever since he returned from England, two conflicting pulls had been struggling within Gandhi for expression. One was the pull of convention, the desire to live up to the standard of an English-educated barrister, and the other was an inner urge towards simplicity. The inspiration for a simple life came from the *Gita* which he read and pondered over every day. The ideal of *aparigraha* (non-possession) grew upon him. He began to reduce his needs, and to pay less and less attention to what passed for standards of the middle class. The drive towards simplicity received a tremendous fillip in 1904 when Gandhi read Ruskin's *Unto This Last* in a train journey from Johannesburg to Durban in 1904. 'The book,' records the autobiography, 'confirmed and strengthened some of my own deepest convictions.' Before the train reached Durban, he had already resolved to adopt the design of the simple and austere life outlined in it. Within a few months the Phoenix Settlement came up; Gandhi could now live and work among people who shared his ideals. Over the next decade in South Africa, the transformation in Gandhi's life, the liberation from the bonds of money, property, and

sex enhanced his capacity for total absorption in public causes. These
changes in his personal life were to tremendously influence his public image
as well as his effectiveness as a political leader.

III

It was fortunate for Gandhi that his religious quest and his fight against
racial discrimination in South Africa started simultaneously. The religious
quest was not only to enable him to tap his inner resources and transform
his personality, but to equip him with the courage and stamina for the
political role he was called upon to play. It so happened that both in
South Africa and India he had to lead a multi-religious following. Thanks
to his religious mentor, Rajchandra, and his own study of major religions,
he had no difficulty in expanding his religious (Hindu) identity to embrace
a national (pan-Indian) identity. He declared that Hinduism satisfied
his soul and suffused his whole being. However, his Hinduism was 'not
an exclusive religion; in it there is room for worship of all the prophets of
the world. It is not a missionary religion in the ordinary sense of the term
... Hinduism tells everyone to worship God according to his own faith
or Dharma and so it lives at peace with all religions.'

Gandhi read books on Christianity and Islam in South Africa. While
in jail in India he read Maulana Shibli's biography of Prophet Muhammad
and also a volume on the companions of the Prophet. These studies led
him to the conclusion that the Quran and the Bible were sacred books
for him just as the Vedas and the Gita were. He found an underlying
unity in the teachings of the major religions. It was impossible, he wrote,
to estimate the relative merits of the various religions of the world, each
of which embodied 'a common motivating force: the desire to uplift man's
life and give it purpose'. As Margaret Chatterjee tells us,[1] Gandhi was
able to nourish his inner life through his friendships with men of other
faiths, and that it was this human contact with living faiths which helped
to 'sustain him and give depth to his experiences'.

Gandhi's advocacy of religious toleration originally stemmed from
his studies in comparative religion and his own spiritual quest, but it
had a practical aspect too when he took up the cause of his countrymen
in South Africa. He had to win and retain the allegiance of the Muslim
merchants who were the backbone of his struggle in Natal and Transvaal.
A time came, especially after the discovery of satyagraha, when Gandhi
began to see his campaign in South Africa as a prelude to a larger struggle
which might have to be waged one day in his homeland. In November

1907 he wrote to Rash Behari Ghosh, the president-elect of the Surat Session of the Indian National Congress that the Indians in Transvaal regarded themselves 'as the representatives in this country, of our Motherland, and it is impossible for us, as patriotic Indians, to keep silence under an insult that is levied against our race and our national honour'. Gandhi took particular pride in the fact that though Indians in Natal and the Transvaal included Muslims, Hindus, Christians, and Parsis, and came from different provinces of India, they were united in resisting injustice to which they were subjected by the colonial regime.

When he returned to India in 1915, Gandhi was hailed as the man who had solved the Hindu–Muslim problem in South Africa. He entertained high hopes of bringing the two communities together in his homeland. He did not know how intricate the web of Indo-British and Hindu–Muslim relations had become during the century and half of British rule in India. For the next thirty years he made strenuous efforts to draw Indian Muslims into the national mainstream, but with limited success. His hope that the 'grand gesture' of unconditional support by the Hindus to the Muslims on the issue of the Ottoman Caliphate would secure their lasting gratitude was not realized. It is not possible to discuss here the growth of Muslim separatism which culminated in the division of the country in 1947.[2] Gandhi has been charged with complicating the problem by introducing religion into politics. There has been much confusion of thought and misinterpretation of Gandhi's position on this. In the very paragraph in which he wrote that politics were not exempt from religion, he made it clear that he was not referring to the organized religion of dogmas, rituals, superstition and bigotry. 'Here religion does not mean', Gandhi wrote, 'sectarianism. It means belief in the ordered moral government of the universe.'

Gandhi's last days were saddened by the partition of India. The battle for Pakistan had been waged and won on the basis of the two-nation theory professed by the Muslim League and Gandhi was reviled as the foremost enemy of Islam, but even in that dark hour in 1947 he held on to his multi-religious world-view and his pluralistic vision of an independent India, the political content of which had been enunciated in the resolution on 'fundamental rights' passed by the Karachi Congress in 1931. That resolution had guaranteed equality before the law to all citizens, irrespective of caste, creed, or sex, and enjoined that 'the State should observe neutrality in regard to all religions'. These provisions were later enshrined in the constitution of the Indian Republic.

IV

While Gandhi's religious and national (pan-Indian) identities were fairly developed and perceived by his adherents as well as his opponents, when in South Africa, his transnational (universal) identity took longer to be recognized. One of the reasons for this time-lag was that Gandhi was engaged in a struggle against European racialism and imperialism; he was seen as the arch rebel against the British Empire. The fact that several other European countries possessed or wanted to possess colonies did not endear Gandhi to them. A few exceptional individuals such as Romain Rolland, C.F. Andrews, and Albert Einstein were quick to recognize Gandhi's stature, but the common image of the Mahatma in the inter-war years oscillated between that of an eccentric saint and that of an astute politician. Curiously, the prejudice against Gandhi in the British bureaucracy in India lasted almost till the end. In February 1947, just six months before the 'transfer of power', Lord Wavell, the last but one Viceroy, in a letter to King George VI, described Gandhi as 'a most inveterate enemy of the British', and in his diary described him as 'a malignant old man'.

Part of the mistrust of Gandhi in the West was due to the impression that he was an enemy of Western civilization. This impression had been fostered in the early decades of twentieth century by his little book *Hind Swaraj*. Written in 1909, on his return voyage to South Africa, after a frustrating visit to England, it was really directed at the young Indian anarchists who wanted to liberate India by using against the West its own weapon of the pistol and the bomb. It covered a wide range. It discussed 'Home Rule', the mainsprings of British authority in India, the parliamentary system of government, the Hindu–Muslim problem, the comparative efficacy of 'brute force' and 'soul force'. Its most striking feature, however, was the broadside against Western civilization. 'The tendency of the Indian civilization', Gandhi wrote, 'is to elevate the moral being, that of the Western civilization to perpetuate immorality. The latter is godless, the former is based on a belief in God.' He went on to denounce railways, law courts, and hospitals, which, he believed, were the gifts of that civilization to India.

This sharp critique of Western civilization in *Hind Swaraj* is baffling if we consider Gandhi's own exposure to it. From 1888, when he left for England to study law, until 1915 when he returned from South Africa, he was continually exposed to British influence apart from the two years (1891–3) he spent in India. In South Africa he lived in the English cities of Durban and Johannesburg. Even as he opposed the policies of the colonial government he made several English friends. In 1915 he confided to Kaka Kalelkar, who was to become his lifelong associate, how much he loved the English language. 'If I have given up anything for national service', Gandhi told Kalelkar, 'it is my interest in English literature. Renouncing wealth and career was no sacrifice; I wasn't really interested in them. But I was completely fascinated by English literature.' He imbibed the British habits of punctuality and understatement. He carefully observed the workings of democratic institutions in South Africa, even though they excluded non-whites from the full privileges of citizenship. He learnt how to use the publicity media, the platform and the press, to air grievances and mobilize public opinion. He read Western writers; and significantly, in the list of twenty books he recommended to the readers of *Hind Swaraj*, all but two were by them.

When Gandhi wrote *Hind Swaraj*, he had much to worry about; his movement in South Africa had reached a dead end, his pleas to British ministers had gone unheeded; he was disturbed by the drift of radical Indian youth towards political terrorism. The tenor of the book seems to have been affected by the state of Gandhi's mind in 1909, but it is wrong to present it, as has often been done, as the definitive statement of Gandhi's thought on every subject. As Rajmohan Gandhi puts it in his book *The Good Boatman*, *Hind Swaraj* is 'a text for its time, not a text for all times' and it is Gandhi's 'first, and not the last word'. The fact is that in this little book Gandhi's real target was industrial civilization and not Western civilization. This becomes clear from his subsequent clarifications. Twelve years later, he wrote in *Young India*, his weekly journal, that nothing could be farther from his thought than that 'we [Indians] should become exclusive or erect barriers. But I respectfully contend that an appreciation of other cultures can fitly follow, never precede, an appreciation and assimilation of our own'. He expressed the same idea more graphically when he said, 'I do not want my windows to be stuffed. I want the cultures of all lands to be blown about my house, as freely as possible. But I refuse to be blown off my feet.'

Some of the insights in *Hind Swaraj* can be better appreciated today in the post Cold-War era, bedevilled, as it is with religious fundamentalism, ethnic violence, terrorism, the nuclear menace and the looming threat of an ecological disaster. It was, however, too extreme a statement for the pre-1914 generation. Gokhale, Gandhi's political mentor and closest friend, who read it in 1912, pronounced it crude, and predicted that Gandhi himself would destroy it after spending a year in India. Gandhi's thesis was thus questioned not only by his Western critics but by Indian nationalists, who looked forward to making India an independent, industrialized, and strong nation-state that would take its place in the comity of nations. The book fostered an image of Gandhi as a vehement opponent of Western, and indeed, 'modern' civilization; his ideas came to be dismissed as pre-modern, obscurantist, and impractical. Gandhi's words and actions in succeeding decades did not justify it. The image was not true, but it has persisted to this day. He tried hard to keep the nationalist struggle free from racial bitterness; his fight, he said, was not against the English people but against the colonial system of which they were as much victims as the Indians.

It has been suggested that Gandhi's religious and 'Indian' image restricted, and perhaps still restricts, his appeal to the people of the West. Syed Hossain, an Oxford-trained Indian nationalist, in his book *Gandhi, The Saint and Statesman* published in 1937, recalled a lecture he had delivered on Gandhi in the United States. After the lecture, someone from the audience got up and said, 'Ladies and gentlemen, we of the Western world cannot follow the leadership of a man who goes about half-naked'. 'The most important thing about Mahatma Gandhi', Syed Hossain replied, 'is not what he wears; the most important thing about Mahatma Gandhi is not even his body; the most important thing about Mahatma Gandhi is his soul. As for the alleged inability of the Western peoples to accept the leadership of someone not conventionally clad, I am reminded that the one whom they call their Master was also clad in nothing more than a loin-cloth at a crucial moment in the history of humanity.'

The cultural block certainly existed, but it did not inhibit the understanding of Gandhi by leaders of Asian and African nationalism like Kenneth Kaunda of Zambia, Kwame Nkrumah of Ghana, and Nelson Mandela of Africa, or of Martin Luther King of the United States. Nor has it prevented earnest pacifists, environmentalists, and anti-nuclear crusaders in Europe and America in recent decades from responding to Gandhian thought.

V

If Gandhi had not gone to South Africa, like many middle-class English-educated Indians, he would in all likelihood have passed through an identity crisis on the question of Westernizing (or 'modernizing') his mode of life. He would, however, have somehow muddled through, as most of his contemporaries did, and made compromises to suit his income and his social situation in Rajkot or Bombay. The identity crisis he experienced on arrival in South Africa in 1893 was, however, qualitatively different.

One wonders whether it ever occurred to Gandhi that the three greatest benefactors of his life were Mr Charles Ollivant, the Political Agent of Rajkot, who had thrown him out of his house, the nameless white railway official who had bundled him out of a first-class carriage at Maritzburg railway station in South Africa, and Mr Michael Coates, the irrepressible missionary at Pretoria who was in a desperate rush to save Gandhi's soul. These three men in quick succession, unwittingly, conspired to trigger the process of self-examination, self-preservation, and self-assertion in the young Gandhi by threatening both his racial and religious identities. In a strange land thousands of miles away from his home, family, and friends, and, in what was evidently a very hostile environment, Gandhi was driven to ask himself: 'Who am I?' The upshot of this self-exploration was that he rediscovered Hinduism, the religion of his birth. He was imbued with a new confidence and new vistas for personal growth. Thanks to his religious mentor, Rajchandra, and his own study of major religions, he expanded his Hindu identity into a multi-religious (pan-Indian) identity that was to prove an inestimable asset in his political role as the leader of the national cause both in South Africa and India. The struggle against European racialism and imperialism would in the ordinary course have generated racial bitterness against the foreign oppressors, but it was minimized, if not wholly eliminated, by Gandhi's transnational (universal) identity, and the ethical framework of satyagraha that ruled out hatred and violence. In retrospect this transnational identity may seem surprising in the leader of the greatest nationalist movement in history. In Gandhi's case, however, it was a logical development. This third identity, like the other two, the religious (Hindu) and the multi-religious (pan-Indian), drew its dynamic from the same source: his inner spiritual core. 'My mission', he wrote in 1929, 'is not merely brotherhood of Indian humanity. My mission is not merely freedom of India, though today it undoubtedly engrosses the whole of my life and the whole of my time. But through the realization of freedom of India, I hope to realize and carry on the mission of the brotherhood of man.' Gandhi was not indulging in a vague humanitarianism. Five years earlier, at the Belgaum Congress, he had declared that what the world desired was not absolutely independent states 'warring against one another', but a federation of friendly interdependent states. He died soon after India became independent, but his passion for peace and cooperation among nations in an embattled world found expression in Jawaharlal Nehru's foreign policy.

Gandhi had developed the three identities in South Africa by the time he had turned forty. They were not mutually exclusive, nor were they projected (or perceived) equally strongly all the time. The national identity was dominant in South Africa and in India, especially during the satyagraha struggles. There were however interludes, such as during 1932–4, when during a period of political lull, Gandhi's religious (Hindu) identity was noticeable in his crusade against untouchability. In periods of political tension, such as during the Second World War, while the British and the Hindus continued to see him as the leader of Indian nationalism, the Muslim intelligentsia, thanks to Jinnah's propaganda blitz, began to see him solely as a Hindu leader. Gandhi took the changing perceptions of the government and of his political opponents in his stride. Neither kudos nor criticism could divert him from his goals and methods.

We have already noted Gandhi's flair for creative transmutation of ideas in the Indian tradition. He did the same with the ideas that came to him from foreign sources. He paid tributes to Tolstoy and Thoreau for their insights into civil disobedience, but the reality is that these great writers only provided Gandhi with a reassurance and confirmation necessary to allow him to proceed along the path on which he had already embarked. Ruskin's *Unto This Last* could hardly have brought about a revolution in Gandhi's lifestyle had he not already been inclined towards it. Besides, in all these cases he went much farther than these great writers did themselves. What was an individual ethic, a matter of conscience for Tolstoy and Thoreau, turned in Gandhi's hands into a tool for non-violent mass action. Similarly, Ruskin's recipes for a simple life, and manual labour (which he never followed in his own life) became in Gandhi's hands a blueprint for community life, and eventually for the radical concept of *Sarvodaya*.

Gandhi did not make claims to profound scholarship. He was, he said, '... not built for academic writings. Action is my domain'. C.F. Andrews aptly described him as the 'Saint of Action, not of Contemplation'. Though Gandhi explained his thoughts in hundreds of articles and letters, he never tried to build them into a system. He talked of his 'experiments with truth', but he sought this truth not in textbooks, but in the challenging context of action and conflict. He had not only to discover the truth for himself but also to find the terms on which he could cooperate with others. In action he revealed a combination of radicalism and realism that confounded both his followers and opponents. To quote N.K. Bose, Gandhi's 'greatness lay ... in his inner restlessness, ceaseless striving and intense involvement in the problems of mankind. He was not a slave to ideas and concepts, which were for him aids in grappling with human problems, and were to be reconsidered if they did not work.'

NOTES AND REFERENCES

1. Margaret Chatterjee, *Gandhi's Religious Thought* (London, 1983), p. 180.
2. For a fuller explanation, *see* B.R. Nanda, *The Making of A Nation, India's Road to Independence* (Delhi, 1998), pp. 69–93 and 172–8.

SEVEN

Gandhi and Vivekananda

For nearly a hundred years Vivekananda has occupied a unique position in the history of India as the prophet of a resurgent Hinduism. He had shot to fame with his address at the Chicago Parliament of Religions in September 1893. His exposition of classical Hinduism thrilled his countrymen, satisfying as it did a deep and long-felt psychological need of the Hindu intelligentsia. Throughout the nineteenth century Hinduism had been on the defensive, believing itself to be beleaguered by erosion from within and assaults from without. 'There is not', wrote the *Friend of India* in 1863, 'an Englishman in India, who would not look upon the entire Christianization of our native subjects as a great political gain. There are few who do not believe that the accomplishment of this result is only a work of time.' Experienced British observers openly said that English education, railways, and modern communications would undermine Hinduism. Professor William Wordsworth of Bombay Elphinstone College warned in 1876 that the activities of missionaries were tending to widen the existing breach 'between the rulers and the ruled'. As the principal target of the missionaries' assault was Hinduism, it was Hindu society that felt threatened in the nineteenth century. Both Christianity and Islam were making converts at its expense. The Hindu response to this challenge was twofold: efforts at internal reform and a reassertion of religious identity. In the mid 1890s there were signs of a religious revival. 'A dozen years ago', *Amrita Bazar Patrika* wrote on 14 October 1895, 'when educated men sat together they talked of politics; now, generally speaking, they talk of religion.'

It was against this background that we should appraise the role of Vivekananda. He sought to purify and revitalize Hinduism so as to fit it to the twentieth century. As his ardent disciple, Sister Nivedita, said, he was the first to formulate the basic character of Hinduism as a system of thought and way of life in the modern age. He expounded the Vedanta of the Upanishads not as a life-negating and other-worldly philosophy, but as 'a universal and practical creed which was to be carried into everyday life, city life, the country life and home life of every nation'. His Vedanta was based on eternal principles and did not depend on any particular book; it embraced all the scriptures of the world; going beyond toleration and brotherhood, it recognized 'God in every soul and God immanent in nature'. He looked forward to a universal religion that would be 'infinite like the God it would preach and whose sun would shine upon the followers of Krishna and of Christ, on saints and sinners alike, which would not be Brahmanic, Buddhist, Christian or Mohammedan, but the sum-total of all these and still have infinite place for development'. There would be no conversions and upon the banner of every religion would be inscribed: 'Help, not Fight', 'Assimilation, not Destruction', and 'Harmony and Peace, and not Dissension'.

To the Hindus, Vivekananda presented Vedanta as an instrument of a spiritual and moral revolution in which reason was to be an active agent of change. He felt India had a strong rationalist tradition, but over the centuries rationalism had been pushed to the background. He ridiculed the mumbo-jumbo of ritual and superstition in which an ignorant and selfish priestly class had entangled the Hindu masses. 'Think of the last six hundred or seven hundred years of degradation,' he said, 'when grown-up men have been discussing for years whether they should drink a glass of water with the right hand or the left, gargle five or six times ... Our religion is in the kitchen. Our God is in the cooking pot.' He blamed the priests for 'doling out ditch water, overlooking the eternal fount of *amrit* (nectar) that lies behind us'. He denounced the degeneration of the caste system and the curse of untouchability. What sense did it make, he asked, in preaching Advaitism, after reducing *bhangis* and pariahs to their degraded condition? He condemned child marriage and called the opponents of the Age of Consent Bill 'religious hypocrites, as if religion consists in making a girl mother at the age of twelve or thirteen'.

Vivekananda had the courage to clash head-on with Hindu orthodoxy. Once, while he was explaining at a meeting in Madras the nuances of Vedanta, somebody from the audience interjected: 'Why, if this was so, it had never before been mentioned by any of the old masters.' 'Because,' Vivekananda shot back, 'I was born for this and it was left for me to do so.' When the code of Manu was invoked, Vivekananda declared that all social rules which stood in the way of unfolding freedom must be destroyed. He wanted to raise the status of women in Indian society; the level of a civilization, he said, was judged by the way it treated its women: 'With 500 motivated men it will take me 50 years to transform India, with 50 motivated women it may take me only a year.' He thought 'the great national sin' was the neglect of the masses. Priestly power and foreign conquest had trodden down the poor of India for centuries. No amount of politics would be of any avail, until the masses were 'well-educated, well-fed and well-cared for. If we want to regenerate India, we must work for them ... I do not believe in a God who cannot give us bread here, giving eternal bliss in heaven.'

As for relations between adherents of different religions, Vivekananda was not for *tolerance*, but for *acceptance* of other forms of worship. 'If you are born a Christian', he said, 'be a good Christian. If you are born a Hindu, be a good Hindu. If you are born a Muslim, be a good Muslim.' Mankind had to realize that religions were but the varied expressions of *The Religion* which is *Oneness*, so that each may choose the path that suits him best. He especially commended the spirit of equality in Islam and, in a letter dated 10 June 1898 to a Muslim correspondent, even envisaged 'a junction of the two great systems, Hinduism and Islam', into 'a Vedantic brain and an Islamic body'.

Vivekananda's pleas for religious harmony did not mean that he agreed with or commended everything that had been said or done in India or elsewhere in the name of any religion, whether Hinduism, Buddhism, Islam, or Christianity. As we have already seen, he did not spare his own co-religionists. He had a knack of applying a sort of shock therapy to jolt the orthodox, the complacent, the arrogant, and the bigoted out of their grooves. Some of his critics in the Parliament of Religions had argued that since the Hindus had never been conquerors of other lands, and were also poor, he had no business to preach his religion in Western countries. Vivekananda told them that he admired the life and teachings of Jesus Christ, but wondered whether they understood the religion they professed. 'All this prosperity', he said, 'all this from Christ! Those who call upon Christ care for nothing but to amass riches! Christ would not find a stone on which to lay his head among you ...'

Vivekananda pooh-poohed the idea that the adoption of Western ideas, Western language, Western food and Western manners would make India as strong and powerful as the Western nations. 'Does the ass in lion's skin,' he asked, 'become a lion?' At the same time he rebuked those of his co-religionists who advocated a revival or restoration of India's past. What he wanted was 'the strength of old India finding new applications and undreamt of expression in the new age'. He longed to see Hinduism imbibe something of 'the masculine vigour and dynamism' that had so fascinated him in the European nations.

II

Gandhi was the most charismatic Indian leader of the twentieth century as Vivekananda was of the nineteenth. They were contemporaries though they never met nor had any interaction while they lived. Their public life began at about the same time: Gandhi's South African odyssey in 1893, the year of Vivekananda's triumph at the Chicago Parliament of Religions. The two men vastly differed in their family background and the educational and social milieu in which they grew up. Vivekananda was a religious leader, the proclaimed heir of the great saint of Bengal, Sri Ramakrishna; Gandhi plunged into the political arena at the age of twenty-four and for the next fifty years led struggles against racialism and imperialism. Vivekananda was only six years older than Gandhi, but died young in 1902 at the age of thirty-nine.

Despite these obvious differences it is possible to detect remarkable similarities between their thought patterns and teachings; so much so that it appears as if it was Gandhi's historic role to carry forward the work for reform and revitalization of Hinduism, which Vivekananda left unfinished.

Unlike Vivekananda, Gandhi's life was not suddenly transformed by contact with a great saint. His religious quest really began soon after his arrival in South Africa, when some missionaries tried to convert him to Christianity. He had a sceptical streak in him and decided to study not only Christianity, but other religions, including the religion of his birth. A decisive influence on him during this formative period, as I have noted in earlier chapters, was that of Rajchandra, a young jeweller, poet, and savant of Bombay, who was (in Gandhi's words) one of the 'three moderns' who had influenced him most, the others being Tolstoy and Ruskin. Rajchandra restored Gandhi's faith in Hinduism, and helped to give a sense of direction to Gandhi's religious quest: it was the way a man lived, not what he professed which made him a good Hindu, a good Muslim or a good Christian.

Gandhi's religious quest triggered off his metamorphosis from an upper-middle-class barrister into Churchill's 'half-naked faqir', a sanyasi, all but in name. Religion transformed Gandhi, but he also transformed religion.

Like Vivekananda, Gandhi threw down the gauntlet to Hindu orthodoxy, and questioned the validity of some centuries-old dogmas and practices. He condemned animal sacrifice, child marriage, the dowry system and the greed of the priests and filth scattered around temples. His severest strictures were reserved for the aberrations of the caste system and its monstrous progeny, untouchability. He reinterpreted, both in theory and practice, several Hindu concepts to suit the changing times. For example, fasting was not merely a necessary ritual for the pious; it could be used as a tool of social action. An ashram was not merely a place for prayer and meditation, but also for training workers for service of the country.

Gandhi worked ceaselessly to break the barriers between various castes, communities, religions, and even nations. Like Vivekananda, he called for a new deal for women, and for the 'naked hungry mass' in the villages. It is interesting that the word *daridranarayan*, which Gandhi often used, was coined by Vivekananda; it was not meant to idealize poverty, but to bring out both the cruel predicament and essential nobility of the poor of India. Like Vivekananda, Gandhi also attempted to shift Hinduism from its predominantly individualistic and other-worldly moorings.

Vivekananda had taken his lessons in religious tolerance from his master, Sri Ramakrishna. Gandhi delved into the scriptures of major religions and discovered an underlying unity in their teachings. 'God's grace and revelation', he said, 'are not the monopoly of any race or nation; they descend equally upon all who wait upon God.' Religion consisted, Gandhi said, not in outward ceremonial, but in encouraging inward response to the highest impulses of which a man was capable. What was important was not what 'we label ourselves, but what we are'; a belief without action was nothing. He regarded all the principal faiths of the world as divinely inspired but felt they were imperfect because 'they have come down to us through imperfect human instrumentality'. Hence the necessity for tolerance, which did not mean indifference towards one's own faith but a more intelligent and purer love for it. 'The need of the moment', he wrote, 'is not one religion, but mutual respect and tolerance of the devotees of different religions.' No religion was absolutely perfect; but every religion was to be judged not by its worst specimens, but by the best it produced. 'If you read the Koran,' Gandhi wrote, 'you must read with the eye of the Muslim; if you read the Bible, you must read with the eye of the Christian; if you read the Gita, you must read it with the eye of the Hindu. What is the use of scanning details and then holding up a religion to ridicule?'

For Gandhi, communal harmony was not an academic issue; it was vital for success of his struggle against the imperial power which claimed that it was the discord between the religious communities that barred India's progress towards self-government.

Like Vivekananda, Gandhi, while deriving sustenance from the un-sullied fount of ancient Indian spirituality, responded to Western influences with judicious discrimination, accepting what was life-giving and rejecting what was deleterious.

In one important respect, Gandhi differed with Vivekananda, and it was fortunate that he did so. Vivekananda had rejected politics. 'The Greeks had sought political liberty,' he had noted in one of his lecture notes, 'the Hindus had sought spiritual liberty.' Vivekananda called for a spiritual and moral revolution to precede a political revolution. He neither used the word nationality, nor proclaimed an era of nation-making. 'Man-making', he said, was his task.

Gandhi's political mission and religious quest began simultaneously when he was in his twenties; his religious convictions gave him the strength and the stamina for a half-century of a crowded political career. He was accused of introducing religion into politics. It is true that he asserted that religion could not be separated from politics, but he also made it clear that he was not referring to the dogmas and rituals but to the essential ethical content in all major religions. He had been, in his younger days, deeply influenced by the call of his political mentor, Gopal Krishna Gokhale. In 1904 in his farewell address to Fergusson College, Gokhale exhorted the Indians of his day, especially the youth, to put aside 'all thoughts of worldly interest and work for a secular purpose with the zeal and the enthusiasm which we generally find in the sphere of religion alone'. The idea of 'spiritualizing politics', as Gokhale put it, of evoking abnegation and self-denial for secular causes, which inspired Gokhale to establish the Servants of India Society, appealed to Gandhi; he applied it to the ashrams he set up in South Africa and India. He however went further, extending the application of this idea to the political field. Satyagraha, his method of resolving conflicts, drew its dynamic from his deeply-held religious and philosophical beliefs. One can be an atheist or agnostic and still practise satyagraha. It is, however, easier for men of religion to accept the assumptions on which satyagraha rests: it is worthwhile fighting, even dying, for causes that transcend one's personal interests, that the body perishes, but the soul lives, that no oppressor can crush the imperishable spirit of man, that every human being, however wicked he may appear to be, has a hidden nobility, a 'divine spark' that can be ignited.

PART II

Freedom's Battle

EIGHT

'And then Gandhi Came'

I t is difficult for us to imagine today how dramatic and unexpected Gandhi's emergence on the political scene in 1919–20 was. He returned to India in 1915 after having spent twenty years in South Africa. For the first few years he appeared to hover on the periphery of nationalist politics. At the annual sessions of the Indian National Congress he was invited to speak on the problems of Indians in South Africa and other British colonies, but he was nowhere near the inner group that shaped Congress policies. His ideas and methods did not quite fit in with those of the Moderates or the Extremists, the two factions whose rivalries paralysed the Congress for over a decade. The Moderate leaders did not like his extra-constitutional weapon of satyagraha, and the Extremist leaders were repelled by his studied moderation towards the government.

The attitude of the British authorities towards Gandhi in these early years was also curiously ambivalent. Personal esteem for him was overlaid by deep suspicions of his motives and actions. They discerned in satyagraha a serious challenge to British rule; they did not see that what was most important to Gandhi was that the challenge had a moral and non-violent basis. Perhaps they saw no particular virtue in being evicted from India non-violently. Their hope that Gandhi's reformist zeal would drain off in innocuous channels of religious and social reform, was not realized. Even before he came out against the Rowlatt Bills in February 1919, Gandhi's relations with the government had practically reached a breaking point. Lord Chelmsford, the Viceroy, wrote home that he proposed to call Gandhi's bluff. There was talk of deporting him, and indeed, he was arrested on 10 April while he was travelling to Delhi by train. The sequel— disturbances in western India and Punjab—shattered official complacency. The following year when he embarked on non-cooperation, the first reaction of the authorities was again to underrate it; the Viceroy described

Gandhi's programme 'so intrinsically foolish that the common-sense of India would reject it'. Nevertheless, the non-cooperation movement gathered momentum until it became within a few months the most formidable challenge to the British Raj since the revolt of 1857.

The emergence of Gandhi was as bewildering a phenomenon to the Indian political élite as it was to the government. Gandhi's announcement of satyagraha against the Rowlatt Bills in February 1919 was promptly denounced by almost all the prominent politicians of the day. When he presented his programme at the special session of the Congress at Calcutta in September 1920, he met with stiff resistance. Tilak was dead, but almost all the front rank leaders, Annie Besant, C.R. Das, B.C. Pal, Jinnah, and even Lajpat Rai, the president of the session, were either sceptical or in open opposition. Bhupendranath Basu, a survivor of the Naoroji–Gokhale era, described non-cooperation as a 'plan of mad men'. 'Your programme', Jinnah warned Gandhi, 'has for the moment struck the imagination mostly of inexperienced youth, the ignorant and the illiterate. All this means complete disorganization and chaos.'

How did Gandhi overcome this solid wall of opposition and come to dominate the Indian National Congress for the next quarter of a century? The hard-pressed British officials tended to conjure up the image of the 'wily Gandhi' exploiting men and situations to build up his leadership. This explanation has been dished up in a new form in recent years by some latter-day historians, who have sought to portray Gandhi as a 'skilful operator' with 'contractors' and 'subcontractors' to build up his influence in the provinces. The truth is more complicated than that. By the end of 1918 both the factions in the Congress were played out, and there was a vacuum of leadership at the top. The Moderates seceded from the Congress, and became a party of leaders without followers. The Extremists, riven by a feud between Annie Besant and Tilak, had also reached a dead-end. Tilak, who had spent the best part of 1919 in England and returned just in time to attend the Amritsar Congress, was planning another Congress deputation to England in February 1920 on the Punjab tragedy. Jinnah made a similar suggestion soon after leading an infructuous Khilafat delegation to London. This was in fact the traditional Moderate strategy of (what the *Amrita Bazar Patrika* once described as) appealing from 'Chota Sahib to Burrah Sahib'. Clearly, both the Moderates and the Extremists were unable to attune themselves to the fast-changing political situation and to channel the growing anti-British feeling.

Gandhi's greatest asset was a new ideology and a new method: he could offer a practical alternative to speech-making and bomb-throwing between which Indian politics had so far oscillated. Gandhi's 'rise to power' in the Congress and in the country was also facilitated by 'the accidents of time and circumstance' such as the deaths of old, established leaders: Gokhale, Pherozeshah Mehta, and Tilak; the post-war social and economic ferment, the Indian Muslims' discontent over the defeat of Turkey and the fate of the Caliphate, and the British bungling over the Rowlatt Bills and the Punjab martial law. To all these must be added the profound impact of Gandhi's personality. 'And then Gandhi came', Jawaharlal Nehru wrote in *Discovery of India*,

He was like a powerful current of fresh air that made us stretch ourselves and take deep breaths; like a beam of light that pierced the darkness and removed the scales from our eyes; like a whirlwind that upset many things, but most of all the working of people's minds.

Gandhi's charisma seemed tailor-made for that generation. Subhas Chandra Bose, who plunged into the non-cooperation movement after turning his back upon the I.C.S., recalled in his *Indian Struggle*:

Gandhi was not too revolutionary for the majority of his countrymen. If he had been so, he would have frightened them, instead of inspiring them, repelled them, instead of drawing them. He wanted to unite them, the Hindu and Muslim, the high-caste and the low-caste, and the capitalist and the labour, the landless and the peasant. By his humanitarian outlook and freedom from hatred, he was able to receive sympathy even in his enemy's camp.

Gandhi spoke in an idiom that the people readily understood; the battle between good and evil, the higher and baser ideals made more sense to them than the niceties of a constitutional debate could ever have done. They loved and venerated him for turning his back on worldly ambitions; his call for sacrifice for the motherland did not sound hollow, because he himself seemed an epitome of renunciation. This direct link with the people gave Gandhi a unique advantage; his influence did not depend upon any office he held in the Congress, and indeed it was independent of the success or failure that attended his campaigns.

Gandhi did not, however, subsist upon his charisma. He had a genius for organization; in a few months he converted the thirty-five-year-old Indian National Congress from an annual three-day spectacle into a broad-based national movement. He shifted the Congress from its old moorings; he restructured it; he gave it a new creed and a new method. He knew how to spot, train, and harness talented men and women for public causes. He picked up promising men of diverse abilities and temperaments:

Jawaharlal Nehru, C. Rajagopalachari, Rajendra Prasad, Vallabhbhai Patel, and others who were to form the vanguard of the national movement in the 1930s and 1940s. They did not share all his ideas on politics and economics; few shared his religious outlook but were tied to him by a deeply emotional bond. With his immense appeal to the masses, and his peculiar relationship with Congress leaders, Gandhi symbolized in his own person the basic unity of Indian nationalism over a quarter of a century, thus providing a prophylactic against the tendency of national movements towards schism. Gandhi visualized the Indian National Congress as a common front against British imperialism. Whenever there was a danger of a split in the Congress, such as between the Swarajists and the 'No-Changers' in 1924, between the protagonists of Dominion Status and Complete Independence in 1928, or between the 'Rightists' and 'Leftists' in 1936, Gandhi's weight was cast in favour of unity. An open rift in the Congress would have been a godsend to the British.

He forestalled the revolt of the youth in the Congress with a blend of patience and generosity by seeing that Jawaharlal Nehru became Congress president in 1929 and 1936, and by his judicious handling of the socialists who, by the time of the 'Quit India' movement, had been converted from trenchant critics into admirers of the Mahatma. He was the high court of private appeal for politicians of various hues, and knew how to soften mutual antipathies and antagonisms. He did not derive his power in the Congress from any office he held. He presided over the Indian National Congress only once, in 1924, and that was out of deference to the wishes of Motilal Nehru and C.R. Das and to smooth the way for the Swarajist sway over the Congress. He was a member of the Congress Working Committee during the non-cooperation movement and occasionally presided over its meetings. However, in 1934 he snapped all formal links with the Congress by ceasing to be even 'a four-anna member', but this did not in any way affect his standing. There was never a dearth of his critics in the Congress, but they knew that if there was a conflict with the Raj, his leadership was indispensable. It was as the author and the sole practitioner of non-violent warfare, satyagraha, that he had entered the political arena in 1919, and it was this role that gave him his unique position.

Napoleon's maxim that the nature of a weapon decides everything else in the art and organization of war was certainly true of satyagraha. Gandhi knew that his political technique was not a magic wand; it required sustained vigilance, effort, and sacrifices which were forthcoming only intermittently in periods of intense political excitement. The politically conscious classes in India wanted quick results; in 1920 they welcomed non-cooperation because Gandhi promised Swaraj within a year. The promise was remembered, but not the conditions for the fulfilment of that promise. Too often satyagraha was viewed by Gandhi's critics as if it was a method of violent warfare; it was forgotten that in satyagraha it was not a question of overwhelming an army corps, bombing or capturing a town, but of initiating certain psychological changes in those who offered it and in those against whom it was directed. The British authorities could not easily be brought to believe in Gandhi's sincerity; nor were they willing to accept the moral basis of his challenge. 'Gandhi is the most astute politician in India', Lord Willingdon wrote in July 1933, 'and the acknowledged leader of the party whose aim is independence ... The Congress may change its tactics, but they will never change their objects.' As late as 1946, Lord Wavell wrote in his journal that Gandhi was an 'exceedingly shrewd, obstinate, double-tongued, single-minded politician'. It was the object of satyagraha to penetrate this wall of prejudice. The successive civil disobedience movements, while lifting the spell of fear that had enveloped the Indian masses for a hundred years, also wore out, however slowly, British rigidity into scepticism and scepticism into fatigue.

Gandhi excluded secrecy, hatred and violence from satyagraha, and called for extreme restraint even in the face of provocation from the enemy. Despite his undoubted magnetism and unrivalled prestige, he could only sporadically command a mass following for his campaigns: in 1920–2, 1930–2, and 1940–2. His overriding concern while conducting his campaigns was to ensure that they were not marred by violent outbreaks. As he wrote to Jawaharlal Nehru after the Chauri Chaura tragedy, he was not prepared to lead a movement that was half-violent and half-non-violent. The ethical nuances and the self-restraint of satyagraha puzzled and even infuriated some of his radical colleagues. However, the rationale for some of his decisions, which have been criticized as tactical blunders, such as the withdrawal of mass civil disobedience in 1922, the Gandhi–Irwin Pact in 1931, the untouchability fast in 1932, and the Bombay talks with Jinnah in 1944 can only be understood in terms of his mode of satyagraha. It was a mode of warfare in which he could lose all the battles but still win the war.

NINE

The Dandi March

On 12 March 1930 Gandhi set out from Ahmedabad, along with seventy-eight volunteers from Sabarmati Ashram, on a 241-mile trek to Dandi on the west coast. The Dandi March, which inaugurated the 'Salt Satyagraha', proved to be one of the most dramatic and successful episodes in the history of the Indian freedom struggle. Curiously, its spectacular success was foreseen neither by Gandhi nor by his colleagues nor by the representatives of the British Raj.

Ten weeks earlier, in the last week of December 1929, the Lahore session of the Indian National Congress, presided over by Jawaharlal Nehru, had declared that its acceptance of dominion status in the previous year had lapsed, and henceforth Swaraj would mean complete independence. At midnight on 31 December 1929 the Congress unfurled the flag of independence on the bank of Ravi, and authorized the All India Congress Committee to launch civil disobedience. Once again, after nine years, the Congress had dared to defy the British Empire.

There was little doubt that, in executing the decision of the Lahore session, the Congress party would be guided by Gandhi. Civil disobedience was, as the Mahatma was wont to say, 'the ultimate sanction', but he made no secret of his opinion that the country was not ready for civil disobedience. There had been serious differences of opinion at the Lahore Congress; senior Congress leaders such as Sarojini Naidu and Madan Mohan Malaviya had counselled caution; so had Dr M.A. Ansari and the nationalist Muslim leaders, who were worried over the communal tension. In contrast to 1919–20, there was no rallying cry like the Rowlatt Bills, no rankling grievance like the Punjab martial law, no emotional bridge for Hindu–Muslim differences like the Khilafat. That violence was in the air was shown by the angry opposition to a resolution moved at the Lahore Congress by Gandhi himself to congratulate the Viceroy, Lord Irwin, on his lucky escape from a bomb attack a few days earlier.

For the Mahatma the basic problem was how to arouse the people and still keep them non-violent. On 10 January 1930, he confided to Jawaharlal Nehru: 'I have not seen my way clear as yet.' The first step he took was to call for the celebration of 'Independence Day' on 26 January. He was gratified by the popular response, but a week later, he wrote to C.F. Andrews: 'The nature of the action is not yet clear to me. It has to be civil disobedience. How is it to be undertaken and by whom besides me I have not yet seen clearly. But the shining cover that overlays the truth is thinning day by day, and will presently break.'

At last the 'shining cover' broke. On 5 February the newspapers reported that Gandhi would begin civil disobedience by defying the salt laws. The salt tax, though relatively light in incidence (in 1930 it amounted to just three annas per head), hit the poorest in the land, but somehow salt did not seem to fit into a struggle for national independence. According to Dr B.C. Roy, who was at Allahabad when the proposal of breaking salt laws became public, Motilal Nehru was amused, even angered, by the apparent irrelevance of Gandhi's plan. To Motilal, as indeed to many other 'intellectuals' in the Congress, it may have seemed that salt had become, like fasting and charkha, another of the Mahatma's hobby-horses.

The first impulse of the British authorities too was to laugh away the idea that the King–Emperor could be unseated by boiling sea water in a kettle. Tottenham, a member of the Central Board of Revenue, described the breach of salt laws 'as Mr Gandhi's somewhat fantastic project'. A committee of senior officers reported that salt did not appear to be a promising field for initiating a no-tax campaign; that the most that could happen was that small quantities of inferior salt would be sporadically produced in some areas and consumed locally; that neither the government revenues nor the price of salt were likely to be affected.

The Government of Bombay told the Government of India that so long as the march was conducted peacefully, there was no provision of law that prohibited it. Moreover, it seemed possible that Gandhi's march might end in a fiasco; even Wedgwood Benn, the Secretary of State for India in the Labour Cabinet, indulged in some wishful thinking: 'If the whole escapade fizzles out in some ridiculous way, I shall be too pleased.'

On 2 March Gandhi communicated his plan to the Viceroy, Lord Irwin. His ambition, the Mahatma wrote, was 'no less than to convert the British people through non-violence'. The prayer meeting in Sabarmati Ashram on the evening of 11 March had a record attendance. 'Our cause is just,' said Gandhi, 'our means the purest and God is with us.' Next morning, at 6.30 the trek began. The seventy-eight satyagrahis, all selected from the inmates of the Sabarmati Ashram, included scholars, newspaper editors and weavers. The people of Ahmedabad turned out in their thousands to cheer them. Gandhi, the eldest member of the volunteer band, walked so fast that the younger men found it difficult to keep pace with him. He rose as usual at 4 a.m., conducted the morning prayers, addressed meetings in villages through which he passed, did his daily quota of spinning, wrote articles for his journals, and letters to his correspondents. He announced that he would not return to Sabarmati Ashram until the salt tax was repealed. He condemned the salt tax, and the alien regime that had imposed it. He appealed to local village officials to resign their posts; the response rattled the local government: by 5 April 140 out of 760 village headmen had resigned.

Like his predecessor, Lord Irwin agonized for weeks over the pros and cons of arresting Gandhi. C. Rajagopalachari, a shrewd observer, had, however, told Gandhi that his arrest was inevitable: 'They [the British] cannot let the conflagration grow on the ground that much salt cannot be made by you. It is not salt, but disobedience you are manufacturing.' Far from proving a fiasco, as some British officials had hoped and Indian sceptics had feared, Gandhi's march electrified the entire country. A thrill of patriotic fervour, which ran through the whole subcontinent, found expression in Jawaharlal Nehru's memorable words:

Today the pilgrim marches onward on his long trek ... but the fire of a great resolve is in him, and surpassing love of his countrymen, and love of truth that scorches, and love of freedom that inspires. And none that passes him can escape the spell, and men of common clay feel the spark of life. It is a long journey, for the goal is independence of India.

Gandhi's imprisonment in early May stimulated rather than slackened civil disobedience. The Government retaliated with an iron ring of ordinances to strangulate the Congress organization, freeze its funds, and choke its publicity channels. Over 60,000 civil resisters were jailed. Ample testimony to the tremendous nationalist upsurge exists in confidential government records of the time and in the private correspondence of the Viceroy and his advisers. For example, Governor Sykes of Bombay lamented that the whole population of that town had been 'carried away on a wave of semi-hysteric enthusiasm,' and Haig, the Home Member in the Viceroy's Executive Council, ruefully acknowledged 'the power and success of the Congress movement'.

The civil disobedience campaign lasted for just twelve months, ending with the Gandhi–Irwin Pact in March 1931. It is not proposed to discuss that pact here, but of one thing there is no doubt. This campaign came closest to Gandhi's conception of a model satyagraha. The earlier mass campaigns of 1919 and 1920 had to be called off in the wake of violent outbreaks, and in 1942, the Mahatma was removed from the scene before he could even launch his struggle. In the Salt Satyagraha of 1930–1 we can see the lineaments of the classic non-violent battle: the careful preparation, the articulation of the moral issue, the intuitive choice of symbols and instruments, the cautious beginning, the slow acceleration and, finally, the successful mobilization of the people without hatred and violence, simultaneously with the willingness to build bridges with the enemy for an eventual meeting of minds.

TEN

'Quit India'

O n 8 August 1942 the All India Congress Committee met at Bombay and passed a resolution calling for the immediate end to British rule in India. The 'Quit India' resolution, as it came to be known, was the culmination of a three-year-long confrontation that had been ongoing, since the outbreak of the Second World War, between Congress and the government.

In September 1939, the Congress had posed two questions to the British government: first, what was to be the shape of the new world order after the war, and would it include the freedom of India? Second, could India have a foretaste of that freedom while fighting for the Allied cause? The Congress could not elicit a satisfactory response to these posers; indeed, they were dismissed as evidence of impractical idealism or cynical opportunism. The Congress leaders were deeply disappointed at the British obduracy, but they, and especially Gandhi, were reluctant to challenge Britain while she was engaged in a life-and-death struggle against Nazi Germany. Gandhi tried hard to balance his passion for Indian freedom with the chivalrous code of Satyagraha, which forbade embarrassment of the adversary in his hour of adversity. He channelled the pent-up frustration of the people through an individual civil disobedience campaign. Though nearly 30,000 Congressmen, personally selected by Gandhi, went to prison in 1940–1, it was designed as a symbolic gesture of defiance. When it was pointed out to the Mahatma that this was an anaemic movement, and had no adverse effect on the British war effort, Gandhi replied that it was not intended to have such an effect. Events, however, soon took a turn that strained even Gandhi's studied patience and restraint.

Early in 1942, in the wake of the swift Japanese advance through South East Asia, the British government despatched Sir Stafford Cripps, a Labour member of the Cabinet, to India to resolve the political deadlock.

The Cripps Mission might have succeeded had it not been hamstrung by a tie-up between the Viceroy Lord Linlithgow and Prime Minister Churchill. For Gandhi, the failure of the Cripps Mission was the last straw. It was clear that even in her desperate straits in the spring and summer of 1942, Britain was unwilling to part with power. Meanwhile Gandhi had his hand on the pulse of the people: he became convinced that if India was not to go the way of Malaya and Burma, something had to be done, and quickly. He concluded that only an immediate declaration of Indian independence by the British government could give the people of India a stake in the defences of their country. That such a demand should be made at a time when the Japanese were knocking at the gates of India seemed wholly unrealistic not only to Britain and her allies, but to some of Gandhi's own trusted colleagues such as Jawaharlal Nehru and Abul Kalam Azad who did not want to do anything that would jeopardize the defence of China and Russia. The crisis in the Congress Working Committee was, however, resolved in July 1942. Gandhi's argument that only an India that felt the glow of freedom could cope with the Japanese peril was accepted, but he also waived, at Nehru's insistence, his objections to violent resistance to the external threat. The Quit India resolution passed by the All India Congress Committee on 9 August envisaged a free India resisting aggression with all the armed and non-violent forces at its disposal in cooperation with the Allied powers and the United States.

In his fateful confrontation with the British government in August 1942, Gandhi made a serious, almost inexcusable, miscalculation. He assumed that Linlithgow would react to the Congress ultimatum, as his predecessors had done in 1921 and 1930, and thus give him time to negotiate with the government to elucidate his stand, and to regulate the form and range of civil disobedience. Linlithgow had, however, no intention of playing the game according to the Mahatma's rules; he had decided two years earlier, in August 1940, to crush the Congress if it threw down the gauntlet to the government during the war. Within hours of the passage of the Quit India Resolution, the government arrested all the leaders of the Congress not only at the all-India, but also at the provincial and even district levels, and clamped down on the Congress organization so as to disable it from functioning.

If Gandhi was guilty of a serious miscalculation, so was Linlithgow; the pre-emptive strike, far from preventing trouble, provoked a violent explosion that shook the Raj. There were clashes with the police in Bombay, Delhi, Pune, Kanpur, Allahabad and many other towns, and countless cases of firing by the police. There were strikes by mill-workers in Bombay,

Jamshedpur, Ahmedabad, Bangalore; students walked out of schools and colleges. Seventeen newspapers in the English and Indian languages suspended publication. The gravest developments from the British standpoint were, however, the uprisings in the countryside in Bihar, UP and Bombay. Most of them were instigated by students who led mobs in attacks on the nearest police stations, post offices, court and school buildings, roads and railways, indeed, on all the visible symbols of foreign rule.

On 31 August 1942 the Viceroy informed Prime Minister Churchill that he was facing 'the most serious rebellion since that of 1857'. The comparison was not quite apt. The Indian sepoys who mutinied in 1857 had some arms, ammunition, and training; the simple village folk of Ballia, Sahasaram, Azamgarh, and other small towns and villages in Bihar and UP, who had risen in revolt at the bidding of boys fresh from schools and colleges, wielded nothing more lethal than staves and stones; their violence was sporadic, unplanned, and suicidal. The British response was predictably ruthless. According to official figures, which could well be underestimates, by the end of 1942 over 66,000 persons had been convicted or detained; the military had fired on 538 occasions.

There was, of course, the underground movement which started in a low key from 9 August. In continued fitfully for over two years. It was led by Congress Socialists, Forward Bloc members, revolutionary terrorists, and even some Gandhians who instigated strikes, burnt government buildings, damaged railway tracks and bridges, organized the cutting of telegraph and telephone wires, and stole or burnt postal boxes. Then there were the parallel governments, such as in Midnapore and Satara districts, which revealed great ingenuity and organization. Doubtless there was in this underground movement ardent patriotism, individual heroism and even romance, but it did not affect the war effort; much less did it pose a serious challenge to the British Raj.

When Lord Linlithgow left India in 1943, he had no doubt that he had crushed not only the 'rebellion', but the Congress. Little did he realize that he had hastened the liquidation of the Raj. In his arrogance he had taken the risk, which none of his predecessors had dared to take, of Gandhi's death in jail when the Mahatma embarked on a 21-day fast to protest against the charge that he was responsible for the violence of the Quit India movement.

Not until after his release from jail in 1944 did Gandhi give his considered verdict on the events of 1942. There was, he said, something to be said for the fact that the people had not remained supine under the blows of the government, but it pained him to discover that those who professed to follow him should have forgotten his fundamental tenet of non-violence. Had he not been saying for twenty years that in satyagraha there was no room for hatred, violence or secrecy? It was wrong to think, he told the Congressmen of Midnapore (who proudly recounted their achievements in the underground movement), that evil resided in bridges and roads and not in men; the destruction of bridges and roads could not change the hearts of men. 'But is not non-violent rebellion a programme of seizure of power?' he was asked. 'Therein lies the fallacy', Gandhi replied. 'A non-violent rebellion is not a programme of seizure of power. It is a programme of transformation of relationships ending in a peaceful transfer of power.'

Gandhi rejected the assertion that it was sabotage and underground activity that had strengthened the national cause or brought freedom to India. That the reverse was true was brought home to him forcibly in 1946 when he trudged through the riot-torn districts of Bihar and Bengal. By then it was evident that the events of 1942 had been in some ways an embarrassing legacy. It was the first large-scale outbreak in which wrecking and burning were indulged in a spirit of, what to the Mahatma was, misconceived patriotism. It lowered the standards of mass behaviour, and set a dangerous precedent when in 1946–7 communal feeling replaced patriotism as the principal ingredient in popular ferment.

ELEVEN

Gandhi and Pan-Islamism

No decision made by Gandhi in the course of his long political career, extending over more than fifty years, has come in for sharper criticism than his support of the Khilafat (Pan-Islamist) movement in the early 1920s. Nationalist historians have blamed him for his gross misjudgement in taking up a purely religious grievance of Indian Muslims, and thus introducing religion into politics. Western and Pakistani scholars have accused him of exploiting Muslim religious sentiment for the Ottoman Khilafat for a political purpose: forging a Hindu–Muslim alliance against the British Raj. Much of this criticism derives from an inadequate appreciation of the roots and ramifications of the Khilafat agitation as well as of Gandhi's role when he was catapulted into its leadership during the years 1920–2.

Curiously, the historical links of Indian Islam with the institution of the Caliphate had been tenuous. The rulers of the Slave dynasty, who had to contend with ambitious nobles and stubborn ulema, considered it politic to seek the blessings of the Abbasid Caliph in Baghdad and even of the shadow Caliphs in Cairo. The Mughal kings needed no such support for the assertion of their legitimacy; as their coins show, they themselves assumed the title of Caliph in India. Sir Jadunath Sarkar, the most eminent historian of Mughal India, was consulted by the Government of India in 1920. He was of the view that 'the claim that the Khilafat of the Ottoman Sultan is something which has remained unchanged for thirteen centuries or that it has universal application which is binding under Muslim law, is flatly contradictory to history'.[1] He pointed out that even Aurangzeb, the most orthodox of Mughal emperors, had not acknowledged the Sultan of Turkey. 'In short,' Sarkar wrote, 'the theory that the Muslim ruler of Turkey is the spiritual head of all Muhammadens is a creation of the late nineteenth century, and merely a result of the growth of a political pan-

Islamic movement as a natural reaction against steady absorption of all sovereign Muslim States by the Christians.'

It was only in the last decades of the nineteenth century that Turkey really began to loom large in the imagination of Indian Muslims. After the extinction of Muslim rule in India, Turkey had become a symbol of the glorious past of Islam. This identification with Turkey did not at first disturb the British rulers of India, when bolstering up Turkey against Tzarist Russia was a plank in British foreign policy. The situation, however, changed in the closing decades of the century, when the disintegration of the Ottoman Empire had begun. Turkey had to contend not only with its traditional enemy Russia, and with the national aspirations of the Slav nationalities under its rule, but with a resurgent imperialism in Europe, which was colonizing large tracts of Asia and Africa. Tunis had been occupied by the French in 1881, Egypt by the British in 1882, Eritrea by the Italians in 1885, the Sudan by the British in 1898. At the same time, the submerged nationalities in the Balkans—the Serbs, the Rumanians, the Bulgars—were struggling to be free; they commanded the sympathy of most countries of Europe. Muslim observers in India and elsewhere could not help feeling that the dice was heavily loaded against Turkey.

With increasing tension in south-eastern Europe, the pro-Turkish feeling in India became a source of anxiety to the British rulers. The Urdu press in northern India tended to see every conflict in the Balkans and to interpret every move on the European chequerboard in terms of a struggle between Islam and Christianity. W.S. Blunt, a shrewd British observer and a vocal champion of Islam, who toured India in the winter of 1883–4, noticed deep resentment caused by the aggression of European powers against Turkey. He was struck by the simmering hatred for England amongst some of the orthodox Muslims, who would have given anything to see the British out of Egypt. It was clear, Blunt wrote, that they would 'welcome any deliverer here, Russian or French, or from the Devil'.[2]

Sympathy for Turkey was not confined to orthodox elements. Badruddin Tyabji, who later rose to be a judge of the Bombay High Court, and presided over the Madras session of the Indian National Congress in 1887, wrote a letter to *Bombay Gazette* in 1879 refuting the stories of Turkish atrocities in Bulgaria.[3] In 1897, when news arrived of Turkish victory over Greece, Muslim homes and mosques throughout India were illuminated. At the turn of the century, Turkey had thus come to occupy a place in the minds and hearts of large sections of the Muslim community, which it had not done during the long centuries of Muslim rule in India. Sir Syed Ahmad Khan, no Turko-phile himself, understood the impulses behind the emotional identification of Indian Muslims with Turkey. 'When there were many Muslim kingdoms', he told Theodore Morison, 'we did not feel much grief when one of them was destroyed; now that so few are left, we feel the loss of even a small one. If Turkey is conquered, that will be a great grief, for she is the last of the great powers left to Islam. We are afraid that we shall become like the Jews, a people without a country of our own.'[4] In fairness to Syed Ahmad Khan, it must be stated that he rejected the theory of a universal caliphate and the claim of Sultan of Turkey to be the religious head of all Muslims. Syed Ahmad's opinion on this subject did not go down well with his community. When his successor at the Aligarh College, Nawab Mohsin-ul-Mulk wrote an article questioning the validity of the concept of the caliphate for Indian Muslims, he was immediately denounced in the Urdu press as a traitor to Islam.[5]

II

The outbreak of the Balkan Wars in 1911 triggered off a chain reaction in south-eastern Europe, northern Africa, and the Middle East, which portended the dissolution of the Turkish Empire. The Muslim press, especially the Urdu press in northern India, reflected the anger and frustration that the Muslims felt. *Al Hilal*, a new journal started by a brilliant young scholar, Abul Kalam Azad, electrified the Muslim community: his high-flown Urdu prose laced with Persian and Arabic quotations, and citations from the Quran and Islamic traditions, his references to the magnificent past of Islam, his denunciation of European imperialism, his sympathy with Turkey in her unequal struggle with the Christian powers of Europe together constituted a heady cocktail for the readers of *Al Hilal*. He was supported in this crusade on behalf of Turkey by the *Comrade* and *Hamdard*, edited by Mohamed Ali, and the *Zamindar*, edited by Zafar Ali Khan.

Most Muslims in India knew little about the history or even the geography of the Middle East or the merits of the Turkish Sultan's claim to the universal caliphate. There was, however, no doubt about the intensity of their emotional identification with the government and people of Turkey. The sympathy for Turkey and bitterness against the European powers touched the deepest chords in the psyche of the Muslim community. Great Britain was not directly involved in the Balkan Wars, and the most that could be said against it was that it did not intervene on behalf of Turkey. In 1914, however, when Turkey aligned itself with Germany and declared a jihad against the Allied Powers, it created a dangerous situation. The Government of India did what it could to soothe the feelings of Indian Muslims; it represented Turkey as a dupe of German intrigue; it issued a communiqué making a solemn promise on behalf of Britain and its allies that the Holy Places of Islam and Jeddah would remain immune from attack or molestation. The loyalty of Muslim princes, landlords, and the upper middle class could in any case be taken for granted, but even the millions of literate and semi-literate Muslims in small towns and villages remained quiescent during the war years. The drastic powers under the Defence of India Rules were invoked to remove the more vocal Pan-Islamists from the scene. The Ali brothers, Mohamed and Shaukat, Abul Kalam Azad, Zafar Ali Khan, Hasrat Mohani, and Mahmud-al-Hasan were jailed or interned, and the Pan-Islamic papers and journals were forced out of circulation.

Not until the end of the First World War, did the Khilafat issue pose a critical situation for the British. Indian Muslims, and the Government of India, were now confronted with the spectre they had dreaded for years: the dismemberment of Turkey. Turkey was defeated and lay prostrate, the Turkish armies had been driven back into their home territory; Constantinople was occupied by Allied troops. When the All India Muslim League met for its annual session in Delhi six weeks after the end of the war, Dr M.A. Ansari, the Chairman of the Reception Committee, warned the British Government that Indian Muslims might not be able to exercise the extraordinary restraint on the Turkish issue they had exhibited during the war. Several eminent ulemas, including Maulana Kifayatullah of Delhi, Maulana Abdul Bari of Lucknow, Maulana Ahmed Saeed of Delhi, and Maulana Azad Subhani of Kanpur had been invited to this meeting. A 'united fatwa' was issued brushing aside doubts on the legitimacy of the Turkish Khilafat and declaring that it was the duty of all Muslims to prevent non-Muslims from taking possession of the Holy Places of Islam in 'Jaziratul Arab', a region which was so defined as to include Syria, Palestine, and the Arab lands.

The agitation on behalf of Turkey soon acquired an institutional basis. In March 1919 some Muslim leaders of Bombay decided to form a Khilafat Committee with Seth Mian Muhammad Haji Jan Muhammad Chotani as President. Six months later, an All India Muslim Conference convened at Lucknow by the Muslim League Council, witnessed a clash between moderate and extremist Pan-Islamists; the former led by the Raja of Mahmudabad opposed the pitting of the Muslim community against the government, but the extremists led by Maulana Abdul Bari won the day. The Conference formulated the demands of the Indian Khilafatists and decided to observe 17 October as an All India Khilafat Day. It also constituted an All India Khilafat Committee. Two months later, an All India Khilafat Conference was held in Delhi; it called on Muslims to boycott the peace celebrations planned by the government. It declared that if the Khilafat was jeopardized by an 'unjust peace', imposed on Turkey, it would be 'the religious duty of all Indian Muslims' to withdraw cooperation from the government. A new organization of Muslim divines, Jamiat al-Ulema-e-Hind, was formed.

The Khilafat propaganda received a boost from the release of Ali brothers, Mohamed and Shaukat, at the end of the year, who had been interned since 1915. Mohamed Ali sailed for England in early February as the head of a delegation to plead for leniency to Turkey. The deputation got little out of Lloyd George, the British Prime Minister, when it met him on 19 March 1920. Lloyd George flatly rejected the case for leniency to Turkey:

I do not understand Mr Mohd. Ali's claim to indulgence for Turkey. He claims justice and justice she will get. Austria has had justice. Germany has had justice—pretty terrible justice. Why should Turkey escape? I want the Muhammadans of India to get it well into their minds that we are not treating Turkey severely because she is Muhammadan; we are applying the same principle to her as we have applied to Austria, which is a great Christian country.[6]

It was clear that the British Government did not intend to intervene on behalf of Turkey at the peace conference. The Central Khilafat Committee was under pressure from the provincial committees to declare non-cooperation with the British government. In February 1920, the Bengal Khilafat Committee called on Muslims to break off all connection with the government. The following month, the UP Khilafat Conference approved a four-stage programme for non-cooperation with the government: the surrender of titles, resignations from government service, the police and the military, and finally non-payment of taxes.

The publication of the Treaty of Sèvres in May 1920 brought the anger and the frustration of the Khilafat leaders to a high pitch. The treaty had left Turkey helpless and mutilated, a 'shadow state' living on the sufferance of powers and peoples who were annexing her riches and territories. On 12 May the Central Khilafat Committee decided to go ahead with its programme of non-cooperation with the government, and decided to call a meeting of the All India Khilafat Conference at Allahabad. It invited Congress leaders who about the same time had assembled at Benares (Varanasi) for a meeting of the All India Congress Committee. Among those who came to Allahabad were Madan Mohan Malaviya,

Motilal Nehru, Annie Besant, Tej Bahadur Sapru, C.Y. Chintamani, and Gandhi.

The pan-Islamist leaders, Dr M.A. Ansari, the Ali brothers, Abdul Bari, and others, realized that after its defeat in the war, Turkey would be in for a stern reckoning at the peace conference unless Indian Muslims could exert overwhelming pressure on the British government. They calculated that this pressure could be immeasurably enhanced if they could secure the backing of the Hindus who formed the majority of the population of India and were politically better organized. It seemed to them that of all the Hindu leaders, Gandhi was the most sympathetic to Muslim sentiment on the Khilafat issue. This impression may appear surprising in view of the fact that Gandhi had returned to India only in 1915 after twenty years' stay in South Africa.

III

During his two decades-long struggle in South Africa, Gandhi had taken little interest in the pan-Islamist movement, but he had achieved a remarkable success in uniting his Hindu and Muslim followers in his campaign against racialism. After leaving South Africa, he continued his efforts to befriend his Muslim countrymen. In October 1914, at a meeting of the Indian Ambulance Brigade in London, at which the Aga Khan was present, Gandhi lauded the contribution made by Muslim participants in his South African struggle; he also hinted that he shared the Muslim anxiety about the future of Turkey.[7] During the war years, while he abstained from active politics in India, he seemed to evoke more respect and affection in the Muslim community than almost any other Hindu leader; this was evidently due to his South African record. On 28 November 1917, the students of the M.A.O. College accorded him an enthusiastic reception when he arrived at Aligarh. They unhorsed the carriage in which he sat and hauled it through the profusely decorated streets of the town. The British Principal of the M.A.O. College did not allow a meeting to be held in the Union rooms, but Gandhi addressed an audience of two thousand on the lawns of the Lyall Library. He denounced communal riots, which had disfigured Bihar recently, and paid a tribute to the Ali brothers, Mohamed and Shaukat, distinguished alumni of Aligarh College, who had been interned by the government without trial. He exhorted the Muslim community not to lag behind Hindus in the struggle for national regeneration. Communal harmony was a recurring theme in Gandhi's speeches during these years. He supported the Congress–League scheme and the Lucknow Pact, though he had no share in framing them. He made it a point to attend the annual sessions of the Muslim League, which were being held during these years at the same place and almost at the same time as the Indian National Congress. In December 1917 he was present at the Calcutta session of the Muslim League, when a resolution on the release of Mohamed Ali was moved. He saw the wild excitement that prevailed when the League leaders indulged in platform oratory; some of them offered to sacrifice their lives for Mohamed Ali; others talked of surrendering honours conferred on them by the government.[8] Gandhi tried to calm them down, and exhorted them not to give in to despair or anger. In Calcutta he saw how intimately the Ali brothers had come to be associated with the Turkish cause, how deeply their detention without trial was resented, and how helpless the Muslim leaders felt in the face of official intransigence. From that moment he decided to whole-heartedly take up the case of the Ali brothers and became the most forceful advocate of their release.

Throughout 1919 Gandhi was deeply involved in the satyagraha struggle against the Rowlatt Bills and its aftermath. He had suspended the struggle in April after the violent outbreaks in Bombay, Ahmedabad, and Amritsar. How to conduct a struggle against injustice without hatred and violence was a problem that taxed his intellectual and moral resources to the uttermost. With one satyagraha struggle on his hands, he was in no hurry to launch another on the Khilafat issue. In March 1919, when he paid a brief visit to Lucknow on his way to Allahabad, Maulana Abdul Bari unburdened himself on the dangers that beset Islam after the defeat of Turkey. Gandhi was sympathetic and explained his method of satyagraha, which he was about to invoke against the Rowlatt Bills. Abdul Bari was attracted by the possibilities of satyagraha for the cause of the Khilafat and suggested steps to promote permanent amity between Hindus and Muslims. Gandhi had, however, little to do with the stepping up of the Khilafat agitation in India in 1918 and 1919, bringing it up high on the agenda of the All India Muslim League, the establishment of the All India Khilafat Committee, and Jamiat al-Ulema-e-Hind, the organization of the Muslim divines. After the publication of the terms of the Treaty of Sèvres in May 1920 Muslim frustration came to a head. Hitherto Gandhi's role had been that of a friendly observer, expressing his sympathy, counselling patience, acting as a meditator with the government. Suddenly in the summer of 1920, the Khilafat cauldron boiled over. The Central Khilafat Committee and some of the provincial Khilafat Committees called for 'direct action' against the British government for its indifference to Turkey's fate. The

Khilafat leaders turned to Gandhi for advice and assistance. Was he not preaching that non-violent resistance, satyagraha, was a superior weapon to violence? When the Congress leaders at the joint Hindu–Muslim Conference at Allahabad in June 1920 hesitated to support a non-cooperation campaign on the Khilafat issue and called for a special session of the Congress to take the final decision, the Khilafat leaders were beside themselves with rage. Gandhi tried to cool their tempers. He pleaded that he had done his best to bring round the sceptics in the All India Congress Committee to his own view on non-cooperation, but had failed. He assured them that the Hindus would be with them so long as they (the Khilafat leaders) remained Indians and did not adopt insane measures or indulge in violence. He considered the call for *Hijrat* (migration) or Jihad impracticable. He told the Khilafat leaders that if they thought they could achieve their object by any means other than satyagraha, they were at liberty to do so. If, on the other hand, they accepted non-violent non-cooperation, he was prepared to sacrifice his life in employing it.[9]

The joint Hindu–Muslim Conference was an eye-opener for Gandhi. He was disconcerted by what he saw of the Muslim temper. 'Impatience may any day be reduced to madness,' he remarked, 'and the latter must inevitably lead to violence. And I wish I could persuade everyone to see that violence is suicidal.' That Gandhi's fears were not groundless is proved by C.I.D. reports submitted to the Home Department of the Government of India for the months of April and May 1920. Thousands were attending public meetings in UP and applauding the most extravagant flights of mosque orators. A curious feature of these meetings was the heckling of the speakers by impatient men who said in effect, 'Enough of words. It is now time for deeds.' Sind was seething with discontent. A provincial conference was held in May 1920. A fatwa was issued by sixteen *pirs* and maulvis making it incumbent upon every Muslim to renounce his titles, *parvanas*, pleaderships, etc. because the Christians 'have killed pigs, walked with boots on, smoked cigarettes, drunk with liquor, in the sacred places of Islam'.[10] The arrival in India of the Afghan Peace Delegation, some of whose members were believed to be pro-Turkish, gave the Pan-Islamists a shot in the arm. Excitement rose to a high pitch. Wild rumours were rife; it was alleged that the study of the Quran was about to be banned in British India, that Mecca and Medina were under British occupation, that the sanctuary of the Kaaba had been destroyed, that Sunday was going to be the day for prayers instead of Friday. Urdu newspapers were publishing inflammatory articles and poems, and proclaiming that India had become a *dar-ul-harb*, that good Muslims had to make the awesome choice between jihad and *hijrat*. The notion that it was possible for Indian Muslims to migrate to Afghanistan, and then to reconquer India was romantic in the extreme, but it obtained wide currency through Khilafat propaganda.[11] It was at about this time that Maulana Abul Kalam Azad issued his famous fatwa in favour of *hijrat*: 'After taking into account all the provisions of the *Sharia*, contemporary events, the interests of the Muslims, and pros and cons [of political issues], I feel satisfied ... the Muslims of India have no choice but to migrate from India ... Those who cannot migrate immediately should help the migrants [*Muhajirin*].' In April and May 1920, *hijrat* began as a trickle, but by June and July it became a torrent. Whole families, and in some cases entire village populations, set out for their El Dorado in Afghanistan.[12]

The frenzied mood of the rank and file may be surmised from a letter written by the secretary of the Khilafat Committee of Badaun, a small town in UP, to the Central Khilafat Committee in Bombay: 'Having seen the peace terms offered to Turkey, the heart is broken into pieces. Every member of the Badaun Khilafat Committee is ready to give up his own life and take the life of every Christian dog. The Badaun Committee has resolved to write to your Central Committee as soon as possible to hoist the Mohammedi flag and to declare a general jihad.'

There was a serious crisis in the Jama Masjid, the largest mosque in Delhi, when the Imam, suspected of pro-British leanings, was not allowed to conduct the Maghrib prayers. His attempt to have the prayers conducted by his son was foiled by militant Khilafatists; the Imam's brother was later assaulted, and there was a near riot.[13]

IV

Gandhi was disturbed, but not surprised by the course of events. He had been urging moderation on the Khilafat leaders, and at the same time warning the government not to flout Muslim sentiment on the Turkish peace terms. He had a lingering hope that the British government would do something to stem the tide of Muslim resentment and frustration. He had toyed with the idea of visiting England to meet the British ministers, but his request for a sea passage was turned down.

What was Gandhi to do? By June the Khilafat barometer had shot up. There was no doubt about the intensity of Muslim feeling. It was not confined to a few fanatical maulanas, or ambitious politicians. The protagonists of the Khilafat included not only known critics of the government, such as Abul Kalam Azad and Ansari, but such staunch loyalists as the Aga

Khan and Ameer Ali, who were presenting to the British government memorials on behalf of the London branch of the Muslim League. Lala Lajpat Rai, who presided over the special session of the Indian National Congress at Calcutta in September 1920, was not far wrong when he said that there could not be more than one person in a million among the Sunni Muhammadens of India who entertained any doubts on the Khilafat issue. Indeed, the Khilafat sentiment cut across sectarian barriers. Jinnah was a Shia, yet at the Lucknow session of the Muslim League in 1916, he urged the government to respect 'Indian Muslims' dearest and most sacred religious feelings on the Khilafat issue'. In 1919 he headed a Muslim League delegation to England to plead on behalf of Turkey and the Khilafat. In his presidential speech at the September 1920 session of the Muslim League, he described the Khilafat 'as a matter of life and death' for Muslims. He did not, however, commit himself to any course of action, leaving the decision to the 'collective wisdom of Mussalmans'. When the Muslim League opted for non-cooperation, Jinnah opted out of the League. He did not embroil himself with the government, but continued in his press statements to support the case for Turkey and the Khilafat. The Director of the C.I.D. in the Simla secretariat, which exercised surveillance over political movements in India, must have been surprised when Abdul Majid, one of his most trusted officers, avowed his sympathy with the Khilafat cause and expressed his antipathy to Sharif Husain, the British protégé in Arabia.[14] If the pan-Islamic feeling was so strong among Western-educated Muslims, its intensity among the semi-literate masses, who were daily exposed to mosque oratory and the fervid prose of the Urdu press, can well be imagined.

Despite the intensity of Muslim feeling, there was little real enthusiasm for the Khilafat issue amongst the Hindu leaders, even in Gandhi's own immediate entourage. Most of them had supported the demand for the release of the Ali brothers and even supported the hartals on Khilafat days, but they did not pretend to understand or sympathize with the pan-Islamic sentiments. 'Pan-Islamism or Pan-Hinduism,' Motilal Nehru wrote to his son in February 1920, 'does not enter in the programme of the Indian nationalists.' Hindu leaders were glad to see that Muslim loyalty to the Raj was wearing thin; they saw in the Khilafat issue another stick with which to beat the British, but the logic of the Khilafat grievance was not clear to them. Some of Gandhi's closest colleagues felt uneasy at his involvement with the Khilafat issue. Vallabhbhai Patel was frankly sceptical. 'Imagine,' he said, 'our fighting for the independence of the Arabs of Arabia and Palestine, Syria and Mesopotamia, when we ourselves are held as slaves under the British bayonets in our own land.'[15] C.P. Ramaswamy Aiyar, the brilliant Home Rule leader from Madras, feared that the Khilafat agitation was likely to throw a whole community off its balance, and in the long run embitter the relationship between Hindus and Muslims by raising hopes that might not be realized.[16] Some Hindu leaders, such as M.M. Malaviya, recoiled at the very idea of involving Hindus in a purely religious crusade of the Muslim community. N.C. Kelkar, a lieutenant of Tilak, did not see why Hindus should embroil themselves in a conflict between the British government and the Muslims.[17] To Rabindranath Tagore, the Khilafat agitation seemed a manifestation of irrational and turbulent politics. C.F. Andrews, one of Gandhi's closest English friends, told him that Hindus and Christians could not support Turkish domination of non-Turkish lands such as Syria, Palestine, Arabia, Armenia, Mesopotamia. 'These lands have been won by the sword', Andrews added, 'and lost by the sword. They have never been peopled by the Turks.'

Gandhi saw the Khilafat issue primarily in moral terms. He felt that as an Indian he was bound to share the sufferings and trials of his fellow countrymen. 'If I were not interested in the Indian Mohammedans,' he wrote, 'I would not interest myself in the welfare of the Turks any more than I do in that of the Austrians or the Poles.'[18] He did not pretend he was qualified to adjudicate on the theological and juridical aspects of the Khilafat issue. It was enough for him that influential Muslim opinion in India was united on it. It was, he believed, the duty of the Government of India to impress on the British government the importance of placating the sentiments of eighty million Indian Muslims in devising the peace treaty with the defeated Ottoman Empire.

Gandhi wanted Hindu support for the movement to be wholly unconditional. 'If twenty-two crores of Hindus intelligently plead for the Muslims on the Khilafat issue,' he wrote, 'I believe they would for ever win the vote of eight crores of Muslims.' He did not deny that the fate of the Khilafat was a Muslim problem, and Hindus were not directly concerned. It, however, seemed to him that this was an opportunity for the Hindus to make a grand gesture, 'a compelling act of love' to their Muslim compatriots.

Gandhi had been on the verge of a confrontation with the government since July 1919 when he had suspended the satyagraha against the Rowlatt Bills. Some of his colleagues wondered why he had not chosen an issue with a wider and secular appeal. His hand, however, seems to have been forced by the intensity of Muslim discontent and the danger of its diversion into self-destructive channels. The Khilafat leadership was the victim of its own propaganda: it was under pressure from its own following, and Gandhi was under pressure from the Khilafat leaders. The programme of non-cooperation was launched on the Khilafat issue in August 1920. However, almost immediately Gandhi embarked on a strategy to bring the Khilafat agitation into the mainstream of nationalist politics. He succeeded against heavy odds in securing the approval of the Indian National Congress at its special session in September 1920 for his programme of non-cooperation.

V

From the autumn of 1920 to the spring of 1922, when he was imprisoned, Gandhi was the leader of both the nationalist struggle for Swaraj and the Khilafat agitation for the revision of the Treaty of Sèvres that had been imposed on Turkey. By linking the Khilafat issue with Indian independence, Gandhi had for the first time brought the Muslim community into the heart of nationalist politics. The Khilafat agitation, which had been sporadic and shapeless at the beginning of 1920, was a force to reckon with a year later. Its impact was felt even in such political backwaters as Sind, Punjab, Bihar, and Madras. It swamped the fourteen-year-old All India Muslim League, leaving its established leadership isolated. It became a major plank in the programme of the two new major Muslim organizations, the All India Khilafat Conference and the Jamiat-al-Ulema-e-Hind.

The advent of mass politics in 1920–1 was as bewildering for the Muslim political élite, consisting of the landed and titled gentry and the professional classes, as it was for its Hindu counterpart. The Muslim élite's response to non-cooperation was on the whole more antipathetic; it was pro-Turkish, but not anti-British. It might feel deeply for Turkey and the future of Khilafat; it might indulge in criticism of the British policy in the privacy of the living-room; it might even contribute secretly to the Khilafat funds, but it was not prepared to risk the consequences of involvement in Gandhi's campaign. The Muslim élite had an ingrained distrust of the Indian National Congress, and indeed of most Hindu leaders. It was proof against Gandhi's asceticism and charisma and determined not to lose British support. Nor was it prepared to lightly fling aside the two levers for Muslim uplift: English education and government employment, which it had cherished since the days of Syed Ahmad Khan, and which were threatened by Gandhi's non-cooperation programme. It is not surprising that most of the Khilafatists who were sucked into non-cooperation were young students, briefless lawyers, petty shopkeepers, poor artisans, and impecunious village maulvis.

The ulema came to hold a position in Muslim society which they had rarely ever occupied before. It is an index of their religious zeal, that they tried to establish separate shariat courts and the collection of *zakat* (a percentage of income) for religious charities on a regular basis. Abul Kalam Azad called for the appointment of a hierarchy of theologians as Amirs in each province and district with an elected Amir-i-Hind for the whole country to administer Islamic law for Muslims. The Amir-i-Hind was to be initially appointed by the organization of Indian ulema, the Jamiat-al-Ulema-e-Hind, but was ultimately to be the nominee of the Sultan–Caliph of Turkey. Abul Kalam Azad seems to have aspired to hold this office.[19] That such a proposal of a 'state within a state' could have been seriously made shows the make-believe world which the Khilafat enthusiasts, especially the ulema, had created for themselves.

It is difficult today to visualize the depth of the emotion aroused by the Khilafat issue. The cry of Islam in peril echoed through thousands of mosques. Some of the eminent Khilafat leaders, such as Mohamed Ali, Zafar Ali Khan, and Hasrat Mohani, were poets; their speeches, laced with Urdu verse, raised emotions at Khilafat meetings to a fever pitch. Not infrequently, the speakers and the audience were seen weeping together at the misfortunes of Turkey and travails of Islam.[20]

'Fatwas' rained upon Indian Muslims. They were enjoined by the ulema not only to save the last Muslim empire from extinction, but to remould their lives in accordance with the teachings of the Prophet. There was scarcely any aspect of life on which Muslim divines could not produce an injunction from their theological repertoire. Even in the domain of politics everything had to be buttressed with scriptural authority. British Councils, courts, and schools were to be boycotted because they were *haram* (forbidden) under the shariat. Titles, honorary offices, and government jobs had to be given up because events in Turkey had made it a sin to hold them. Mohamed Ali argued that the Quran permitted Hindu-Muslim unity, and this unity was 'not only highly necessary, but obligatory in view of our present condition'.

The religious overtones of the Khilafat agitation, which made it susceptible to fanaticism and violence, were a source of constant concern to Gandhi. Restraint in speech did not come easily to most Khilafat leaders. After hearing Maulana Zafar Ali Khan at a meeting in Lahore, Mahadev Desai, Gandhi's secretary, wrote in his diary, 'The Maulviji's tongue is sharp and incisive as a dagger.' The concept of ahimsa did not go down well with the Khilafatists: it smacked of cowardice or unmanliness. Most Khilafat leaders thought it necessary to continually justify non-violence to their followers. Shaukat Ali affirmed that though for Muslims, the ultimate choice lay between jihad and *hijrat*, they had 'for the time being' decided to follow Gandhi and adopt non-violent non-cooperation.

Gandhi had not inducted the ulema into the Khilafat movement. They were there before he was invited to guide the movement. He found them embarrassing allies, ever verging on fanaticism and violence. It required all his patience, skill, and firmness to restrain them. When bad news from Turkey inflamed Muslim opinion, and the Khilafatists were straining at the leash, Gandhi counselled patience and restraint. 'Mere ignorant, thoughtless and angry outbursts of violence,' he warned, 'may give vent to pent-up rage, but can bring no relief to Turkey.' The best help that the people of India could give to Turkey was to liberate themselves from the British yoke, so that India could have a voice in the comity of nations. What can a 'paralytic do to help others,' Gandhi asked, 'except to try to cure himself of paralysis.' Even though the Khilafat agitation was originally a religious, and indeed an exclusively Muslim issue, Gandhi tried to impart to it a secular orientation. The programme of non-cooperation including the boycott of legislative councils, courts, schools and foreign cloth, the building up of alternative educational and judicial structures, the extension of hand-spinning and hand-weaving, was meant for *all* communities.

Gandhi offered his method of non-violent resistance to the protagonists of Khilafat in 1920, as he had offered it to the peasants of Champaran in 1917 and the textile workers of Ahmedabad in 1918. His immediate concern was to prevent the Khilafat agitation from turning into a violent explosion; he lifted it from the religious to the political plane and linked it with the Indian demand for self-government. The goal of Swaraj he placed before the country was secular, as was the programme of non-cooperation with the symbols and institutions of alien rule. In the course of his countrywide tours, he addressed thousands of meetings of Hindus as well as Muslims. Sometimes he had the rare honour, for a non-Muslim, of being asked to speak in mosques and *idgahs*. He did not pander to popular prejudices, giving no encouragement to religious obscurantism; he described purdah as a curse of Muslim women, and warned the Muslim community against resort to such desperate and suicidal expedients as *hijrat*. He studiously refrained from playing on the religious feelings of Muslims; indeed he insisted on a reasoned and sober presentation of the Khilafat issue.

Gandhi had two principal aims in lending his support to the Khilafat movement: to prevent it from turning violent and to draw the Muslim community into the orbit of the nationalist movement. He achieved a great measure of success in his first aim; but not in the second. The 'grand alliance' between the Congress and the Khilafat organizations did not mature into a permanent Hindu–Muslim accord. Gandhi's hope that the Hindus' unconditional support would secure the lasting gratitude of their Muslim compatriots remained unrealized. The period of the 'grand alliance' was much too short to offset the decades-long conditioning of the Muslim intelligentsia against Indian nationalism. Since the days of Syed Ahmad Khan they had been taught to believe that there was an essential antagonism between the interests of Hindus and Muslims, that the future of the Muslim community was linked with the continuance of British rule, that its replacement by a representative form of government would place Muslims at a permanent disadvantage vis-à-vis Hindus.

The basic weakness of the Congress–Khilafat alliance was that it was the outcome of a temporary alienation of Indian Muslims from the British government because of its refusal to rescue Turkey from the consequences of its defeat in the world war. The non-cooperation movement succeeded in forging a common front between the two communities, but while Hindus were animated by the aspirations for Swaraj, the Muslims' over-whelming concern was the fate of Turkey and the Caliphate. Gandhi and his colleagues in the Congress do not seem to have realized the risks inherent in such a situation. Shrewd British observers, however, even at the height of the Khilafat movement, felt confident that the alienation of the Muslim community was a passing phase and could be reversed. Both the Viceroys, Lord Chelmsford and Lord Reading, who headed the Indian administration during this period, repeatedly urged the British government to do something to assuage Muslim opinion in India by working for substantial modifications in the peace treaty in favour of Turkey. They were strongly supported by Montagu, the Secretary of State for India, but Prime Minister Lloyd George could not be deflected from his anti-Turkish and pro-Greek stand.

'I am most anxious,' Load Reading telegraphed the Secretary of State for India in September 1922, 'to get the Moslems in line with us. But we must get back to the position of Britain, the friend and protector of Muslims. We must be able to rely on the Moslem; we must not have him arrayed against us, and if only you and I can restore the former position in this respect, we shall have taken a great step for the pacification of India and the restoration of our authority and prestige.'[20A]

In the event, Turkey was saved not by British diplomacy but by Turkish arms. Kemal Ataturk won decisive victories over the Greeks in 1921–2.

A peace conference was summoned at Lausanne in November 1922. The Treaty of Lausanne (July 1923) recognized complete Turkish sovereignty over all the territories included in the present-day Turkish Republic. Turkey, alone among the defeated powers of the First World War, was thus able to alter the peace terms imposed on her. The news of Turkish victories thrilled Indian Muslims, but their jubilation did not last long. The Turkish Parliament, under the direction of Kemal Ataturk, first separated the institutions of Sultanate and Caliphate, and then abolished both of them. Ignorant as they were of the cross-currents of Turkish politics, Indian Muslims were stunned by the course of events. They received news of the abolition of the Caliphate with utter disbelief. The Turks, the guardians of the Khilafat, had themselves destroyed it. The ulema were beside themselves with rage; the Khilafat politicians were crestfallen, the Muslim masses were confused. The new Turkish regime set out to make a clean break with Turkey's imperial and Islamic past: its orientation was ostentatiously nationalist, secular, and modern. It was anxious, as the British Ambassador to Turkey told Prime Minister Lloyd George, to shed its pan-Islamic baggage, and to reshape its domestic and foreign policies to suit the interests of the new Turkish nation-state.

Indian Muslims were to discover that the issue of the Caliphate was not, as they induced themselves to believe, a question of Islamic doctrine, but of power politics; it was intertwined with national and tribal rivalries and the dynastic ambitions of Arab chieftains. The solidarity of the Islamic world on which they had been fed proved to be a myth.

M.A. Ansari, one of the foremost leaders of the Khilafat movement, recalled in the evening of his life that, with the collapse of the Khilafat, 'the Indian Muslims' dream had crashed on their head'. 'The pan-Islamism, that was once an ideal', he wrote, 'is now a vague grievance, what was once a hope and an inspiration, is now a sorrow.'[21] The same sense of remorse was implicit in the remark of Syed Raza Ali, the president of the Bombay session of the Muslim League in December 1924, who called upon Indian Muslims to switch their attention to 'the internal problems of our motherland, and not to be disturbed by what was going on in a distant land. Extra-territorial patriotism is a most noble and inspiring sentiment if kept within reasonable limits.'[22]

Thirteen years later, Professor Shafa'at Ahmad Khan, in his book *The Indian Federation*, described the Khilafat movement 'as a destructive force in which subconscious impulses, lofty idealism, youthful indiscretion and desire for power and leadership were mixed in a most incongruous manner' and which was 'devoid of constructive thought and was purely negative in its aims, methods and policy.'[23] Muslim critics of the Khilafat movement in later years did not try to explain why such a 'negative' movement took such a firm and pervasive hold of the Muslim community in India and became an emotional issue for millions of Muslims of all classes. On the other hand, some of them were tempted to blame Gandhi and the Hindus. This is what the poet, Sir Mohammad Iqbal, did when he described the Khilafat movement as 'an act of foolishness on the part of Indian Muslims, and a surrender to the Hindus'. A Pakistani writer in 1948 even alleged that the hijrat movement was a trap cunningly laid by Hindus for unsuspecting Muslims.[24]

The denouement was certainly a deep disappointment for Gandhi when he was freed from jail in 1924. His success in drawing the Muslim masses into the nationalist mainstream proved short-lived. Several of the Khilafat leaders had broken off their connection with their allies of the non-cooperation movement. Maulana Abdul Bari blamed Hindu–Muslim riots on the Hindus, charged Gandhi with partisanship, and switched his righteous indignation from the British to the Hindus. He ended up, as he had begun, as a loyal supporter of the Raj. Another prominent Khilafat leader, S.D. Kitchlew, lost no time in plunging into movements for *tabligh* (conversion) and *tanzim* (unification) of the Muslims as a counterblast to the Hindu movements of *shuddhi* and *sangathan*. Hasrat Mohani, the firebrand of the Khilafat days, became sharply critical of Gandhi and the Indian National Congress, and exhibited a quaint mixture of pan-Islamism, communalism, and communism; he joined the Muslim League, supported the division of the country, and then stayed back in India to raise the only dissenting voice when the constitution of the Indian Republic was put to vote in the Constituent Assembly in 1949.

The most dramatic change in the post-Khilafat period came, however, in the Ali brothers. Unlike most of their colleagues in the Khilafat movement, they did not accept the Turkish abolition of the Caliphate as a fait accompli. They had never been gifted with much tact and restraint at the best of times, but in the post-Khilafat period they became increasingly isolated. They opposed proposals for the transfer of the office of the Central Khilafat Committee (which had already come under the cloud of charges of embezzlement) from Bombay to Delhi or to any place in northern India. They fell out with most of their comrades in the Khilafat movement. They got embroiled in bitter controversies with Zafar Ali Khan and Kitchlew. They were temperamentally very different from Abul Kalam Azad and Ajmal Khan, but they alienated even Ansari, who had long been their devoted friend and physician. When Ansari was manhandled at a meeting of the Central Khilafat Committee, he accused Shaukat Ali of 'condoning the atrocious deed of violence under his very nose'.[25]

As for Mohamed Ali, it must be said to his credit that during the two years of Gandhi's incarceration, he tried to work with the Congress leaders. Even after Gandhi's release from jail, it seemed for a time that the Ali brothers would be able to work with him. It was in Mohamed Ali's home in October 1924 that Gandhi went through his twenty-one day fast for Hindu–Muslim unity.

The Ali brothers were under great strain at this time. Mohamed Ali lost a much loved daughter; Shaukat Ali passed through a serious illness. Their mother, whom they adored, fell ill and died; they were short of money. Their break with Gandhi came, however, when they became increasingly bitter and partisan in their attitude to communal issues; their motto seemed to be 'my community, right or wrong'. They professed to see in every disturbance a Hindu conspiracy, and in every Hindu leader an enemy of Indian Muslims. In the end they were levelling charges of communalism even against Gandhi and Motilal Nehru.[26] After the brief interlude of the Khilafat agitation, they reverted to the grooves of pre-1914 politics.

When Gandhi launched civil disobedience in 1930, Mohamed Ali said it was a movement not for complete independence for India but for the enslavement of seventy million Indian Muslims.[27] The answer to this charge was given by Ansari: 'To say that Satyagraha was aimed not so much against the government as against the Muslims is a piece of monstrous falsehood.'

In January 1931, in a letter which he addressed from his deathbed to Ramsay MacDonald, the British Prime Minister, Mohamed Ali explained that he belonged 'to two circles of equal size which are not concentric—one is Indian and the other is the Muslim world'.[28] This indeed was the tragedy of Mohamed Ali's life. 'We are not nationalists,' he wrote, 'but super nationalists, and I as a Muslim say that God made man and Devil made the nation.' It was this basic conflict between a vague pan-Islamism and Indian nationalism in his mind which he could not resolve. He spent the better part of his life chasing the Khilafat mirage. Later he talked vaguely of 'a federation of faiths in India' and 'cultural federalism'. In his letter to the British Prime Minister, to which reference has been made, he argued that Muslims had ruled India for a thousand years, and Hindus were determined to rule India in a spirit of revanche, that he would not favour 'replacing the "nation of shop-keepers" by their Indian counterpart, the *bania*'.[29] He propounded a theory of hostages. He demanded

Muslim majorities in the legislatures of Bengal and the Punjab, and the creation of more Muslim-majority provinces as 'our safeguard, for we demand hostages as we have willingly given hostages to Hindus in the other Provinces where they form huge majorities.'[30]

Mohamed Ali, of course, died long before Jinnah's two-nation theory came to be formulated, but be certainly reinforced the flight from secular nationalism which took Muslim separatism to a point of no return.

Shaukat Ali usually took his cue in politics from his brother; after Mohamed Ali's death he rapidly travelled downhill. Gandhi observed, during the Second Round Table Conference, how Shaukat Ali faithfully toed the Tory line.[31] In February 1932 the Viceroy, Lord Willingdon, was glad to see 'Shaukat Ali in a most amazingly loyal frame of mind'.[32] Six months later, Shaukat Ali applied for the revival of his pension for his past service in the Opium Department before he plunged into the Khilafat agitation. 'Along with other Indian Muslims,' he wrote to the Viceroy, 'both of us [Ali brothers] felt very strongly against the British policy of weakening Muslim States. But I am glad that there has been a great change since then, and I hope never again such a catastrophe would happen and force a Muslim to give up his loyalty to the temporal power for the sake of his faith and religious conviction.'[33] Despite all these disappointments, the Khilafat agitation brought Gandhi and the Congress some valuable allies. One of these was Hakim Ajmal Khan who had been a founder-member of the All India Muslim League and Chairman of its Reception Committee at the Delhi session in December 1919, and became one of the foremost leaders of the Khilafat movement. He did not revert to sectarian politics and remained untouched by the communal taint of the twenties. Like Ajmal Khan, Dr M.A. Ansari had, since his younger days, been a member of the Muslim League. He was an ardent pan-Islamist too, and in the highest echelons of the Khilafat movement. Nevertheless, thanks to his exposure to the non-cooperation movement and association with Gandhi, he outgrew sectarian politics and maintained his secular outlook till his death in 1935. No less remarkable was the transformation wrought by the non-cooperation movement in Maulana Abul Kalam Azad. Here was an ardent pan-Islamist and a learned theologian—whose writings, studded with quotations from the scriptures, gave little inkling of his latent rationality and modernity—suddenly maturing into a secular and nationalist politician. After the eclipse of the Ali brothers, and the deaths of Ajmal Khan and Ansari, Azad became in the late thirties and early forties the most outstanding nationalist Muslim leader in India.

The Indian National Congress had not been able to secure the enthusiastic participation of the Muslim community in its proceedings and activities during the first thirty years of its existence. The conclusion of the Congress–League Pact in 1916 was indeed an acknowledgement of this. It is true that a few prominent Muslim politicians, such as Rasool in Bengal, Mazharul Haq in Patna, and Mohammad Ali Jinnah in Bombay took part in Congress activities in those years. It would, however, be difficult to contest the opinion of Professor Mujeeb in his book, *Indian Muslims*, that 'till 1919 there was no Muslim leadership that could be definitely identified as representing the common Indian interests'.[34] Mujeeb was not sure, however, whether Muslim alienation from the Congress was due to the inability of Muslim leaders to adopt a form of political expression other than in religious terms, or whether they sensed that Muslims would be unresponsive to a secular approach. Mujeeb's poser had been answered many years earlier by Shibli Numani, the eminent Arabic scholar and poet and colleague of Sir Syed Ahmad Khan, and the mentor of Abul Kalam Azad: 'The followers of the Prophet do not respond to the call of nationhood. Appeal to them in the name of religion and you will see what a splendid response you get.'[35] How prophetic! Both the mass agitations in the twentieth century that swept Indian Muslims in the Indian subcontinent, for the Khilafat and for Pakistan respectively, were waged with the cry of religion in danger.

NOTES AND REFERENCES

1. Quoted in a memorandum entitled 'Misrepresentations in connection with the Khilafat question' enclosed with Home Dept's circular letter no. 382 dated 10 Feb. 1920 to all Local Governments. L/P+S/10/798, India Office Library (henceforth I.O.L.)

2. Quoted in P. Hardy, *The Muslims of British India* (London, 1972), p. 176.

3. H. Tyabji, *Badruddin Tyabji* (Bombay, 1952), pp. 50–1.

4. Theodore Morison, 'Muhammedan Movements' in *Political India, 1931–2*, edited by. Sir John Cumming (London, 1932), pp. 95–6.

5. Matiur Rahman, *From Consultation to Confrontation* (London, 1970), pp. 227–8.

6. Minutes of Procs. at a Deputation from the Indian Khilafat Delegation to the Prime Minister at 10 Downing Street, on 19 March 1920, L/P+S/10/798, I.O.L.

7. *Collected Works of Mahatma Gandhi* (henceforth *C.W.M.G.*), vol. xii, p. 536.

8. Home Pol, B., Jan. 1918, no. 487–90, National Archives of India (henceforth N.A.I.).

9. Home Pol, April 1920, no. 103, N.A.I.

10. Home Pol, June 1920, no. 78, N.A.I.

11. Gail Minault, *The Khilafat Movement* (Delhi, 1982), p. 106.

12. Grant, Chf Comm., N.W.F.P. to Chelmsford, 15 August 1920, Chelmsford Papers.

13. Home Pol Dept., April 1920, no. 103, N.A.I.

14. Note dt. 26 April 1918 by A. Majid in Home Pol, May 1918, Procs. no. 15, N.A.I.

15. Indulal Yajnik, *Gandhi as I know him* (Delhi, 1943), p. 131.

16. *New India*, 22 April 1920.

17. Home Pol, Aug. 1920, Procs. no. 35, N.A.I.

18. *CWMG*, vol. xvii, p. 475.

19. Abdul Razzaq Malihabadi, *Zikr-e-Azad* (Calcutta, 1960), p. 37.

20. Gail Minault, 'Urdu Political Poetry During the Khilafat Movement' *in Modern Asian Studies*, 8, 4, (1974), pp. 459–71.

20A. Viceroy to Secretary of State for India, September 1922, *Reading Papers*.

21. Halide Edib, *The Conflict of East and West in Turkey* (Delhi, 1935), p. vi.

22. A.M. Zaidi, *Evolution of Muslim Political Thought in India*, vol. II (Delhi, 1980), p. 298.

23. Shafa'at Ahmad Khan, *The Indian Federation* (London, 1937), p. 330.

24. A.B. Rajput, *Muslim League, Yesterday and Today* (Lahore, 1948), p. 37.

25. Ansari to Shaukat Ali, 14 May 1929 *in* Mushirul Hasan (ed.), *Muslims and the Congress* (Delhi, 1979), pp. 65.

26. A.M. Daryabadi, *Muhammad Ali: Zaati Diary Ke Chund Warq*, vol. 1, (Hyderabad, 1943), p. 155.

27. Afzal Iqbal, *The Life and Times of Mohamed Ali* (Delhi, 1978 edn), p. 371.

28. Ibid., p. 381.

29. Ibid., p. 384.

30. Ibid., p. 382.

31. Mahadev Desai to Jawaharlal Nehru, 16 Sept. 1931. Jawaharlal Nehru Papers, N.M.M.L.

32. Willingdon to Hoare, 15 Feb. 1932, Templewood Papers, I.O.L.

33. Shaukat Ali to Erick Miéville, P.S. to the Viceroy, 10 Aug. 1933, Home Pol., File no. 151 of 1933.

34. M. Mujeeb, *Indian Muslims* (London, 1967), p. 528.

35. Quoted in S.M. Ikram, *Modern Muslim India and the Birth of Pakistan 1858–1951*, (Lahore, 1965), p. 138.

TWELVE

Abdul Ghaffar Khan: the 'Frontier Gandhi'

In the history of the nationalist movement Khan Abdul Ghaffar Khan is in a class of his own. For eighteen years he was in the highest echelons of the Indian National Congress under Gandhi's leadership. In his background, temperament, and style, he differed from other Congress leaders such as Jawaharlal Nehru, Vallabhbhai Patel, C. Rajagopalachari, Rajendra Prasad, and Abul Kalam Azad, the chief lieutenants of the Mahatma in the political field. Vinoba Bhave exemplified the ethical and spiritual side of the Gandhian ideology; Jamnalal Bajaj was the pivotal figure in the constructive programme; J.C. Kumarappa assisted Gandhi in the campaign for the regeneration of rural India, and Thakkar Bapa immersed himself in the crusade against untouchability. Abdul Ghaffar Khan was associated with the boldest experiment in non-violence as a tool of social and political action. His evolution into an outstanding practitioner of non-violence in the Indian subcontinent, next only to Gandhi, is a phenomenon that amazed his colleagues and baffled his opponents. There was, however, nothing inevitable about this evolution; indeed it is surprising that it took place at all and was the result of a few happy accidents in the early years of his life.

The first accident was the location of the hostel of Edward Memorial Mission High School, where Abdul Ghaffar Khan studied, in Peshawar, in proximity to the bungalow of Rev. E.F.E. Wigram, the British principal of the school. Abdul Ghaffar was impressed by the way Wigram and his devoted band of missionaries rendered selfless service to all those who came to them for help. He thought of emulating their example when he grew up.

The second accident was that, after being commissioned into the prestigious Guides Regiment, even before he had passed the matriculation examination, Abdul Ghaffar resigned when he saw a British subaltern insulting an Indian cavalry officer. He came to the conclusion that no self-respecting Indian could serve in the British Indian army under such humiliating conditions. If he had listened to his father's pleas not to resign, Abdul Ghaffar may well have ended up as a major, or perhaps even as a colonel, in the Guides Regiment.

The third 'accident' that changed the course of Abdul Ghaffar's life occurred just when he was about to leave for Britain, where his elder brother Khan Sahib was studying medicine. Abdul Ghaffar's admission to an engineering college had been arranged and his sea-passage booked, but his mother said she could not bear the thought of parting from her youngest son. Ghaffar Khan's plans of taking an engineering degree from a British university went up in smoke. Little did he know that he was destined for a larger role in life than that of an executive engineer in the public works department.

The fourth accident occurred in the years immediately preceding the First World War when there was a strong wave of pro-Turkish and anti-British feeling amongst Indian Muslims in northern India and especially in the North West Frontier Province (N.W.F.P.). Abdul Ghaffar was swept off his feet by the writings of Abul Kalam Azad in his journal *Al-Hilal*. He came under the spell of some fervent advocates of pan-Islamism such as Maulana Mohamed-ul-Hasan of Deoband, Obaidullah Sindhi, and Haji Sahib of Turangzai, the protagonists of the Ottoman Caliphate who were trying to establish centres in trans-border areas. Mohamed-ul-Hasan went to Mecca and was arrested, Obaidullah Sindhi disappeared into Afghanistan and Central Asia, and Haji Turangzai disappeared into the trans-border area. Abdul Ghaffar was disappointed and returned to his village Utmanzai. He was among the eighteen thousand *muhajir*s (migrants) who migrated from the N.W.F.P. to Afghanistan in the belief that India had ceased to be a holy land for Muslims. In Afghanistan he had an audience with King Amanullah Khan, and was surprised to find him ignorant of Pakhtun, his mother tongue. This migration, *hijrat*, proved a fiasco. Fortunately, Ghaffar Khan was saved from further frittering away his energies in fighting for a lost cause by his induction into the mainstream of Indian nationalism. He had his first brush with the British authorities in April 1919 when he addressed a meeting in his village Utmanzai to protest against the Rowlatt Bills passed by the Imperial Legislative Council. The village was surrounded by British troops; a punitive fine of Rs 30,000 was imposed and three times as much was collected. Abdul Ghaffar was arrested on a concocted charge of tampering with telegraph wires and sentenced to six months' imprisonment.

II

In December 1921 Abdul Ghaffar attended the annual session of the Indian National Congress at Nagpur, which put a final seal of approval on Gandhi's programme for non-cooperation with the British government. Abdul Ghaffar did not immediately plunge into the non-cooperation movement. His involvement in nationalist politics was as yet fitful. What really obsessed him was the wretched condition of the Pakhtun masses in the 'settled districts' of the N.W.F.P. He felt that they were in dire need of education and social reform. In 1921 he established an 'Azad High School' in his village, with Pushtu as the medium of instruction and a curriculum which had some relevance to the immediate surroundings of the students. This was to be the first of a chain of schools in the countryside. The British authorities at once became suspicious of Abdul Ghaffar's motives in start- ing the school. Sir John Maffey, the Chief Commissioner, summoned his father Behram Khan. Behram Khan was a big landlord and was in the good books of British officials, some of whom greeted him as their *chacha* (uncle). Maffey's fear was that if Abdul Ghaffar Khan was allowed to open schools and work for social reform, it might stir discontent against the government. Abdul Ghaffar did not heed the pleas of his father nor the warnings of the Chief Commissioner and refused to close down the school. He was arrested under section 40 of the Frontier Crimes Regulation Act and sentenced to three years' imprisonment. He suffered with fortitude, as he put it, 'the tortures of solitary imprisonment, heavy chains on his hands and feet, dirt, filth, lice and hunger and most of all insults'. After his re- lease he went on a pilgrimage to Mecca, and visited Palestine, Lebanon, Syria, and Iraq. The West Asian tour was an eye-opener to him. He saw Turkey under Kemal Ataturk, Egypt under Zaghlul Pasha, Iran under Reza Shah, and Arabia under Ibn Saud moving away from pan-Islamism and developing national consciousness. On return to India, Abdul Ghaffar severed his ties with the Khilafat organization, which had in any case been reduced to a moribund party, and decided to work for the uplift of his own people. Ninety-eight per cent of Pathans were illiterate; they were not even aware that Pakhtun was their language; wherever they went they adopted the local language. In May 1928 he started *Pakhtun*, a monthly journal, under his editorship. Ghaffar Khan's heart was in the promotion of education and social reform, but he realized that the British authorities would not allow him to work even in this field. He needed political clout if he was to survive even as a social reformer. He had outgrown the politics of his province, which were centred on the discredited Khilafat cause, municipal elections, and factional disputes. He was groping his way towards the mainstream of nationalist politics. In September 1929 he convened a meeting at Charsadda in Peshawar district and founded the Frontier Provincial Youth League. All members of the League were to enrol themselves as members of the Indian National Congress, and the League was to send delegates to a session of the All India Youth Congress. As an adjunct of the League, he organized a volunteer corps and named it 'Khudai Khidmatgars' (Servants of God), every member of which was to take a vow:

I am a Khudai Khidmatgar (servant of God), and as God needs no service I shall serve Him by serving His creatures selflessly. I shall never use violence, I shall not retaliate or take revenge, and I shall forgive anyone who indulges in oppression and excesses against me. I shall not be a party to any intrigue, family feuds and enmity and I shall treat every Pakhtun as my brother and comrade. I shall give up evil customs and practices. I shall lead a simple life, do good and refrain from wrong doing ... I shall expect no reward for my services. I shall be fearless and prepared for any sacrifice.

Abdul Ghaffar decided to cast in his lot with the Indian National Congress. There was no other political party which dared to challenge the British authorities. In December 1929, he attended the annual session of the Congress at Lahore along with over a hundred delegates from his province. He had already met Gandhi and Jawaharlal Nehru a few months earlier at the Lucknow meeting of the All India Congress Committee. Abdul Ghaffar's elder brother, Dr Khan Sahib, who had studied medicine in Britain when Nehru was a student in Cambridge and London before the First World War, gave Ghaffar Khan a letter of introduction to Nehru. Ghaffar Khan's attendance at the Lahore Congress was to be a turning point in his life. Jawaharlal Nehru's declaration of 'complete independence' on the bank of the Ravi on the midnight of 31 December 1929 had an electric effect on Ghaffar Khan. He hurried back to his province to prepare for the civil disobedience campaign which Gandhi was to launch. He had been deeply moved by Gandhi's emphasis on non-violence. Suddenly, he no longer seemed a firebrand: his criticism of the government was now in measured language; so much so that a police officer noted that Ghaffar Khan's propaganda was 'unobjectionable'.

III

The inauguration of the Salt Satyagraha by Gandhi on 12 March 1930, when he began his 241-mile march for Dandi on the sea coast, had a dramatic effect on the N.W.F.P. On 23 April, Abdul Ghaffar addressed a meeting in his native village, Utmanzai, and then left for Peshawar with some of his lieutenants. All of them were arrested and sentenced to three years' rigorous imprisonment. This did not dampen the spirit of the rank and file Khudai Khidmatgars in their campaign for non-payment of land revenue and picketing of shops selling liquor and foreign cloth. The reaction of the authorities to the popular upsurge was sharp, almost panicky. They unleashed a reign of terror. They banned the entry of visitors from other provinces. They did not shrink from whipping young boys and setting fire to the houses of Khudai Khidmatgars. The most serious incident during this period was firing by the troops in Kissa Khani Bazar at Peshawar on 23 April 1930. Abdul Ghaffar Khan had been arrested earlier in the day; the news had taken Peshawar by storm and a crowd collected in Kissa Khani Bazar. Indian troops were brought to the scene, and when they refused to fire on an unarmed crowd, British soldiers were requisitioned. Unofficial estimates of those killed in the firing ranged between two and three hundred; many more were wounded. It was a tragedy reminiscent of the Jallianwala Bagh massacre at Amritsar in April 1919.

An idea of the ruthless repression which the Frontier Province went through in 1930–1 can be formed from two reports, one of which was prepared at Gandhi's instance by Verrier Elwin, the British anthropologist, and the other by Devdas Gandhi, the Mahatma's son, after visiting the N.W.F.P. early in 1932.[1] The vindictiveness of the treatment meted out to Congress and Khudai Khidmatgar volunteers was unprecedented. Columns of troops were sent to surround villages from which Khudai Khidmatgars went to the towns to picket foreign cloth shops; if any Khudai Khidmatgar was found, he was beaten up. If a fine was imposed on the whole village for its Congress sympathies or if there was a case of non-payment of revenue, the police raided the houses of Khudai Khidmatgars and took whatever they could. Abdul Ghaffar himself was put through solitary confinement and rigours of jail life which no other Indian political leader had to suffer. Some of the punishments imposed on Khudai Khidmatgars were ingenious and deliberately designed to break their nerve. They were kept on short rations. They could not get more than one blanket to cover themselves in the bitter Frontier winter. In one case a prisoner was tortured by burning a hornet's nest in his cell. Some of the prisoners were locked up for twenty-four hours in stinking cells devoid of ventilation. Some were stripped to the waist and made to carry heavy loads of stone up and down a hill. A 16-year-old landlord, Mazulla Khan, was clapped into prison as a defaulter because he refused to pay land revenue amounting to two thousand rupees; his motor-car, tonga, horse, three buffaloes, crops, and land worth a lakh and a half were seized. As if this were not sufficient, an attempt was made to terrorize villages by bombing from the air.

For Abdul Ghaffar Khan there were some compensations too, especially after he was transferred to Gujarat jail. His fellow prisoners included Dr M.A. Ansari, Dr S.D. Kitchlew, and Gandhi's son, Devdas. It was in this jail that Abdul Ghaffar read the Gita, the Bible, and the Guru Granth Sahib. Pandit Jagat Narain, a fellow prisoner, ran a Gita class. Abdul Ghaffar started a Quran class. Among the books he read in prison was Gandhi's autobiography. He developed a strong empathy with the Mahatma; he began to fast and observe silence once a week.

It is not difficult to understand the reasons for the exceptional severity of the repression of the Khudai Khidmatgars by the British authorities. They considered the Frontier Province as the most vulnerable part of the British Empire. At the back of their minds was a constant fear of propaganda and incursions from Afghanistan and Soviet Russia, and raids by the unruly trans-border tribes. A British newspaper, the *Daily Mail*, graphically summed up these fears: 'The Frontier is an outpost of the Soviet Republic ... the spearhead of an attack on India ... with the Russian gold pouring in across the Khyber Pass. The Muslims being armed with the Russian weapons ... their leader is the terrible Abdul Ghaffar Khan, a jail-bird and relentless enemy of the British.'[2]

The British authorities believed that it was possible to control the Pathans with an adroit mixture of bribery and coercion. They were so much obsessed with the idea of 90 million Muslims confronting 200 million Hindus in an irreconcilable feud in the subcontinent that they had taken it for granted that the Frontier, with its overwhelming Muslim majority, was immune to nationalist infection from the rest of India. It is not therefore surprising that they were alarmed at the sudden emergence of Abdul Ghaffar Khan's Khudai Khidmatgar organization and its alliance with the Indian National Congress. They resorted to the draconian Frontier Crimes Regulations to crush the movement. They could do so with impunity because there were hardly any judicial checks on them; nor was there any newspaper or journal in the N.W.F.P. to expose their excesses.

What was surprising, however, was not the severity with which the government dealt with the Khudai Khidmatgars, but the courage and forbearance with which they bore lathi charges and even bullets. They did not retaliate. This was a curious phenomenon because Pathan society was notoriously violence-prone. Abdul Ghaffar had no more than six months between the formation of Khudai Khidmatgar organization and the commencement of Gandhi's Salt Satyagraha, but he was able not only to imbibe Gandhi's method of non-violent resistance but to impart it to his followers. The government was not convinced that the Pathans would remain non-violent; in any case, the defiance of the Raj in the 'settled districts' was a bad example to the trans-border tribes. The Viceroy, Lord Irwin, was told that the popular disaffection was due to local causes. He thought of sending Maulana Shaukat Ali, the Khilafat leader, to wean Abdul Ghaffar Khan (who had once been a Khilafatist) from the Congress, but Sir Fazl-i-Husain, the Muslim member of the Viceroy's Executive Council, opposed the proposal. 'It would be better for Shaukat Ali not to go', he wrote, as the 'alliance between the Congress and Abdul Ghaffar Khan was unnatural and was bound to break up in time'. A similar view was taken by the Secretary of State for India, Wedgwood Benn, who wrote to Lord Irwin, 'My impression is that Ghaffar is not really with the Congress, and that if Muslim situation can be eased, his objectionable activities may be curbed especially if personal contact is established'.[3] So obsessed were the British rulers with what they believed to be the fundamental clash of interest between Hindus and Muslims that they could not understand the strength of the bonds between Abdul Ghaffar and Gandhi.

IV

According to Pyarelal, Gandhi's secretary, Abdul Ghaffar Khan was drawn to the Mahatma because he found in him a 'kindred spirit, a man of faith and prayer dedicated to a pure and ascetic life'. But even before they met, circumstances were conspiring to bring Abdul Ghaffar into the orbit of the Congress and the Mahatma. From his youth he had an overwhelming urge to uplift his people, the Pakhtuns, especially the poor peasants and artisans among them. He wanted to make them aware of their cultural heritage, to revive their language, to educate them, to wean them away from their violent feuds and to liberate them from the stranglehold of the mullahs and the landlords, the 'big Khans', who were thriving on the bounty of the British rulers. This is why he formed his volunteer force, the Khudai Khidmatgars. He was not really interested in politics, but he found that the autocratic government of his province would not let him even undertake social and educational work. To survive in public life he needed the support of a political party; he alone could not take on the imperial power. He sounded the Muslim League, the Muslim Conference, and other Muslim parties, but, dependent as they were upon official patronage, none of them was prepared to embroil itself with the government. They told Abdul Ghaffar Khan's emissaries that they could not oppose the British who were 'protecting' Muslims from the Hindus. Abdul Ghaffar Khan came to the conclusion that the Indian National Congress was the only party in the country which could stand up to the British.

It was his instinct for self-preservation that had led Ghaffar Khan to seek an alliance with the Congress. What he may not have foreseen was the tremendous impact that Gandhi's ideas and methods were to make on him. However, long before the Lahore Congress, Abdul Ghaffar's mind had been turning towards non-violence through his study of the Quran. He was also deeply moved by the lives of the early Caliphs, their piety, austerity, and compassion for their fellow men. The inspiration for the oath which he prescribed for Khudai Khidmatgars came from the Islamic scriptures, but its text was such that Gandhi could have adopted it *in toto* for members of his ashram. For Ghaffar Khan, non-violence was as yet an individual ethic; its possibilities as a tool of social and political action came home to him only when he attended the Lahore Congress in December 1929. The idea of a civil disobedience campaign under Gandhi's leadership appealed to him, but he knew how formidable a task it was to inculcate non-violence in his people. Many years earlier Winston Churchill, who had served as a subaltern in the north-west frontier of India, had graphically described in his book *My Early Life* (1897) the Pathans' addiction to violence: 'Every man is a warrior, a politician and theologian. Every large home is a real feudal fortress ... Every family cultivates its vendetta, every clan its feud ... Nothing is ever forgotten, and very few debts are left unpaid.' Another Briton, Verrier Elwin, an anthropologist and missionary, who visited the N.W.F.P. at Gandhi's instance in early 1932, wrote in his report to the All India Congress Committee that the Pathan 'was naturally violent and revengeful; possessed arms and for thousands of years had lived by the law of retaliation'.[4] Elwin added that non-violence was 'a very new idea' and the Khudai Khidmatgars 'were not saints', but it was a miracle that on 'so uncompromising a soil, Abdul Ghaffar had been able to cultivate the flower of non-violence'. During he civil disobedience campaign in 1930 in N.W.F.P. there were some minor incidents, such as pelting of stones at the police, but they were rare, and became rarer in later campaigns. The remarkable restraint and discipline of Khudai Khidmatgars, surprised and delighted the nationalist leaders in India, but disconcerted the British authorities. They saw in this highly organized volunteer force a threat to the Raj, which must be nipped in the bud. How grave the threat seemed and how drastic the official response was can be deduced from the annual report, *India in 1930–1*, which was presented to the British Parliament:

In August 1930 martial law had to be imposed and kept in force until the following January ... the troops had to be employed in helping the civil authorities to uphold the administration throughout the Settled Districts in the province. The task of the military was usually to surround the disaffected towns and villages under cover of darkness in order that the civil officers might effect arrests at daybreak, and frequently it proved necessary to maintain cordons round the centres of disaffection for days at a time ... Hitherto, the Frontierman had tended to concentrate his attention solely on his feuds with his neighbours ... so far as he was concerned at all with external affairs it was with those of Muslim countries of the West rather than those of India. On this occasion, however, it is unquestionable that much of the trouble was directly due to the activities of the Congress party; and the extensive influence which this organization proved itself to have acquired over a predominantly Muslim population ... as a result of the operations of the Red Shirt organisation [Khudai Khidmatgars] for whose creation Khan Abdul Ghaffar Khan was largely responsible ...

The report took note of a strange phenomenon during this period. The unruly trans-border tribesmen in the course of their raids in the 'settled districts' abstained from looting, in their customary manner, the villages they had passed through, and one of the tribes, the Afridis, when negotiating a settlement with the authorities,[5] 'put forward demands for the release of Mr Gandhi and the repeal of the special ordinances in India'. It was not surprising that the government was alarmed at the prospect of the Congress agitation penetrating into the trans-border area. During the negotiations with Gandhi in March 1931, the Viceroy, Lord Irwin, tried hard to exclude the Frontier Province from the truce between the government and the Congress, but Gandhi did not agree. Ghaffar Khan and the Khudai Khidmatgar leaders were released and attended the Karachi Congress. Three months later, he was Gandhi's guest at Borsad in Gujarat. This was the first opportunity for, what Gandhi called, 'heart to heart' talks between them. Gandhi was delighted to meet the Pathan leader and in a letter to the Viceroy's private secretary described him as 'a truthful man, an out and out believer in non-violence'.[6] In Gandhi's lexicon there was no higher compliment!

V

The terrible ordeal which Abdul Ghaffar and his followers had undergone during the satyagraha struggle in 1930 and his meeting with Gandhi at Borsad cemented the alliance of the Khudai Khidmatgars, or the Red

Shirts as they came to be known because of the colour of their clothes, with the Indian National Congress. In August 1931, the Congress Working Committee approved of the adoption of the Khudai Khidmatgar organization. Abdul Ghaffar became responsible for all the Congress activities in the N.W.F.P. This led to a transformation of the Congress in that province; its headquarters were shifted from Peshawar, the capital of the province, to the village of Utmanzai; it ceased to be only an urban movement; its activities now came to be focused on the rural population. The tentative alliance of the Congress and Khudai Khidmatgars in 1929 had grown into a merger in 1931. How complete the merger was is indicated in a letter written by Abdul Ghaffar's elder brother, Dr Khan Sahib, to Jawaharlal Nehru:

In every village flies a Congress flag which possesses an office; every car which carries an office-bearer carries a Congress flag; all people who are working with us are Congress[men]; our chief object here is to unite all different communities into Indians, not theoretically but practically. Our purpose is one, and that is the freedom of India, which I know for certain is yours. Our volunteers are organized bodies waiting for orders from the Congress and will show you when the time comes that they are for national freedom and nothing else ...[7]

After the collapse of the uneasy truce between the Congress and the government in January 1932, when civil disobedience was resumed, the response of the Frontier Province to Gandhi's call surpassed that of all other Indian provinces. According to an official record of convictions for civil disobedience between January to September 1932, the Frontier Province with a population of just three million accounted for 5557 convictions in comparison to 1620 in the Punjab, which had five times the population of the former. Even Bengal, politically the most active province, with a population of 62 million recorded no more than 10,952 convictions.[8]

Abdul Ghaffar Khan had been arrested even before Gandhi returned from the Round Table Conference. The Congress was subjected to the severest repression in its history by the new Viceroy, Lord Willingdon, who succeeded Lord Irwin. In September 1932, when Gandhi undertook a fast in Yeravda prison in Poona to protest against separate electorates for untouchables in the British Prime Minister's Communal Award, Abdul Ghaffar, himself a prisoner in a Bihar jail, fasted on all the seven days of Gandhi's fast. Two years later, when Abdul Ghaffar Khan and his elder brother Khan Sahib were released but not allowed to enter their home province, Gandhi invited them to Wardha. They felt at home in Gandhi's ashram. Abdul Ghaffar Khan shared the simple meals from the ashram kitchen, accompanied Gandhi during his morning and evening walks, and read the Quran at the evening prayers. He learnt to spin and resolved to promote hand-spinning and weaving as a cottage industry in the villages of his province. The British authorities did not let Abdul Ghaffar enjoy this peaceful spell at Wardha very long. In December 1934 he was arrested, prosecuted for a speech he had delivered soon after his release from jail, and sentenced to two years' imprisonment.

Not until August 1937, after six years in exile, did Abdul Ghaffar return to the Frontier Province. He was relieved to find that the Khudai Khidmatgars had survived the hammer blows of the Willingdon regime. In the general election under the new constitution while the Congress won 19 out of 50 seats in the provincial legislature, it swept the polls in the Pakhtun-majority districts and especially in the rural areas, and also won all the non-Muslim seats. A Congress ministry headed by Dr Khan Sahib took office. Gandhi was now able to visit the Frontier Province. In the course of three visits in 1938 the Mahatma came into intimate contact with the Khudai Khidmatgar movement. It struck him as a bold and promising experiment in mass application of non-violence. Abdul Ghaffar told Gandhi:

Violence has been the real bane of the Pathans. The entire strength of the Pathans is today spent in thinking how to cut the throat of his brother ... I am convinced, as far as the Frontier Province is concerned, the non-violent movement is the greatest boon that God has sent us ... I say this from experience of the miraculous transformation that even the little measure of non-violence that we have attained has wrought in our minds. We used to be so timid and indolent. The sight of an Englishman would frighten us. Your movement has instilled fresh life into us ... We have shed our fear and are no longer afraid of an Englishman or for the matter of that, anyone.[9]

Most contemporaries tended to attribute Abdul Ghaffar's hold over his people to his charisma. He himself had a simpler explanation: 'The Pathan will go to hell', he said, 'if you win his heart, but even to heaven, you cannot force him to go. Such is the power of love over the Pathan.'[10]

After his visits to the Frontier in 1938, Gandhi's optimism was at its peak. There were, he wrote, over a hundred thousand Khudai Khidmatgars in the N.W.F.P., 'more numerous, more disciplined than the Congress volunteers in the whole of India'. How wonderful it would be, he added, if they could carry the message of non-violence to the turbulent trans-border tribes, set an example to other provinces of India, and indeed to the world, in the efficacy of non-violence in neutralizing anger, hatred, and violence. Gandhi seems to have been unconsciously encouraged in these agreeable thoughts by the temporary détente between the government and the Congress between 1937 and 1939, and the existence of a Congress ministry in the Frontier Province which made it possible for the Khudai Khidmatgar organization to function unhindered for the first and last time in its history under Abdul Ghaffar's personal direction. Little did Gandhi know that his dream of a non-violent utopia in the N.W.F.P. would soon be shattered by the gathering storm in Europe.

VI

The outbreak of Second World War in 1939, the resignation of the Congress ministries, the Quit India movement, and imprisonment of Congress leaders exposed Abdul Ghaffar Khan's following to a joint assault by the British authorities and the Muslim League.[11] We know now how the Governor of the N.W.F.P., Sir George Cunningham, recruited mullahs for anti-Russian, anti-German, and anti-Japanese propaganda, and also used them to malign the Congress. As part of this propaganda, it was made out that Abdul Ghaffar Khan was rendering India and Islam a disservice by commending non-violence to the brave and warlike people of the Frontier. It was alleged that the Congress was trying to bring about a Hindu Raj in collusion with the Axis Powers. In 1943 Governor Cunningham inducted a Muslim League ministry through the backdoor; it was not difficult because, of the 50 members of the provincial legislature, seven Congress members were in prison and another seven seats had fallen vacant. The installation and bolstering of Muslim League ministries in Muslim-majority provinces was in any case part of British policy during the war; it was also followed in Sind and Assam. In the N.W.F.P., for the next two years, the field was clear for the Muslim League to make propaganda for the partition of India. When Abdul Ghaffar Khan and his colleagues returned to the political scene in 1945, after six years in the wilderness, they could see that the League's communal propaganda had had its effect on Muslim officials and students in the province.

The 1946 elections showed that the League had increased its influence in the non-Pakhtun districts. Its volunteers, consisting mostly of mullahs and students spread out in the villages. They posed the choice for the Muslim voter: 'Are you going to vote for the mosque or the temple?' They dubbed Abdul Ghaffar Khan a Hindu because he was known to have fasted and observed silence on certain days, as Gandhi did. They denounced the doctrine of non-violence on the ground that it would sap the strength of the warlike people of the Frontier. The election was fought on the issue of Pakistan, in a highly surcharged atmosphere, but despite its long years of absence from the political scene, the Congress won 21 out of 38 Muslim seats. The Muslim League won 17 seats but 11 of them were from the non-Pakhtun districts of Hazara and Dera Ismail Khan. The Congress won all the non-Muslim seats and a majority of the Muslim seats in the Pakhtun districts. It formed a ministry; but it was unable to settle down to work. After the statement of Prime Minister Attlee on 20 February 1947 which set 30 June 1948 as the deadline for transfer of power, the Muslim League decided to topple the non-League ministries in Punjab and the N.W.F.P. It launched a civil disobedience campaign, but not against the government, nor did it have anything in common with Gandhi's campaigns. The demonstrations in the Frontier were led by students and the Muslim League's National Guards, some of whom had even a supply of explosives. They heightened the communal tension, which led to riots and panic in the minority communities and caused the Khan Sahib ministry no end of embarrassment.

Meanwhile, the tripartite negotiations between the British government, the Congress, and the Muslim League had been proceeding on their tortuous course. The Cabinet Mission Plan proved stillborn. The formation of the Interim Government had not broken the political deadlock. Lord Wavell, the Viceroy, was at the end of his tether. The British government sent a new Viceroy with a new mandate for an early solution of the constitutional issue. The result was Mountbatten's partition plan of 3 June 1947 to set up two sovereign states in the subcontinent. Abdul Ghaffar Khan's response to this decision has been immortalized in the title of Pyarelal's book *Thrown to the Wolves*. There is evidence in British official records to indicate that a separate Muslim-majority state in the north-west of India fitted in with the post-war imperial strategy of Great Britain in the Cold War era, which was just beginning. In a minute dated 11 May 1946 for the British Chiefs of Staff, General Auchinleck, the Commander-in-Chief of the Indian Army, put forward the view that between India (which was expected to be less friendly to Britain following the transfer of power) and Pakistan (which was expected to be more cooperative) it was in British interests that the latter should include the N.W.F.P. and Baluchistan within its borders.[12] Three months earlier, the then Viceroy, Lord Wavell, had sent a plan to the Secretary of State for India for the partition of India, in which a separate state consisting of the Muslim-majority areas of the N.W.F.P., Baluchistan, West Punjab, and Sind was recommended for British strategic purposes. To attribute the Partition wholly to the machinations of the British rulers, would, however, be erroneous. The final plan for the transfer of power was the result of the clash of wits, and wills, between the leaders of the Congress, the Muslim League, and the British government. The acceptance of this plan by the Congress, 'as the lesser evil', shocked Abdul Ghaffar Khan: he felt he had been badly let down by his Congress colleagues. Like Gandhi, he was totally opposed to Partition, but if it became inevitable he preferred the option of an independent Pakhtun state. In May 1947 Nehru had rejected an earlier draft of Mountbatten's plan granting the alternative of independence to any province or princely state on the ground that it would lead to the Balkanization of the country. Having done that, Nehru, and the Congress, could hardly ask for an exception in the case of the Frontier Province. The Congress leadership sympathized with Abdul Ghaffar in his predicament, but felt helpless. Abdul Ghaffar Khan felt that a referendum in the N.W.F.P. would be held in a communally surcharged atmosphere which was not conducive to a sane verdict. He announced that since the option of independence had been denied, he and the Frontier Congress would boycott the referendum.

Gandhi was somewhat puzzled over Abdul Ghaffar's demand for an independent state of Pakhtunistan. He thought Abdul Ghaffar's real goal had always been autonomy for the N.W.F.P., as for other Indian provinces, with freedom to manage internal affairs within a federal Indian polity. The fact is that in the summer of 1947 Abdul Ghaffar and his followers feared that even after the transfer of power, the British influence in Pakistan would continue in one form or another, and the Pakhtuns would come under Punjabi domination. It is possible that Abdul Ghaffar Khan raised the demand for a separate Pakhtun state 'as a bargaining counter to salvage as much as possible of the Khudai Khidmatgar movement in the desperate situation of 1947'.[13] This was a gamble that did not pay off. After the referendum, which he had boycotted, Abdul Ghaffar quickly retraced his steps. Even though Khan Sahib's ministry was dismissed within a week of the inauguration of Pakistan, while still enjoying a majority in the Legislative Assembly, the Khudai Khidmatgars and their allied organizations declared that they accepted Pakistan as their own country and pledged to serve it loyally. They redefined their demand of Pakhtunistan to mean 'full freedom for the Pakhtuns to manage their own affairs as a unit, within the Pakistan state'.

Abdul Ghaffar Khan's conciliatory gesture failed to dispel the mistrust and hostility of the Pakistani leadership. Gandhi heard disquieting reports and was concerned about the safety of the Khan brothers. He wrote to Abdul Ghaffar to leave the Frontier Province and to develop the non-violent technique from India. 'This', he added, 'you can do here with me, or otherwise. What that otherwise can be, I do not know.' Gandhi felt that the only other alternative for Abdul Ghaffar was to remain where he was, and to let the Pakistan authorities do their worst.

Abdul Ghaffar chose to stand by his people in Pakistan in their hour of trial. On 23 February 1948 he attended the first session of the Pakistan Parliament at Karachi, and took the oath of allegiance to Pakistan. He was invited to tea by Jinnah who was the President of the Constituent Assembly, as well as the Governor-General. Jinnah embraced him and said: 'Today I feel that my dream of Pakistan is realized.' Next day, he invited Abdul Ghaffar to dinner. Abdul Ghaffar told the Quaid-i-Azam that his was essentially a movement for social reform, and that it was the unrelenting hostility of the British administration in his province that had forced him into politics. Jinnah heard with interest the hand-spinning and hand-weaving programme of the Khudai Khidmatgar organization and said that he would order two hundred thousand spinning wheels for them. Abdul Ghaffar Khan returned to the Frontier and asked his followers to launch an intensive programme of constructive work. In April 1948 Jinnah paid his first official visit to the Frontier, but did not meet Ghaffar Khan, evidently on the advice of the British Governor, the Muslim League Chief Minister, and senior bureaucrats of the province.

In June 1948 Abdul Ghaffar Khan was arrested, charged with sedition, and sentenced to three years' rigorous imprisonment. Between 1948 and 1965, he spent fifteen years in Pakistani jails. In his autobiography, he recalled the hardships of his jail life and the savage repression to which his faithful Khudai Khidmatgars were subjected. He contrasted the attitude of the government of Pakistan with that of the British rulers before 1947: 'The British had never looted our homes, but the Islamic Government of Pakistan did. The British had never stopped us from holding public meetings or publishing newspapers, but the Islamic Government of Pakistan did both. The British had never treated the Pakhtun women disrespectfully, but the Islamic Government of Pakistan did.'[14] That Abdul Ghaffar Khan was not exaggerating is confirmed by the verdict of Swedish historian, Erland Jansson, who had access to Pakistani, Indian, and British sources. He describes the dismissal of the Congress ministry and the vendetta against the Khudai Khidmatgars 'as the first steps in a development where provincial and national politics were reduced to a sham .... From the political degeneration which began in the N.W.F.P. in August 1947, Pakistan has never been able to recover'.[15]

VII

Abdul Ghaffar Khan had told a British writer, Robert Bernays, in 1931: 'The Government of India misunderstands my movement. I do not hate the British. I only want some reforms for the N.W.F.P. The British have put me in prison, but I do not hate them. My movement is social as well as political. I teach the Red Shirts to love their neighbours .... The Muslims are a warlike race, they do not easily take to non-violence; I am doing my best to teach it to them.' He spoke in the same vein to successive British Chief Commissioners and Governors in Peshawar, in his first speech in the Pakistan Constituent Assembly in 1948, and to Jinnah privately, but he was not believed. The British hated and feared him. 'Large, rugged, bearded, obviously hostile, silent, in rough khadi', is how the Viceroy, Lord Wavell, described him in his private journal when he met him at the Simla Conference. Jinnah could hardly control his anger when he first saw him in the Congress delegation in a meeting with the Cabinet Mission. As late as 1980, Sir Olaf Caroe, a former Governor of the N.W.F.P., in profile of Abdul Ghaffar Khan in his book *The Pathans* (1983), portrayed him as a calculating politician who exploited 'Congress brains and Congress money' for his own ends.[16] His opponents, the British officials and the Muslim separatists, had a deep-rooted distrust of his motives. In contrast, we have the pen-portrait of the Pathan leader in Jawaharlal Nehru's autobiography published in 1936: 'He was, and is, no politician as politicians go; he knows nothing of the tactics and manoeuvres of politics. A tall, straight man, straight in body and mind, hating fuss and too much talk, looking forward to freedom for his Frontier Province people within the framework of Indian freedom. It was surprising how this Pathan accepted the idea of non-violence, far more so in theory than many ...' Gandhi described him as a 'man of truth' with a deeply spiritual nature, who 'would die serving the Pathans with his last breath'. The fact is that Abdul Ghaffar Khan's mind was more akin to that of a Sufi saint than a politician. He did not like the title of 'Frontier Gandhi' bestowed on him by the people. 'There is only one Gandhi,' he said, 'who is the general of us all.' When he was offered the presidency of the Congress, he declined, saying that he had always been a soldier and would like to die as a soldier. Abdul Ghaffar's combination of rock-like firmness on principles and candour disconcerted his political opponents, who were unable to appreciate his burning zeal to uplift the Pathan masses caught in a tangled web of poverty, illiteracy, and violence. They missed his greatest achievement, the non-violent mobilization of the most violence-prone race in the Indian subcontinent. He had the mortification of seeing his life-work destroyed before his own eyes by the partition of the subcontinent. The British kept him in prison for fifteen years; their Pakistani successors for another fifteen years. They suspected him of cunning; he could well have repeated a Sufi saint's answer to the charge; 'Yes, I have cunning, but it is the cunning of truth.'

Notes and References

1. File P. 17 A.I.C.C. Papers.
2. D.G. Tendulkar, *Abdul Ghaffar Khan: Faith is a Battle* (Bombay, 1967), p. 131.
3. National Archives of India (N.A.I.) Home Pol. (Confidl.) 33/8/31, pt I.
4. File P. 17/1931, A.I.C.C. Papers.
5. D.G. Tendulkar, op.cit., p. 74.
6. Gandhi to H.W. Emerson, 16 March 1931, N.A.I., Home Pol 33/8/31, pt I.
7. Dr Khan Sahib to Jawaharlal Nehru, 16 Oct. 1931, A.I.C.C. papers P. 17/1931.
8. N.A.I., Home Political (Confidl.) 5/72/1932.
9. D.G. Tendulkar, op. cit., p. 253.
10. Pyarelal, *Thrown to the Wolves* (Calcutta, 1966), p. 120.
11. Erland Jansson, *India, Pakistan or Pakhtunistan?* (Upsala, 1981), p. 119.
12. N. Mansergh (ed.), *Transfer of Power*, XII, pp. 800–6.
13. Erland Jansson, op.cit., p. 242.
14. *My Life and Struggle: Autobiography of Badshah Khan* (as narrated to K.B. Narang) (Delhi, 1969), p. 208.
15. Erland Jansson, op. cit., p. 243.
16. Olaf Caroe, *The Pathans* (Karachi, 1983), p. 433.

THIRTEEN

Gandhi and the Capitalists

The eighteen accused in the Meerut Conspiracy Case, who included the founding fathers of the Communist Party of India, in their long statement before the court, declared that Gandhi's civil disobedience campaigns were a means of sabotaging 'revolutionary movements', that the Indian National Congress under his leadership shied away from violence as it did not wish to overthrow foreign rule, and that Gandhi was really working for a compromise in the interests of the Indian bourgeoisie.[1] This statement was in accord with the thesis presented to the Second Communist International by M.N. Roy in 1920, and his subsequent commentary on the non-cooperation movement. Roy made a pointed reference to the instinct of 'preserving property rights [which] betrays the class affiliation of Gandhi in spite of his pious outbursts against the sordid materialism of modern civilization'.[2]

Young Roy had left his country during the First World War. He had little first-hand information about the conditions in India in the early 1920s; nor had he met Gandhi. However, his thesis of a direct nexus between Gandhi and Indian capitalists became a leftist dogma which was taken up, elaborated, and propounded by numerous writers to our own day;[3] it has inspired at least two beliefs that have had an astonishingly long life. One of these is that the capitalists kept Gandhi and the Congress flush with funds; the other is that, as a quid pro quo, Gandhi astutely checked the revolutionary aspects of his struggle against the Raj to suit the vested interests of the capitalists.[4] From these beliefs has stemmed the leftist thesis that there was an alliance between Gandhi and Indian capitalists, and that he regulated the intensity of his satyagraha against the British at their bidding and in their interest.[5] A balanced critique of the leftist thesis would require a close examination of these beliefs, and this is what this essay seeks to do.

I

The financial position of the Congress in the years preceding the First World War was, in the words of the historian of the Indian National Congress, 'never very sound'.[6] The irony of the situation, as a Poona journal put it, was that 'those who can and ought to pay for the Congress have not the will, while those whose heart is in the movement are most of them too poor to pay'.[7] The main expenditure in those early years was on holding annual sessions, which had to be met from the delegates' fees, supplemented by donations. The Congress was rarely able to meet its commitments to its branch in London, the British Committee of the Congress, whose chairman Sir William Wedderburn, while complaining of 'the want of pence', met the deficit from his own and his friends' pockets.[8]

From 1920 the Congress was dominated by the personality of Gandhi. Despite his indubitable charisma, and the great reverence in which he was personally held by all sections of society, it is significant that hardly any capitalist, with the exception of A.D. Godrej, Omar Sobhani, and Jamnalal Bajaj, contributed to the Tilak Swaraj Fund. Not a single industrialist signed the satyagraha pledge against the Rowlatt Bills in the spring of 1919. So, far from supporting Gandhi, the prominent industrialists of Bombay banded together to form an Anti-Noncooperation Committee, with Purshotamdas Thakurdas and Chimanlal Setalvad as secretaries, and the Tatas as financiers. Gandhi knew some of the industrialists, and treated them, as indeed he treated everybody else, with courtesy, but he had no illusions about them. In a letter 'To the Millowners' published in the *Bombay Chronicle*, he wrote that the merchants whom he was urging to boycott the sale of foreign cloth had 'frightened me by saying that the result of their response will simply mean that you millowners will immediately send up the prices and fling up in the face of the nation the law of supply and demand in support of the inflation of price'.[9]

Gandhi's appeal to the industrialists 'to conduct their business on national rather than on purely commercial lines' fell on deaf ears. He discovered that the industrialists were not susceptible to such appeals; they were hard-headed men, not easily swept off their feet by patriotic slogans. Some of them, such as the Tatas in Bombay and the Mukherjees of Martin Burn in Calcutta, were socially integrated with the European business community, and were dependent upon official patronage for orders from the railways and other government departments, and for access to markets abroad. Then, there were men like Sir Purshotamdas Thakurdas, 'the cotton king of Bombay', and Lala Shri Ram, the Delhi industrialist, who were 'moderate nationalists', to whom Gandhi's methods of satyagraha and civil disobedience were anathema. Finally, there were industrialists like G.D. Birla, whose nationalist sentiment was heightened by their sense of resentment at British discrimination against Indian trade and industry. Birla was perceptive enough to see that Gandhi's struggle would ultimately weaken the Raj and help to loosen the grip of British capital on the Indian economy. He sincerely wished Gandhi and the Congress to succeed in wresting power from the Raj, but he did not want to get himself embroiled in the struggle.

Birla and his friends stayed out of the non-cooperation movement; in the mid-1920s they sought the support of the Congress Swarajists, led by Pandit Motilal Nehru, in the Central Legislative Assembly to extract concessions from the government. This support was willingly given. Motilal was glad to extend a helping hand in the fight for protection for nascent Indian industries against foreign competition as well as for an equitable rupee–pound ratio. What Motilal saw of the cynical opportunism of the Indian capitalists in these years deeply shocked him. He found that their patriotic fervour cooled off as soon as their immediate objectives were achieved. They had the temerity to suggest a meeting with top leaders of the Congress before they made any contributions to the funds of the Swaraj Party for the forthcoming elections. Motilal turned down their suggestions with withering scorn. In a letter to a Bombay mill-owner, Lalji Naranji, he wrote on 21 April 1928:

It is very kind indeed of Sir Fazulbhoy Currimbhoy and Mr Stones to condescend to see the Mahatma, Dr Ansari and myself and hear what we have to say. Please tell them with my compliments that on the conditions mentioned by you, we have no alternative but to decline the honour. Allow me, however, to congratulate you and other mill-owners of Bombay on the new phase of devotion and loyalty to the government and the banks it controls, so rapidly developed after abolition of the excise duty and the fight for 1/4 (1s 4d). I have been thinking over the matter ever since I received your telegram, and it is now my considered opinion that the Congress should welcome this change in the attitude of the mill-owners. An alliance between the Congress and the capitalists, who are bent on profiting by the sufferings of the nation, is an impossible one. The more suitable field of work for the Congress is among the workers and not the owners of the mills. But I was misled by the patriotic talk of some of my personal friends among the mill-owners. Mahatmaji never believed in an alliance with the latter and I have now told him that he was right and I was wrong.[10]

Three days later, Gandhi himself confided to Jawaharlal Nehru (who was in Europe at the time) that the Bombay mill-owners 'wanted to have a deal with the Congress. But I am not sorry for the abortive negotiations. They have cleared the atmosphere.'[11] Nehru himself has discounted, in his *Discovery of India* written in 1944, the 'frequent assertion' that the Indian National Congress was heavily financed by the big industrialists:

This is wholly untrue and I ought to know something about it, as I have been general secretary and president of the Congress for many years. A few industrialists have financially helped from time to time in the social reform activities of Gandhiji and the Congress, such as, village industries, abolition of untouchability and the raising of depressed classes, basic education, etc. But they have kept scrupulously aloof from the political work of the Congress, even in normal times, and much more so, during periods of conflict with government. Whatever their occasional sympathies, they believed, like most sober and well-established individuals, in safety first. Congress work has been carried on almost entirely on the petty subscriptions and donations of its large membership.[12]

Gandhi prided himself on the fact that while Madan Mohan Malaviya knew how to secure donations from the princes, he himself specialized in collecting contributions from the poor. The Mahatma valued the coppers of the poor as much as the magnificent gifts from the rich. He was sometimes disconcerted by the niggardliness and cynicism of the richer donors. In 1940 he issued an appeal over his own signature for five lakh rupees for erecting a memorial to that great Christian friend of India, C.F. Andrews. After about a month he found that only a small sum had come in. He issued another appeal. Again a few thousand rupees trickled through. Gandhi then talked to Vallabhbhai Patel, who told him that money could not be collected for memorials even by a Mahatma by merely issuing appeals in the press. He suggested that Gandhi should go to Bombay and stay there for a week. Much against his will, Gandhi went to Bombay in response to Patel's invitation, and was able to collect five lakhs. Thereafter he never issued any appeal for funds to erect memorials. 'I have had a very sad experience about C.F. Andrews' memorial', he told Shriman Narayan, Jamnalal Bajaj's son-in-law, 'I am not prepared to burn my fingers once again.'[13]

Gandhi never expected much from the Indian capitalists and preferred the Congress funds to come from its supporters at the grassroots. The idea that a central organization, such as the All India Congress Committee (AICC), should finance provincial or district Congress committees seemed to him utterly wrong. On the contrary, it was for the district committees to finance the provincial committees, and for the latter to contribute funds to the functioning of All India Congress Committee.

Above all, the strictest economy was essential in disbursing public funds. Gandhi felt:

We may not build a pucca building when a thatched cottage would do. We may not use a motor-car when a bullock cart would serve the purpose, and we must avoid the bullock cart when the journey can be made on foot. Similarly the rigidest economy should be exercised in regulating the expenses of feeding workers.[14]

The fact of the matter is that the support which the national movement drew from the business class came largely from small merchants and petty shopkeepers who closed their shops when hartals were declared, occasionally attended public meetings addressed by Congress leaders, and openly or secretly contributed their mite to Congress funds. As for the big merchants and the industrialists, their watchword was 'safety first'. In 1921 they ostentatiously refrained from contributing to the Tilak Swaraj Fund; if the target of one crore was finally attained, it was not through the donations of a few tycoons, but by a massive campaign to rope in thousands of small merchants and professional men, and farmers and workers in towns and villages. According to Hare Krushna Mahtab, the veteran Congress leader of Orissa, the contribution of twenty-three thousand rupees from that province to the Tilak Swaraj Fund was made by 'door to door collections in all the districts. Even the copper pice were accepted. Everywhere there were small collections. There were no donations say of even Rs. 100'.[15] The experience of most provinces was probably the same, except that of Bombay and Bengal; but even in these two provinces it was the merchants rather than the industrialists who loosened their purse-strings to help complete the quotas of collection fixed for these provinces.

The bulk of the Tilak Swaraj Fund was spent, as it had been meant to be spent, on the non-cooperation movement, on subsistence allowances to lawyers who had given up their practice, on national schools, and on the promotion of khadi and other planks in the Congress programme.

By 1927 the Tilak Swaraj Fund was dwindling and the general secretaries of the Congress were stressing the urgency of collecting money for the efficient running of the central office of the AICC.[16] Among the steps suggested by them were raising the fee for Congress delegates to the annual sessions from one rupee to ten rupees, and the levy of a fee on members of the AICC, besides contributions from provincial Congress committees. This, however, led to no substantial improvement in the financial position of the Congress. All it was able to do was to arrange its annual sessions with the customary éclat. The AICC and the provincial Congress committees operated on shoestring budgets.

In 1936 the AICC, through its travelling inspectors, compiled some information about the offices of the provincial Congress committees which makes interesting reading. The Maharashtra Congress Committee paid Rs 15 a month as rent for its office, and employed a secretary for Rs 60 a month and an accountant for Rs 30;[17] its total assets were Rs 2,892. Some of the other provincial committees were much worse off. The Central Provinces Congress Committee at Nagpur paid a monthly rent of Rs 5; it had no paid staff, and its assets amounted to Rs 406.[18] The Kerala Congress Committee at Cochin had free accommodation for its office, and employed an office secretary at Rs 20 a month; its cash balance was Rs 49. The Karnataka Congress Committee at Dharwar paid Rs 15 a month as rent for its office and boasted of Rs 21 in the bank, besides a cash balance of Rs 4. Incredible as it may seem, in March 1937, Jawaharlal Nehru, the Congress president, was hard put to it to finance the Bombay branch of the Civil Liberties Union, which was under the charge of his brother-in-law, Raja Hutheesing. Nehru expressed his anguish to a friend in Bombay:

It is a standing wonder to me how a person will gladly spend a hundred rupees or more in entertaining me, and many thousands of rupees on a marriage function or another, and yet be averse to give a small donation for public work. Can we not get a number of people to give a small subscription of Rs 10 or 15 a month for this Union?[19]

A year earlier, Govind Ballabh Pant had confided to Rajendra Prasad, one of the three members of the Central Parliamentary Committee, that the prospects of securing funds for provincial elections in the United Provinces locally were dismal.[20] The letter was intercepted and brought to the Viceroy's attention. Lord Linlithgow's comment was: 'Finance in all probability is going to be the limiting factor for the electoral and agrarian activities of the Congress. We ought to watch their moneybags with constant attention.'[21]

At about the same time Bhulabhai Desai, who had borne the brunt of organizing election campaigns for the Central Assembly in 1934, was entertaining the liveliest scepticism about support from the industrialists. Desai told Birla that the provincial elections in the subcontinent on an extended franchise would need at least ten lakhs, and that it was 'the duty of the upper middle classes, the businessmen and the industrialists to provide it'. Desai complained that though the Indian industrialists had profited from the swadeshi movement, they had 'hardly any sense of shame which would make them feel small that they are in no way interested or helpful in any patriotic work at all'.[22] Birla was clearly of the view, as Desai noted in his diary on 20 February 1936, 'that the upper middle class and the industrialists are not at all taking their share of the burden of India's freedom. If others could be persuaded, Mr. Birla is willing to bear his share of the burden .... He agreed it should be a voluntary contribution and not a matter of begging for favours'.[23] A few days later, when the captains of Indian industry, Walchand Hirachand, Purshotamdas Thakurdas, Padampat Singhania, Kasturbhai Lalbhai, and others, assembled at Bombay for a meeting of the Federation of Indian Chambers of Commerce and Industry, all that Bhulabhai could secure from them was the promise to contribute ten to twelve thousand rupees to partially offset the deficit of twenty-five thousand incurred by the Congress in the central assembly elections two years earlier.[24]

The fact is that the reluctance of the capitalists to contribute to Congress funds, at least until 1937, was based on careful calculations. The political and economic programme of the Congress, however conservative it might have seemed to its socialist and communist critics, struck the princes, landlords, and capitalists, whose interests were tied up with the status quo of the Raj, as much too radical. It is significant that in the provincial elections in 1937, the Congress won only four out of the thirty-seven seats reserved for landholders, and of the forty-six seats for commerce and trade organizations, only three went to the Congress. In the 1920s and 1930s, and indeed even in the early 1940s, the result of the conflict between the Indian National Congress and the British government was by no means a foregone conclusion. Those who joined the Congress camp, did so with their eyes open; they knew they were incurring the displeasure of the authorities and might have to pay a heavy price for it.

II

The hard choices that confronted big businessmen during these turbulent years can be best illustrated by contrasting the careers of Ghanshyam Das Birla and Jamnalal Bajaj, both Marwaris, and in their own ways close to Gandhi.

Bajaj had plunged into the political arena at Gandhi's instance in 1920, and never looked back. His supreme loyalty was to Gandhi and the causes that he periodically espoused. Jamnalal's resources were smaller than those of the great magnates of Bombay and Calcutta, but he made substantial contributions to Congress funds and to Gandhi's social reform activities. As a member of the Congress Working Committee, and indeed its treasurer, Jamnalal took full responsibility for its policies, and repeatedly courted imprisonment in 1923, 1930, 1932, 1939 and 1940.

In contrast, G.D. Birla's attitude towards Gandhi and the Congress was ambivalent. In the evening of his life Birla recalled:

There was not much in common between us so far as our mode of life went. Gandhiji was a saintly person, who had renounced all the comforts and luxuries of life. Religion was his main absorption and this interest drew me irresistibly towards him. His outlook on economics, however, was different. He believed in small-scale industries, charkha, *ghani* and all that. On the other hand I led a fairly comfortable life and believed in the industrialization of the country through large-scale industries .... He not only tolerated my independence of thought, but loved me all the more for it, as a father would his child.[25]

Birla had started his life as a jute and gunny broker; he lived to found one of the largest industrial empires in independent India. As a young entrepreneur in Calcutta, he was a protégé of Lord Ronaldshay, the Governor of Bengal, who nominated him to the Bengal Legislative Council in the hope that he would have a sobering influence on the younger members of the Marwari community with nationalist proclivities.[26] Birla kept the non-cooperation movement at arms length, not permitting politics from deflecting him from his onward march in the field of trade and industry. In 1924, he explained to Jamnalal his reasons for abstention from active politics:

I am enmeshed in business. My revered father and elder brother do not like my abandoning business. I do everything to please them. This is also my dharma ... However, if any financial help or personal service is required by Mahatmaji, I shall be happy to render it. My situation is peculiar: I want one thing and do another.[27]

In the late 1920s Birla entered the Central Legislative Assembly, not as a member of the Congress party, but of the Nationalist Party, led by Lajpat Rai and Malaviya. He remained in the good books of the government, and was nominated to the Indian Fiscal Commission, the Royal Commission for Labour, and the International Labour Conference. At the same time, he was in intimate touch with the nationalist leaders, especially Gandhi, to whose 'constructive' activities he made generous contributions. When, however, Gandhi launched the Salt Satyagraha in 1930, Birla steered clear of it. Lord Willingdon once described Birla as 'one of those men who would only do anything, if it suited his own pocket'.[28] This was a grossly unfair judgement because Birla sought to safeguard not only the interests of his own family, but those of Indian trade and industry as a whole. For decades the scales had been loaded in favour of the British-owned companies in India, who formed the Associated Chambers of Commerce in 1921. Birla played a leading part in building up a rival body, the Federation of Indian Chambers of Commerce and Industry, which came into existence in 1927.

It was part of Birla's strategy to alienate neither the Congress nor the government. He cultivated contacts with high-ranking British officials in India and Britain; this was not difficult for him because of his known proximity to Gandhi. In his correspondence with British statesmen, he made it a point to disavow any connection with the Congress. He claimed that he was 'not a Congressman but a Gandhi man'.[29] He shrewdly played upon the hopes and fears of the British viceroys and secretaries of state. He told them that Gandhi was their best bet for a peaceful solution of the Indian problem; he alone stood between order and chaos.[30] Birla even made a distinction between Gandhi and the Congress, and floated the idea that if the Congress became too radical a body, the British might be able to do business with Gandhi. This was a fatuous distinction, because Gandhi would never have been a party to the destruction of the Congress which he had built up as an instrument of the nationalist struggle against foreign rule.

We get an insight into Birla's strategy in a letter he wrote to Sir Samuel Hoare, the Secretary of State for India, a few weeks after the British government had clamped down upon the Congress and locked up its leadership in jail:

I should like you to know me as I really am. I need hardly say that I am a great admirer of Gandhiji ... I have liberally financed his khadi production and anti-untouchability activities. I am also a believer in khadi as a supplementary occupation for the Indian masses. I have never taken any part in or financed the civil disobedience movement. But I have been a very severe critic of the financial policy of the government and so have never been popular with them. Even today I do not see eye to eye with the policy of the government.[31]

Birla offered his cooperation to the government, if it was prepared to revise its fiscal and economic policies to suit Indian industry. He even hinted that the fact that the Congress had been outlawed was no bar to cooperation between the British government and 'progressive opinion not identified with the Congress'. He suggested a dialogue between Indian and British businessmen. 'So far as we are concerned', he told Sir Samuel, 'you will find us always ready to work for the economic interest, leaving aside sentiments and politics.'[32] 'Never had,' says Claude Markovits, 'such a clear offer of collaboration been extended by Indian big business to the government, and this while Gandhi and the entire Congress leadership were in jail.'[33] No wonder then that a few months later, the liberal leader Srinivasa Sastri was asking Kodanda Rao, 'Has Birla been turned away from Gandhi's policy? That is a shrewd blow.'[34]

This was the time of the Ottawa and Modi–Lees pacts when Indian capitalists were bending over backwards to placate British business for temporary gains which would help them to get out of the economic depression.

Jamnalal Bajaj had a first-hand experience of Birla's astute diplomacy during the Jaipur state imbroglio in 1938. When the tension between the state authorities and the Praja Mandal was building up, and Jamnalal, on the advice of Gandhi and Vallabhbhai Patel, was planning a struggle for the assertion of elementary political rights in the state, he sought the assistance of Birla, who also claimed to be a native of Jaipur state and professed to take an interest in its welfare. Birla offered to use his influence with Sir Bertrand Glancy, the political adviser to the Viceroy, and with Young, the inspector-general of police in Jaipur, to arrive at a *modus vivendi*, and advised Jamnalal to be patient and not to precipitate a crisis by defying the orders of the state authorities.

The movement, which had started on the issue of the recognition for the Praja Mandal, became in the meantime a part of the wider struggle for the people's rights in princely India under the aegis of Gandhi and the Congress. Birla took no part in this struggle. It is doubtful if he had any real influence with the officers of the political department. It is surprising that Jamnalal could not foresee that Birla, who had kept clear of satyagraha struggles in British India, would not burn his fingers in princely India. After the worst was over, Jamnalal approached Birla to join the executive committee of the Jaipur Praja Mandal. Birla's response was an unequivocal refusal: 'You have written to me that I or my son Lakshmi Niwas should join the executive committee of the Praja Mandal. This advice is ill-conceived. This work is against my nature and I do not want to put my foot into something for which I have no natural enthusiasm.'[35]

Birla was aware that Jamnalal was acting in the Jaipur affairs in consultation with Gandhi, but he did not take his cue in politics from Gandhi or from anyone else. In Birla's scheme of things, economics took precedence over politics. Gandhi and the Congress might be interested

in the primacy of Indian self-government, but Birla's eyes were riveted
on the short and long-term prospects of Indian industry. This was so even
when the Second World War took a critical turn, and the prospect of a
major political crisis loomed large. Birla wrote to his friend Purshotamdas
Thakurdas:

We should watch one thing very carefully. In the name of War Industrialization
we should not allow the government to do anything to put up new industries
under the control of British interests. I fear this might be the result. Already I
have heard that aeroplanes and motor-cars may be manufactured, but perhaps
not by Indians but by Englishmen.[36]

In fairness to Birla, it must be acknowledged that he was not alone
in his calculating attitude towards the nationalist movement. Most
capitalists in India, in keeping aloof from the national movement, were
governed by a concern for their family fortunes. It must also be conceded
that he was playing not only for his own hand, but for Indian trade and
industry pitted against foreign capital; and even though he did not finance
the political activities of the Congress, he gave generous support to the
Mahatma's non-political work. Birla was shrewd enough to project the
interests of the entire capitalist class in India. He had access to some of
the top leaders of the Congress, including Gandhi, but he knew that there
was no question of buying over, manipulating, or pressuring the national
leaders.

Some other industrialists were infinitely more cynical and opportu-
nistic in their outlook. Ramkrishna Dalmia, who was building up his
commercial empire in Bihar, contributed twenty-seven thousand rupees
to the election fund of the Congress in that province in 1937. However,
as a quid pro quo he insisted on having a say in the selection of Congress
candidates, expected Congress support for his own election without standing on a Congress ticket, and clandestinely financed some candidates
opposing the Congress.[37] In so far as Dalmia perceived a prospect of
acquiring political influence by contributing to election funds in 1937,
he was more prescient than most of his fellow capitalists; but he did not
really tilt towards the Congress until 1945 when the liquidation of British
power was imminent.

III

Gandhi had no illusions about the motives of Indian capitalists, with some
of whom (such as G.D. Birla, Ambalal Sarabhai, and Kasturbhai Lalbhai)

he had cordial personal relations. He used them, as in the Round Table Conference in London in 1931, to spike the guns of British capitalists and financiers. Birla appointed himself as the Mahatma's spokesman in discussions with British officials in India and in England, but they did not take long to discover that the Marwari industrialist was not as influential in shaping Congress policies as he made out. His published correspondence gives an exaggerated impression of his actual role in political developments. He certainly had access to Gandhi, and his influence was always cast in favour of restraint, of avoiding a confrontation with the British Raj, or of seeking a truce. There were however powerful Congress leaders, such as Jawaharlal Nehru, and Congress Socialists, such as Jayaprakash Narayan, who brought a contrary pressure to bear on Gandhi. The fact is that every possible point of view, from the most conservative to the most radical, was represented in the All India Congress Committee, and even in the Congress Working Committee. Gandhi listened to everyone but made up his own mind; on what appeared to him as fundamental issues, he did not hesitate to strike out a line even against his closest colleagues.

Some historians have been misled by the fact that Birla and his fellow capitalists wrote letters to Gandhi or pleaded in person for a particular course of action at a certain time. This does not prove that Gandhi acted at their bidding; he took his own decisions on critical issues such as the launching of non-cooperation in 1920, the withdrawal of civil disobedience in 1922, the signing of the Gandhi–Irwin Pact in 1931, the withdrawal of civil disobedience in 1933, the acceptance of office in 1937, and the Congress policy during the Second World War. In 1938, the Mahatma told off Birla when the latter sought his support for a bargain with Lancashire for its supposed advantages in economic terms: 'What you say is correct from the economic point of view; but I look at it, and I ought to look at it, as a purely political issue. We cannot enter into any agreement with Lancashire, which will bind us to buy their cloth.'[38]

The fact that Birla was Gandhi's host in Delhi or Calcutta does not prove anything. The attitude of the Birla family towards Gandhi was one of respect and affection, which were reciprocated by the Mahatma, who maintained his personal links with individuals, irrespective of political or social differences. When Kanji Dwarkadas wrote to Gandhi that he should not stay with Birla, Gandhi told him that his political views were not affected by his personal relations with people. This indeed was true.

There is little evidence to indicate that Birla or his friends were, during Gandhi's lifetime, able to garner any substantial economic benefits because of their association with him. Indeed, in the framework of the imperial rule until 1947, Gandhi had no patronage to dispense. The Indian industrialists certainly gained (for example, in protective tariffs) from the nationalist pressure against foreign capitalists and financial interests in India; but this was an inevitable by-product of the nationalist movement.

NOTES AND REFERENCES

1. B.R. Nanda, *Gandhi and His Critics* (Delhi, 1985), p. 131–2.
2. Sibnarayan Ray (ed.), *Selected Works of M.N. Roy*, vol. I (Delhi, 1987), p. 370.
3. Hiren Mukherjee, *Gandhiji: A Study* (New Delhi, 1978), p. 183.
4. E.M.S. Namboodiripad, *The Mahatma and the Ism* (New Delhi, 1958), p. 111.
5. A.R. Desai, *Social Background of Indian Nationalism* (Delhi, 1976), p. 368.
6. S.R. Mehrotra, *Towards India's Freedom and Partition* (Delhi, 1979), p. 77.
7. Ibid.
8. B.R. Nanda, *Gokhale, Indian Moderates and the British Raj* (Delhi, 1977), p. 158.
9. *Bombay Chronicle*, 6 July 1921.
10. Motilal Nehru to Lalji Naranji, 21 April 1928, Purshotamdas Thakurdas Papers (henceforth P.T. Papers), file no. 40/IV, N.M.M.L., New Delhi.
11. Gandhi to Jawaharlal Nehru, 24 April 1928, Navajivan Trust, *C.W.M.G.*, vol. XXXVI, p. 258 (Ahmedabad, 1958).
12. Jawaharlal Nehru, *Discovery of India* (Calcutta, 1946), p. 589.
13. Shriman Narayan, *Window on Gandhi and Nehru* (Bombay, 1971), p. 19.
14. *C.W.M.G.* (n. 11), vol. XLVI, p. 160.
15. Interview with H.K. Mahtab, Oral History Transcripts, N.M.M.L., New Delhi.
16. Annual Report for the year 1927, presented by the general secretaries to All India Congress Committee in A.M. Zaidi and S.G. Zaidi, *Encyclopaedia of the Indian National Congress* (New Delhi, 1976), vol. IX, p. 323.
17. A.I.C.C. Papers, file no. 46, N.M.M.L., New Delhi.
18. Ibid.
19. Jawaharlal Nehru to J.A.D. Naoroji, 27 March 1937, Jawaharlal Nehru Papers, N.M.M.L., New Delhi.
20. Govind Ballabh Pant to Rajendra Prasad, 11 May 1936 in Home Pol, file 4/45-1936, N.A.I., New Delhi.
21. Ibid.
22. Bhulabhai Desai Diary, entry of 2 Feb. 1936, N.M.M.L., New Delhi.
23. Ibid., 20 Feb. 1936.

24. Ibid., 25 Feb. 1936.

25. G.D. Birla, *In the Shadow of the Mahatama* (Calcutta, 1953), p. xv.

26. Lord Ronaldshay, Gov. of Bengal to Secy of State Montagu, 6 Jan. 1921, Montagu Papers, I.O.L., London.

27. G.D. Birla to Jamnalal Bajaj, 27 Oct. 1924, in Ramakrishna Bajaj (ed.), *Patra Vyavahar* (Jamnalal Bajaj's correspondence in Hindi) (Delhi, 1958), vol. 1, p. 68.

28. Lord Willingdon to Sir Samuel Hoare, 21 March 1932, Templewood Papers, I.O.L., London.

29. Lord Linlithgow's note of interview with G.D. Birla, enclosed with his letter to Secy of State Zetland, 10 Aug. 1936, Linlithgow Papers, I.O.L., London.

30. Linlithgow to Zetland, 10 August 1936, op. cit.

31. G.D. Birla to Sir Samuel Hoare, 14 March 1932, Templewood Papers, I.O.L., London.

32. Ibid.

33. Claude Markovits, *Indian Business and Nationalist Politics, 1931–38* (Hyderabad, 1985), p. 33.

34. Srinivasa Sastri to Kodanda Rao, 10 Oct. 1933, Kodanda Rao Papers, N.M.M. & L., New Delhi.

35. G.D. Birla to Jamnalal, 20 April 1940, Bajaj (ed.), *Patra Vyavahar*, (n. 27), vol. VIII, pp. 105–6.

36. G.D. Birla to Purshotamdas Thakurdas, 25 June, 1940, P.T. Papers, file no. 177.

37. B.R. Tomlinson, *The Indian National Congress and the Raj, 1929–42* (London, 1976), p. 83.

38. Gandhi to G.D. Birla, 17 April 1938, *C.W.M.G.* (n. 11), vol. XVII, p. 31.

FOURTEEN

Mahadev Desai

In a series entitled 'Collaborators', a Bombay weekly[1] published three articles under the banner headline: 'Mahatma Gandhi's Secretary was an Informer'. The writer of these articles based this astounding allegation on a few extracts from correspondence exchanged between the Viceroy Lord Linlithgow and Amery, the Secretary of State for India during the early years of the Second World War. This correspondence was not a discovery made by the writer. Scores of research scholars have had access to it in the India Office Library in London or on microfilm in Indian libraries. Only his ignorance of the political background and of Gandhi's philosophy and methods led him to some fatuous conclusions. He cited letters written by Mahadev Desai to Sir John Gilbert Laithwaite, the private secretary to Lord Linlithgow, the Viceroy. With one of these, dated 28 September 1939, Desai enclosed a copy of an article by Gandhi, which was scheduled to appear in the next issue of the Mahatma's weekly journal, *Harijan*. The second letter, dated 12 October 1939, contained Desai's comments on the meeting of the All India Congress Committee which had just concluded after passing a resolution on the Congress policy towards the war.

The import of these letters, with which he makes much play, can be best understood against the backdrop of the global crisis triggered by the outbreak of the war in Europe on 3 September 1939. The Viceroy had failed to take Indian leaders into confidence before declaring India a belligerent, but he endeavoured to make up for this omission soon afterwards. He telegraphed Gandhi that he wished to see him. The Mahatma, who took the first train to Simla, told Lord Linlithgow that his own sympathies were with England and France, that he was inclined to offer his unconditional support to the Allied cause in the struggle against Nazi Germany, but as a man of non-violence, the utmost he could offer was his moral support. The Congress Working Committee, which met soon afterwards, could not bring itself to accept Gandhi's lofty ideas of unconditional and wholly non-violent support to the Allied cause. It expressed its willingness to cooperate in the war against Nazi Germany, but the cooperation had to be between equals. The Congress put two basic posers to Britain: to define the shape of the world order for which the war was being waged, and to give India a foretaste of the freedom and democracy for which she was being called upon to fight.

On 26 September 1939, Gandhi had another interview with the Viceroy. A week later, Jawaharlal Nehru and Dr Rajendra Prasad met Lord Linlithgow. On both sides there was a desire not to terminate the *modus vivendi* of the preceding two years during which Congress ministries had been functioning in eight provinces. The British government naturally desired popular support for the war effort, or at least a political truce in wartime. The Congress, chastened by the thought of the incalculable hazards of the war, was prepared to bury the hatchet; its mood was well expressed in a letter Jawaharlal Nehru wrote to the Viceroy on 6 October 1939: 'I want to tell you how much I desire that the long conflict between India and England should be ended and they should cooperate.'

It was during this period of tense expectancy and heart-searching on both sides in the early weeks of the war that Mahadev Desai wrote the letters quoted in the articles. Desai's letter of 28 September simply forwarded the text of an article which was to appear in the next issue of *Harijan*. He told Laithwaite that he was sending it without telling Gandhi, there being scarcely any need to take the Mahatma's permission for sending a copy of an article which the whole world would be able to read two days later. Desai might also have felt that if the article was taken as coming from the Mahatma himself, that might suggest an additional overture to the government. In any case, Reuter and the Associated Press, the two major news agencies operating in India, had standing instructions from the government to immediately telegraph copies of articles by Gandhi in *Harijan* or other publications to Simla and London.

Desai's second letter, written on 12 October 1939, drew Laithwaite's attention, and therefore the Viceroy's, to the responsive mood in the All India Congress Committee which had met to consider the war crisis, and the studied moderation of Jawaharlal Nehru, who had rebuked young radicals for adopting extreme postures, referred to negotiations with the Viceroy, and assured that 'if there be an agreement, it will be an honourable one'. There was nothing secret about the proceedings of the All India Congress Committee; indeed, Nehru's speeches were reported at length in newspapers on 10 and 11 October. Desai had sent his letter post-haste to Laithwaite as the British declaration on Congress demands was imminent; indeed it came on 17 October. Gandhi pronounced the declaration as 'profoundly disappointing' and made it clear that the Congress would 'rather go into the wilderness than accept it'. There were further meetings between the Viceroy, on the one hand, and Gandhi and the Congress leaders, on the other, but the gulf remained unbridged. The Congress Working Committee directed the Congress ministries in the provinces to resign, and called upon Congressmen to prepare for a struggle under Gandhi's leadership. This proved to be the final breach between the Congress and the government and lasted seven years.

It is amazing that a fantastic structure of 'conspiracy' and 'betrayal' on the part of Mahadev Desai should have been built on the fragile foundation of a few innocuous letters which gave away no secrets and only drew the attention of the Viceroy and his advisers to Gandhi's views which were already in print or soon going to be in print. Seven months before the war broke out, Desai had visited Delhi and met Laithwaite, the Viceroy's Secretary. On 7 February 1939 Lord Linlithgow wrote to the Secretary of State for India that Laithwaite had a meeting with Mahadev Desai 'who had come to Delhi for a talk with, I understand, the Mahatma's blessings'. This particular meeting was about the Rajkot imbroglio. It is clear that the Viceroy and his private secretary took Mahadev Desai to be what he truly was: Gandhi's personal envoy. There was a stream of correspondence between Gandhi's ashram in Sevagram and the Viceroy's House in Delhi/Simla during the winter of 1940–1. Some of them were written by Gandhi, others by Mahadev Desai from Sevagram. At the other end, the correspondents included the Viceroy, Lord Linlithgow, Laithwaite, and Tottenham, the additional secretary Home Department. So far as the Mahatma was concerned, his object was to educate the Viceroy about the nuances of satyagraha, in the form of individual civil disobedience, which he was conducting at that time. In November 1940 Desai was deputed to visit Delhi, where he interviewed high British officials, including Laithwaite, with whom he had an interview for nearly two hours. In his note on this interview, Desai recorded: 'Laithwaite had Bapu's latest letter on the table. Referring to it he said, "Let me send word to Mr. Gandhi through you that though technically we are at war, our relations are as friendly as they used to be. In sending reply through me His Excellency was just observing the form, but everything that comes to me will be immediately placed before His Excellency and he is glad that Mr. Gandhi will keep him fully informed."'

It may well be asked why Gandhi was taking such pains to expound his strategy and Congress policies to the head of the administration with which he was 'at war'. The truth is that in Gandhi's philosophy of satyagraha, the enemy was not regarded as an eternal enemy, but a potential friend. It was the duty of the satyagrahi to reason with the adversary, to try to dispel his prejudices, to disarm his suspicions, to appeal to his dormant sense of humanity and justice, and, eventually, to try to prick his conscience by inviting suffering at his hands. As Gandhi told a correspondent in April 1939, the satyagrahi's object was 'not avoidance of all relationship with the opposing power', but 'the transformation of the relationship'. In South Africa, Gandhi had negotiated, fought, and finally reached an agreement with General Smuts. His parting gift to his chief antagonist was a pair of sandals which he had himself stitched. Smuts repaid this chivalrous gesture many years later when, in the shadow of the Quit India movement and in the midst of official British propaganda maligning Gandhi, he told a press conference in London: 'It is sheer nonsense to talk of Mahatma Gandhi as a fifth columnist. He is a great man. He is one of the great men of the world.' In India, through a quarter of a century, Gandhi corresponded with all the Viceroys—Chelmsford, Reading, Irwin, Willingdon and Linlithgow—keeping his lines of communication open even while he engaged them in non-violent battle. In July 1942, just when he was contemplating the launching of the Quit India movement, he sent his English disciple, Mirabehn, to Simla where she met Laithwaite, the Viceroy's Secretary, to explain to him how the Mahatma's mind was working at that critical moment.

The writer of the articles is entitled to his views, however superficial and preposterous they might be. What is surprising is that such a hotchpotch of ignorance and prejudice should have passed editorial scrutiny. There must be some limits to the quest for scoops.

The myth about the pre-1947 Congress being financed and dominated by Indian capitalists was fostered by British propagandists and leftist ideologues, but has little basis in fact, and can be easily exploded.[2]

What would one say about the scholarship of a writer, who, in the year 1993, asserts that most of the men 'commanding respect and responsible positions in the Indian National Congress' were 'the King's men', that 'big business houses' funded and controlled the Congress, that through these business houses, the British managed the Congress leadership including Gandhi, that while Gandhi manipulated the Congress party, he himself was being manipulated by British agents in his entourage.

The British were not fools; they knew the Indian National Congress for what it was under Gandhi's leadership: the implacable enemy of foreign rule. From 1919 till 1947 the Congress was throughout in opposition, and periodically in a state of war with the imperial power, except for two years from 1937 to 1939 when the Congress had accepted office in eight provinces on its own, not British, terms. No British Viceroy or Secretary of State was so naïve as to imagine that he was capable of manipulating Gandhi or the Congress High Command. Indeed, most British officials in India and politicians in England would have endorsed the opinion of Lord Willingdon, who told Sir Samuel Hoare, the Secretary of State, in July 1933: 'Gandhi is the acknowledged leader of the party whose aim is independence'. Thirteen years later, in July 1946, even on the eve of the liquidation of British rule, Lord Wavell, the last but one Viceroy, wrote to King George VI that Gandhi was 'quite single-minded on the one objective from which he had never swerved in the last 40 years, the elimination of the hated British influence from India'.

As for Mahadev Desai, his place in history is assured. From the day he joined the Mahatma in 1917, until his death in 1942, he was his eyes, ears, and authentic voice. He was not only a supremely efficient aide, but one of the greatest journalists this country has produced. There are thousands of articles in the back files of *Young India* and *Harijan*, which bear eloquent testimony to his patriotism, his scholarship, and his total identification with Gandhi. His was the life of an ascetic, pledged to the rigorous vows of Gandhi's ashram. He received a bare subsistence allowance of Rs 75 a month for the upkeep of his family; he had no bank account of his own, and lived and died in voluntary poverty. He had no political ambition either; it is a remarkable fact that he was as close to Jawaharlal Nehru as to Vallabhbhai Patel. His greatest service to his own generation, in the words of Verrier Elwin, was 'to make Gandhi real to the millions. He made Gandhi the best-known man in the world, certainly the best-loved'. For posterity, Desai preserved a day-to-day record of Gandhi's thoughts and activities covering a quarter of a century. His diaries, of which several volumes have been published, make fascinating reading. He was undoubtedly one of the great diarists of our time; had he not predeceased Gandhi by six years, he might have been a great biographer too.

Notes and References

1. *Sunday Mail*, 4–10 April 1993.
2. See Chapter 13 Gandhi and the Capitalists.

FIFTEEN

Gandhi and National Integration

From 1919, when Gandhi emerged as the dominant figure in Indian politics, till his death twenty-nine years later, if there was one thought that possessed him above all others, it was the freedom and unity of India. His entry on the Indian political stage came rather late in life, in his fiftieth year, but the flame of his patriotism had been kindled long before when, as a budding politician in South Africa, he was leading the struggle of the small Indian community in Natal and the Transvaal for basic human rights. The issues on which he fought had ostensibly little in common with the central issues of Indian politics. He did, however, gradually learn to view even his battle in South Africa as a prelude to a larger struggle which he might one day wage in his homeland. In his correspondence with Dadabhai Naoroji, Gopal Krishna Gokhale, and other Indian leaders, Gandhi took pains to place the Indians' fight in South Africa on a moral plane as a test of Indian honour and patriotism; it was much more than the defence of the vested interests of the few hundred thousand Indians who had emigrated to British colonies overseas. He was carefully following the course of events in India and the world, and drawing lessons for his countrymen in his weekly journal, *Indian Opinion*. 'The Japanese by sheer force of character,' he wrote on 7 January 1905, 'have brought themselves into the forefront of the nations of the world. They have shown unity, self-sacrifice, tenacity of purpose, nobility of character, steely courage and generosity to the enemy. Whether in South Africa or in India we have to copy our neighbours.'

Gandhi took particular pride in the fact that his adherents in Natal and the Transvaal, who included Muslims, Hindus, Sikhs, Christians, and Parsis, and hailed from different parts of India, were united in their resistance to the unjust laws of the colonial regime. In *Hind Swaraj* (1909) he stressed the imperative need for harmony among the various communities.

He warned them against the machinations of 'selfish and false religious teachers' who deliberately fostered suspicion and hatred, as well as against the tactics of the colonial rulers. 'The English have not taken India', he wrote, 'we have given it to them. They are not in India because of their strength, but because we keep them.'

Gandhi's own views on religion had evolved during his long sojourn in South Africa. He had discovered an underlying unity in the teachings of all religions. There were numerous passages in the Quran which he thought could be acceptable to Hindus, just as there were passages in the Gita to which Muslims and Christians could take no exception. He had no doubt that the quarrels between Hindus and Muslims harmed both; the best thing for them was to avoid conflicts, and simply refuse to be provoked. After all, it took two to make a quarrel. 'An arm striking in the air without resistance', Gandhi wrote, 'will be disjointed.' It was foolish and futile to blame the British for fomenting dissensions. It was for the various religious communities to forge a unity which was proof against the machinations of the 'third party'.

It was during these early years in South Africa that Gandhi became aware of the social gulf between Hindus and Muslims and was continually thinking of ways of bridging it. He did not see why festivals, such as Diwali, Dussehra, and the Id, could not be jointly celebrated. *Indian Opinion* carried a report in its issue of 16 November 1907 about 'a gathering of Hindus ... in the building of Mr Abdool Latif in Grey Street in Durban to celebrate Diwali'. We learn that just then Gandhi was visiting Durban. Two years later, Gandhi was the guest of honour at a dinner in London arranged by Indian students belonging to different religions and provinces to jointly celebrate Vijaya Dashmi (Dussehra).

There were other divisions too in the Indian community in South Africa of which Gandhi became conscious, such as that between caste Hindus and the so-called untouchables. He saw the incongruity of Indians protesting against racial discrimination by the Europeans, while they tolerated discrimination based on accident of birth against millions of their own countrymen. 'We who resent the pariah treatment in South Africa,' Gandhi wrote on 23 December 1905, 'will have to wash our hands clean of this treatment of our kith and kin in India, whom we impertinently describe as "out-castes".'

It was again in South Africa that Gandhi first noticed the barriers that divided rich and poor Indians, between the opulent merchants and the anglicized barristers on the one hand and the indentured labourers on the other.

Thus, it was during his political apprenticeship in South Africa, when he had not yet turned forty, that Gandhi acquired insights into the strengths and weaknesses of the Indian society which were to stand him in good stead when he assumed the reins of the struggle in his homeland against the Raj.

Jawaharlal Nehru once compared Gandhi's first impact on Indian politics and society to a 'hurricane'; there is no doubt that it tremendously extended and deepened the national consciousness of the people of India. Gandhi's whirlwind tours carried his message to millions of people who had hitherto been beyond the pale of politics. Political awakening ceased to be the privilege of the English-educated urban classes of the three coastal presidencies of Bombay, Bengal, and Madras. Gandhi himself became a living embodiment of Indian nationalism. The diary of Sir Thomas Jones, Secretary to the British Cabinet, refers to an interesting interview with one Dr Mann, who had just retired from the post of Director of Agriculture, Bombay, and returned to England in 1924. 'How many of the 310 millions in India', Sir Thomas asked, 'have heard of Gandhi?' 'Three hundred and nine millions', replied Dr Mann. Gandhi had, however, no illusions about the message of national unity having gone home as widely and deeply as was necessary. On the contrary, he would have agreed with S.N. Banerjea's description of India when he entitled his autobiography, published in 1925, as 'A Nation in Making'. The Mahatma's initial insights into the centrifugal factors in Indian society acquired in South Africa were further strengthened by his experience during the three decades when he stood at the centre of the political storms in the homeland. During these years he travelled from one end of the country to the other, and acquired at first hand a unique knowledge of the psychology of the Indian people. Not even the Buddha and Sankaracharya could have known as intimately every nook and cranny of this country as Gandhi did. He carefully diagnosed the ills of Indian society. He also believed that he had discovered the remedies; but the only means he had of re-educating the people was through his speeches and writings. Unfortunately, his words did not carry the same weight all the time with all sections of the people. He, however, never faltered in his indefatigable crusade for communal unity, for eradication of untouchability, for propagation of a national language, and for a new deal for the long-suffering rural masses that could form a durable foundation for Indian nationalism. His writings and speeches, even though they were responses to contemporary situations and problems, contained exhortations and warnings, which we can ignore even today at our peril. One of these was about the incalculable hazards of political violence in the Indian context.

They [revolutionaries] can and do applaud [Gandhi wrote in 1942] the actions of Mustafa Kemal Pasha and possibly de Valera and Lenin, but they do not realise that India is not like Turkey, or Ireland or Russia, and that revolutionary activity is suicidal at this stage of the country's life, if not for all times in a country so vast, so hopelessly divided, and with the masses so deeply sunk in pauperism and so fearfully terror-stricken.

There were intellectuals and radical politicians in Gandhi's lifetime who made no secret of their suspicion that he had a bee in his bonnet about non-violence. However, as we look around us today, non-violence seems not a lofty principle, but the only possible foundation on which a viable democratic polity can be sustained in our multi-religious and multi-lingual society.

SIXTEEN

Tragedy and Triumph:
Gandhi and the Partition of India

The last two years were the saddest and the most heroic of Gandhi's life. He was shocked and bewildered by the drift towards the partition of India and the explosion of violence that preceded and followed it. He first saw its ravages when he visited Calcutta in October 1946 after, what the *Statesman* described as 'the Great Calcutta Killing'. He confessed to 'a sinking feeling at the mass madness which can turn a man into a brute'. He was on his way to eastern Bengal where, in the Muslim-majority district of Noakhali, local hooligans, exploiting poor communications and encouraged by fanatical mullahs and ambitious politicians, had burnt properties of the Hindus, looted their crops, desecrated their temples, abducted their women, and made forcible conversions. Thousands of Hindus had fled from their homes.

Gandhi found the atmosphere in eastern Bengal charged with suspicion and fear. He embarked on a village-to-village tour, not to apportion blame for the riots, but to create conditions in which the two communities could again live together peacefully. He confided his strategy to his secretary, Professor N.K. Bose, 'The first thing is that politics have divided India today into Hindus and Muslims. I want to rescue people from this quagmire and make them work on solid ground where people are people. Therefore, my appeal here is not to the Muslims as Muslims nor to the Hindus as Hindus, but to ordinary human beings who have to keep their villages clean, build schools for their children, and take many other steps so that they can make life better.'[1] He lifted the question of communal peace from the plane of politics to the plane of humanity. 'Everyone of us', he said, 'is equally guilty of what anyone of us has done.' He deprecated the habit of providing a moral alibi by blaming the riots on goondas. 'Who are the goondas?' he asked, and answered, 'We are responsible for their creation as well as encouragement.' When the Hindus pleaded for

Hindu pockets in Muslim areas and for police and military reinforcements for their safety, he told them that the only protection a minority could really count on was that provided by neighbours to neighbours. Nor did he accept the specious pleas of Muslim politicians that the accounts of the riots in eastern Bengal had been fabricated by the Hindu press to discredit the Muslim League ministry. 'Thousands of people,' Gandhi said, 'were hardly likely to become homeless and penniless simply to spite the ministers in Calcutta.'

While Gandhi was busy with his pilgrimage for peace in East Bengal, the peasantry of Bihar wreaked terrible vengeance on their Muslim neighbours for the crimes committed on the Hindu minority in East Bengal. He moved over to Bihar, where his refrain was the same as it had been in Bengal: the majority must repent and make amends; the minority must forget and forgive and make a fresh start. In Bihar, however, he was in a position to pull up the Congress ministry, and call upon Nehru and Patel, who were in the Interim Government, to take the sternest measures. While he was agonizing over the violence in Bihar, news arrived of serious riots in the Muslim-majority districts of West Punjab.

Gandhi was dismayed by this prairie fire of religious frenzy and barbaric violence which was rapidly spreading across the subcontinent. All his life he had laboured for the day when India would attain freedom and set an example to the world in non-violence. The chasm between what he had cherished in his heart and what he saw was so great that he could not help feeling a deep sense of failure. His first impulse was to blame himself. Had he been unobservant, careless, indifferent, impatient? Had he failed to detect in time that while people on the whole had been overtly non-violent in the struggle against foreign rule, they had not really imbibed his message of non-violence?

With hindsight, we can see that Gandhi was exaggerating his own responsibility and the failure of his method. The violence that erupted in 1946–7 was in its scale and intensity in an entirely different category from the sporadic communal riots of the inter-war years on such issues as cow-slaughter and music before mosques. It had its origin in the hatred and tensions which the Muslim League's seven-year-long campaign for Pakistan had aroused in its champions as well as its opponents. The basic plank in this campaign was that Hindus and Muslims had nothing in common in the past or the present. While the negotiations on the new constitution for India after the British departure dragged on in the summer of 1946, the masses were seized with vague hopes and fears. No one could say with any degree of certainty whether India would survive as one country or would be carved up into two or more states, whether Punjab and Bengal would be divided, whether the princely states would be integrated into an Indian federation or become independent kingdoms. The Adivasis of central India and the Nagas of Assam suddenly found champions for independence which they had never claimed before; there was talk of a 'Dravidastan' in the south (which Jinnah applauded), and a thousand-mile corridor to link the two wings of a future Pakistan. The Nizam of Hyderabad was intriguing with the Portuguese to secure access to the port of Goa to enable him to set himself up as an independent sultan. The rulers of several other states, such as Travancore and Bhopal, entertained similar grandiose ambitions. All this could not but excite popular fantasy; the turbulent elements in the country began to see in the coming transfer of power a period of power vacuum such as had occurred in the twilight of the Mughal Empire.

In the winter of 1946–7, Gandhi considered the restoration of peace as the most important and urgent task for the country. He believed that this could best be done at the grass roots. He sought to purge fear, hatred, and violence from the hearts of the people and to instil mutual trust and tolerance. His walking tours, prayer meetings and speeches acted as a soothing balm on the hapless victims of the riots. What dismayed him, however, was the way mass madness was escalating from Calcutta to eastern Bengal, from eastern Bengal to Bihar and west Punjab.

Gandhi steeled himself to roam the riot-torn areas until the flames of hatred and violence had been quenched. His colleagues and followers in the Indian National Congress appreciated the loftiness of his mission, but were sceptical of its success. As Nehru told Mountbatten, the Mahatma was 'going round with ointment trying to heal one more spot after another on the body of India, instead of diagnosing [its] cause and participating in the treatment of the body as a whole'. This assessment would have been endorsed by Vallabhbhai Patel, Rajagopalachari, Rajendra Prasad, and other leaders who perceived the riots as the fallout of the gravest political crisis which the country had ever faced; a crisis which indeed seemed to be the culmination of the sixty-year triangular contest between British imperialism, Congress nationalism, and Muslim separatism.

To the historian, it seems surprising that Gandhi should have been so shocked by the Congress leadership's acceptance of the partition of the country. Since March 1940, when Jinnah first propounded his two-nation theory and demanded the secession of the Muslim majority areas in the east and the west, the Congress had been continually softening its stand under the impact of the League's strident propaganda and the confrontation with the British rulers. Soon after the Lahore session of the Muslim League in 1940, while rejecting the two-nation theory, Gandhi wrote in *Harijan* that he knew 'no non-violent method of compelling the obedience of eight crore Muslims to the will of rest of India ... The Muslims must have the same right to self-determination that the rest of India has. We are at present a joint family. Any member may claim a division'.[2]

Two years later, the Congress Working Committee in its resolution on the Cripps' proposals declared that it 'cannot think in terms of compelling the people of any territorial unit in the Indian Union against their declared and established will'. In 1944, in his protracted talks with Jinnah, Gandhi not only accepted the possibility of the partition of the country, but discussed the mechanism for effecting it. Then finally, in the summer of 1946, the Congress accepted, of course after much heart-searching, the Cabinet Mission Plan with its loose three-tier structure and a central government limited to three subjects: foreign affairs, defence, and communications, the durability of which was open to doubt. When such a federal government was suggested for the two wings of Pakistan in 1970, Z.A. Bhutto compared the lot of such a government to that of 'a widow without a pension'.

The Cabinet Mission Plan proved stillborn. The Congress accepted the Plan, but with its own interpretation of the 'Grouping Clause' which differed from that of the Muslim League. The Muslim League withdrew its acceptance of the Plan and refused to join the Constituent Assembly. When the Viceroy, Lord Wavell, formed an Interim Government headed by Jawaharlal Nehru, the League announced 'Direct Action' on 16 August 1946. Rattled by the holocaust that followed in Calcutta and East Bengal, Lord Wavell inducted the Muslim League into the Interim Government, but with results that were just the opposite of what he had hoped for. The Interim Government, rather than becoming more representative and effective, was paralysed by the conflict between its Congress and League members. The Viceroy did not have a clue as to what he should do, and proposed a 'Breakdown Plan' for British military evacuation of the sub-continent, province by province. Prime Minister Attlee considered it a counsel of despair, and decided to appoint a new Viceroy to devise and implement a scheme for more orderly termination of British rule in India.

On 20 February 1947 the British government issued a momentous statement announcing 'their definite intention to take the necessary steps to effect the transfer of power into responsible Indian hands by a date not later than June 1948'. This statement could well have acted as a 'shock therapy' to bring the contending parties together. It had just the opposite effect because of the provision in it that if on 'the appointed date' there was no single government for the whole of British India, power might be transferred 'in some areas to the existing Provincial Governments or in such other ways as may seem most reasonable'. The Muslim League, which had ministries only in Bengal and Sind, took this to mean that it just had fifteen months to capture the provincial governments in the remaining provinces (Punjab, N.W.F.P., and Assam) which it claimed for Pakistan. It unleashed a campaign of 'direct action' in the form of demonstrations, which resulted in widespread communal disturbances in West Punjab in March 1947. The response of the Congress Working Committee came in a resolution demanding the partition of Punjab, as a signal to the Muslim League that it would not be allowed to get away with the Hindu-majority districts of Punjab and Bengal if it insisted on the secession of Muslim-majority areas in the east and the west. The logic which the League applied for the partition of India could as well justify the partition of these two provinces.

By the time Lord Mountbatten arrived in India towards the end of March 1947, the Congress leadership was trying to reconcile itself to Pakistan as 'the lesser evil'; the choice was narrowing down to partition or civil war. While the new Viceroy was hammering out a scheme acceptable to the Congress, the League and the British government, Gandhi was watching the course of events as a helpless spectator. It hurt him to see that he was unable to carry his conviction to his closest colleagues and even to the rank and file of the Congress. It has been suggested that he was isolated and even betrayed by Nehru and Patel who were 'avid for power'. As for Gandhi's isolation, it was largely self-inflicted; he chose to carry on with his humanitarian mission in Bengal and Bihar instead of returning to Delhi where fateful decisions were being taken. More important was the fact that his views seemed utopian and impracticable not only to Nehru and Patel, but to almost all members of the Congress Working Committee on whom the burden of decision rested. They knew that they were not the only players in the making of events. For a quarter of a century, the Congress had been calling for the end of foreign rule. The British withdrawal had now been decided and dated. Partition could only be avoided if a viable alternative could be devised with the concurrence of all the three parties, the British government, the Congress, and the Muslim League. This alternative was not in sight.

Gandhi was thinking hard on how to pull back the country from the precipice of partition. In his second meeting with Lord Mountbatten on 1 April 1947 he proposed that Jinnah should be invited to form a government of his own choice to which the Congress would extend its support. The proposal 'astounded' the Viceroy, but it was also rejected out of hand by Patel and Nehru who had been driven to despair by their experience of working with the League representatives in the Interim Government; in any case, they were certain that such unilateral gestures would not melt Jinnah's heart. Mountbatten did not convey Gandhi's proposal to Jinnah, but it is doubtful whether the League leader's reaction would have been different from what he had said about a similar proposal made by the Mahatma in August 1942:

If they [the Congress] are sincere I should welcome it. If the British Government accepts the solemn declaration of Mr Gandhi and by an arrangement hands over the government of the country to the Muslim League, I am sure that under Muslim rule non-Muslims would be treated fairly justly, nay, generously; and further the British will be making full amends to the Muslims by restoring the Government of India to those from whom they have taken it.[3]

When Gandhi's proposal to hand over power to Jinnah did not find favour, he put forward a basic proposition: there should be no surrender to threats of violence; there must be peace before there was Pakistan. He argued that the communal polarization in the country was not a permanent phenomenon, that the British had in any case no moral right to impose partition on an 'India temporarily gone mad'. The British, he said, could depart from India, but they had no right to divide it.

In the first half of 1947, most political observers would have agreed with Gandhi on the urgency of ending communal violence, but they believed its root cause was political. It was the problem of unity versus partition that had unhinged the minds of the people, and this problem had to be resolved in Delhi and London. Gandhi's approach was different. He sought to work upon the people at the grass-roots, and convince them that they could live together as good neighbours as they had done for centuries. His tours of Bengal and Bihar had met with a measure of success, but he was handicapped by the fact that his voice did not carry the weight with the Muslim community that it had once done. Had his efforts at restoring amity been supplemented by someone who commanded the allegiance of the Muslim community, his task would not have been half as difficult. Had Jinnah toured eastern Bengal or West Punjab, he might have helped in stopping the rot. Such an idea would have simply been laughed out of court by the League leader. 'In politics', he once said, 'one has to play one's game as on the chessboard.'[4] However deplorable communal violence was, it became the strongest argument in his brief for Pakistan. The Quaid-i-Azam's reiteration of 'Congress tyranny' and 'Hindu Raj' for a decade had succeeded in producing amongst his followers and even colleagues a curious blend of paranoia, combativeness, and bravado.[5] The League leaders were wont to ridicule Gandhi's non-violence; whether or not they believed in violence, they appeared to believe in the threats of violence. Jinnah himself had inaugurated his 'direct action' campaign in August 1946 with the remark: 'Today we have forged a pistol and are in a position to use it'.[6] In so far as these threats were designed to rouse the Muslims, frighten the Congress and impress the British, they succeeded; both the Congress and the British were in the end driven to the conclusion that partition was the only alternative to chaos. When riots broke out, the League leaders were reluctant to condemn the misdeeds of their co-religionists, and heaped all the blame on the Hindus, the Congress, and the British. In November 1946, George Abell, the Private Secretary of the Viceroy, wrote after a meeting with Jinnah's deputy, Nawabzada Liaquat Ali Khan, that he 'got the clear impression that the League could not afford to let the communal feeling in the country to die down'.[7] The restoration of peace thus became an intractable problem. The Interim Government at the Centre was a house divided against itself; in the provinces the British Governors and senior I.C.S. officers, conscious of their imminent departure, had neither the will nor the ability to cope with large-scale disorders. There was a real danger of the police and the army being infected with the communal virus.[8] It was the stark choice between partition and civil war that drove the Congress leaders to accept the former.

Latter-day commentators have been asking why Gandhi did not fast to prevent partition. Fasting was certainly one of the ultimate weapons in Gandhi's armoury of satyagraha; he had used it on certain occasions to exercise moral pressure. This pressure was, as a rule, directed not against those who differed with him, but against those who loved and believed in him; he sought to prick the conscience of the latter and to convey to them something of his inner anguish when things went wrong. The fast dramatized the issues at stake; ostensibly it suppressed reason, but in actuality it was designed to free reason from inertia and prejudice that hindered a meeting of minds. Gandhi did in fact have recourse to fasting at Calcutta in September 1947 and at Delhi in January 1948. These two fasts have been rightly reckoned among the greatest miracles of modern times; they had the magical effect of quenching the flames of hatred and violence. These fasts were, however, undertaken *after* Independence and were in reality directed by Gandhi against his own co-religionists. To prevent partition, there was no point in Gandhi's fasting or starting civil disobedience against the British, who were not susceptible to such moral pressure, and were in any case leaving the country. Nor would there have been any point in his undertaking a fast in West Punjab or East Bengal where he had been painted for years as an enemy of Islam. The leaders of the Muslim League were proof against the nuances of satyagraha; they would at once have denounced Gandhi's fast as a trick to cheat them of the prize of Pakistan which lay within their grasp.

Gandhi's proposition that the British had no right to partition India, but should leave India to her fate was acceptable neither to the Muslim League nor to the British. It had been Jinnah's unwavering strategy since 1937 to seek the realization of his objectives with the help of the British;[9] for him the correct sequence was: 'partition first and independence afterwards'. In 1946–7 the Labour Government had decided not to let Jinnah exercise a veto on the freedom of India, but it could not ignore him either. After all, he had obtained a decisive mandate in the general election of 1946 in which he had won, on the issue of Pakistan, all the Muslim seats in the Central Assembly and 90 per cent of the Muslim seats in the provincial legislatures. Prime Minister Attlee advised Jinnah to 'enter the Constituent Assembly and try to resolve the problem through mutual negotiations by argument and compromise'.[10] Jinnah, however, insisted on partition, undaunted even by the prospect of the division of the Punjab, Bengal, and Assam. With the looming threat of civil war, the Labour government could not afford to leave India, as Gandhi said, 'to its fate'. Such a momentous decision, as the liquidation of British Empire in India, needed the support of public opinion and approval of both Houses of Parliament in Britain. Churchill and the Conservative Party would never have allowed any solution that was not acceptable to Jinnah and the Muslim League.

On 1 June 1947, a day before Mountbatten formally presented his partition plan to the Indian leaders, Gandhi's secretary Pyarelal heard him murmuring to himself: 'I find myself all alone. Even the Sardar and Jawaharlal think my reading of the situation is wrong and peace is sure to return if partition is agreed upon ... They wonder if I have not deteriorated with age. I can see clearly that the future of independence gained at this price is going to be dark. Everybody is today impatient for independence. Therefore, there is no alternative.'[11]

Nehru, Patel, Rajagopalachari, Rajendra Prasad, and other Congress leaders were not the only ones who were persuaded that though the partition was an exorbitant price, it was worth paying for a lasting peace in the subcontinent. The Muslim League was congratulating itself on its victory against heavy odds in achieving 'homelands for the Muslim nation'. The British government was relieved at the prospect of an orderly transfer of power. Gandhi alone was troubled by feelings of disillusionment, despair, and deep foreboding. Two years before, in a flash of self-revelation, he had told an American editor: 'I am not a man who sits down and thinks out problems syllogistically. I am a man of action. I react to a situation intuitively. Logic comes afterwards.'[12]

In the summer of 1947, the Mahatma's intuition clashed with the logic of politicians and administrators; hence the 'communication gap' between them. Interestingly, his intuition had brought him instantly to the same conclusion eight years earlier when the then Viceroy, Lord Linlithgow, had first broached the subject of Pakistan with him. The Viceroy wrote after a meeting with the Mahatma in March 1939,

Before we concluded, I thought it well to mention the Pakistan project to him, and to ask him whether he thought it had any life in it. He said, he understood, not, but that that might come ... he doubted if it [the Pakistan project] would stand any detailed examination, though it had no doubt wide possibilities. I asked whether by that he meant that it might represent an upsurge running back into the depths of the Muslim world. He said that might indeed be the case in certain circumstances, but even if Pakistan admitted of realization, it would never settle the communal question in India or represent more than a sharp division which might in due course give rise to a major calamity.[13]

Gandhi was once asked what he would do after India attained freedom. 'If India becomes free in my lifetime', he replied, 'and I have energy still left in me, I will take due share, though outside the official world, in building up the nation on a strictly non-violent basis.' In 1947, just when the bloodless revolution against British rule, which he had led for a quarter of a century, was succeeding, the country was torn by internecine strife. Sad at heart, he did not participate in the celebrations in Delhi on 15 August, spending that day in Calcutta, fasting and praying. His presence provided an immediate healing touch to Calcutta, which had been tense since 'the Great Calcutta Killing' of the previous year, but he remained apprehensive. His worst fears were confirmed when a fortnight later a Hindu mob, inflamed by the news of massacres and migrations from West Pakistan, went on the rampage. Gandhi himself escaped a murderous assault when attempting to pacify the rioters. He immediately went on a fast, which he broke only when the representatives of both the communities solemnly pledged that they would see that Calcutta remained peaceful. The fast had a magical effect in restoring sanity in Bengal. The 'One-man Boundary Force', as Mountbatten described Gandhi, succeeded in achieving in Bengal what 50,000 troops under Major-General Rees were unable to achieve in the Punjab. Suhrawardy, the former League Premier of Bengal who had ridiculed and obstructed Gandhi's peace mission in Noakhali in the winter months of 1946, was a chastened man after 15 August 1947 and begged Gandhi not to go to eastern Bengal but to work for communal harmony between Hindus and Muslims in Calcutta. In his memoirs, he explained why he joined Gandhi's peace mission,

if the Muslims of Calcutta and environs were massacred or driven away, there would be repercussions in East Bengal and the Hindus would be similarly treated. There were almost four times as many Hindus in East Bengal as Muslims in West Bengal ... The result could be that the Muslims of Bihar, Assam and United Provinces certainly and elsewhere probably would be slaughtered or driven out to make room for refugees. There would be a terrible holocaust all over the country.[14]

Gandhi saved West Bengal and East Pakistan from a holocaust. He could not accomplish a similar feat in the west because by the time he reached Delhi in September 1947, the worst had already happened in West Pakistan and East Punjab, both of which had nearly completed, what is now called, 'ethnic cleansing'. Nevertheless, Gandhi's presence in Delhi from September 1947 to January 1948 helped to stem the tide of violence. During these months hundreds of thousands of Hindu and Sikh refugees from West Pakistan were fleeing and seeking refuge in Delhi, U.P., Bihar, and other provinces. Had the Nehru government not taken the firm steps it did, and had Gandhi not quenched the flames of hatred and revenge through his endless vigil, his fasts, and eventually his martyrdom, a Hindu backlash of the type, which Suhrawardy had feared for East Pakistan, might have created a new stream of refugees that would have overwhelmed West Pakistan. Gandhi could not prevent the division of the country, but he had done all he could to mitigate its ravages.

NOTES AND REFERENCES

1. N.K. Bose and P.H. Patwardhan, *Gandhi in Indian Politics* (Bombay, 1967), p. 7.
2. *Harijan*, 6 April 1940.
3. Jamil-ud-Din-Ahmad, *Some Recent Speeches and Writings of Mr Jinnah* (Lahore, 1946), p. 447.
4. Ibid., p. 87.
5. Several speakers at the Convention of Muslim League Legislators in April 1946 had adopted a menacing posture. Sir Firoz Khan Noon said: 'If we

find that we have to fight Great Britain for placing us under one Central Government or Hindu Raj, then the havoc which the Muslims will play will put to shame what Chengiz Khan and Halaku did.' (*Dawn*, 11 April 1946). Abdur Rab Nishtar, who was to become a member of the Indian government later in the year, was reported to have said: 'The real fact is that Mussalmans belong to a martial race and are no believers in non-violent principles of Mr Gandhi.' (*Dawn*, 26 March 1946).

6. Asked if the proposed Direct Action would be violent or non-violent, Mr Jinnah said, 'I am not going to discuss ethics'. (*Dawn*, 1 August 1940).

7. George Abell to Wavell, 18 Nov. 1946, in N. Mansergh (ed.), *The Transfer of Power*, volume IX (London, 1980), no. 49.

8. On 30 June Gen. Auchinleck asked Cariappa, the seniormost Indian officer, to get the views of the officers on the question of the defence problems of a politically divided India. Cariappa reported, 'Officers representing Pakistan collectively said one army for India was desirable, but was not practicable in the present circumstances.'

    Cariappa to Auchinleck, 15 July 1947, quoted by Partha Sarathi Gupta, 'Imperial Strategy and the Transfer of Power 1939–51' *in* Amit Kumar Gupta (ed.), *Myth and Reality: The Struggle for Freedom in India, 1945–47* (Delhi, 1987), p. 22.

9. Jinnah told the annual session of the Muslim League in 1943: 'Pakistan we want—and that commodity is available not in the Congress market, but in the British market.'

10. Attlee to Jinnah, 23 July 1946, N. Mansergh, (ed.), *The Transfer of Power*, vol. VIII (London, 1979), pp. 110–11.

11. Pyarelal, *Mahatma Gandhi, The Last Phase*, vol. II (Ahmedabad, 1958), pp. 210–11.

12. Pyarelal, *Mahatma Gandhi, The Last Phase*, vol. I (Ahmedabad, 1956), p. 120.

13. Lord Linlithgow's minute of 15 March 1939, Linlithgow Papers.

14. M.H.R. Talukdar (ed.), *Memoirs of H.S. Suhrawardy* (Delhi, 1987), p. 108.

PART III

Towards Understanding Gandhi

SEVENTEEN

Gandhi and Nehru

Millions of words have been written by and on both Mahatma Gandhi and Jawaharlal Nehru. Their lives and work are inextricably intertwined with over half a century of Indian history. In this essay, I propose to do no more than touch on a few basic questions. What did Gandhi and Nehru stand for? Do their objectives and methods have any relevance, as we struggle with our problems today? To say that the relationship between Gandhi and Nehru was that of a master and a disciple would not be correct. Nehru was not a blind follower, nor did Gandhi expect unquestioning obedience from him or, for that matter, from anyone else. They were separated not only by twenty years in terms of age, but by deep intellectual and temperamental differences. That Nehru, with his enthusiasm for humanism, science, and technology, should have taken to a Mahatma with his spinning wheel, prayers, and inner voice was an enigma to contemporary critical observers. Nevertheless, the fact remains that the partnership between these two men of exceptional energy and integrity lasted for over twenty-five years, surviving numerous strains and stresses, to which it was subjected by the vicissitudes of politics and life. The secret hope cherished by high British officials (and even by some of the Indian radicals) that Jawaharlal would break with the Mahatma and form a separate party remained unrealized. Deep down, both these leaders knew that, despite occasional differences on tactics and methods, they had the same unalterable aim, namely, the freedom of India. Neither of them was prepared to press differences of opinion to breaking point. Gandhi often went more than half way to meet Nehru's views, and the latter, in the last resort, was not averse to a compromise to prevent a split in the party. In 1928, at the Calcutta session of the Indian National Congress, when there was a clash between the Old Guard and the younger generation of Congress leaders on the issue of Dominion Status versus

Independence, young Nehru accepted the compromise formula suggested by Gandhi.

There were numerous other occasions when Nehru was assailed by doubts about Gandhi's policies: in 1929, on the Dominion Status declaration of Lord Irwin; in 1931, on the Gandhi–Irwin Pact; in 1932, on Gandhi's fast against separate electorates for the untouchables; in 1934, on the withdrawal of the civil disobedience movement; in 1937, on the formation of Congress ministries in the provinces; in 1942, on the Quit India movement; and finally, in 1947, on the partition of the country. Contrary to a widespread impression, it was not always Nehru who gave in. In 1942, in the weeks preceding the adoption of the 'Quit India' resolution by the All India Congress Committee, Nehru was able to effect a major shift in Gandhi's attitude to the retention of Allied troops on Indian soil. In 1947, Gandhi, against his own better judgement, let Nehru and the majority in the Congress Working Committee have their way on the division of India, as embodied in the Mountbatten Plan. It was a deliberate gesture of self-abnegation to keep the party and the country united at a critical time.

In later years, with the advantage of hindsight, Nehru came to realize that the Mahatma's political instinct had often been sounder than the arguments with which he clothed his decisions. It is instructive to compare the *Discovery of India*, written in 1944, with the *Autobiography*, written ten years earlier; in the intervening decade, Nehru's criticism of Gandhi's policies had become visibly muted. As Nehru himself bore the burden of leading the party and the government after 1947, he was better able to appreciate the dilemma of the Mahatma in the pre-Independence days. 'A political leader,' Nehru told Norman Cousins, the editor of *Saturday Review*, 'cannot function like a prophet. He has to limit himself to the people's understanding of him.' Part of the difficulty arose from Gandhi's peculiar idiom, which was aimed at the masses and grated on the ears of the Western-educated élite. Nor was it always easy to immediately grasp the full, long-term implications of Gandhi's strategy. For instance, Nehru once asked Gandhi why he had chosen to campaign against untouchability rather than make a frontal assault on the caste system. 'If untouchability goes', Gandhi replied, 'the caste system goes'. Gandhi thus deliberately attacked the caste system at the point where it was most vulnerable. 'A tremendous revolutionary force in the right direction', was how Nehru described Gandhi to Tibor Mende, the (Hungarian-born) French journalist, in 1955.

II

It was the cause of the Indian freedom that brought Gandhi and Nehru together, and which kept them together. The national awakening long antedated the arrival of Gandhi on the Indian political stage. It had found expression in the brilliant advocacy of Dadabhai Naoroji and Mahadev Govind Ranade, the pointed thrusts at British imperialism by Bal Gangadhar Tilak, the passionate prose of Aurobindo Ghose, and the stately eloquence of Gopal Krishna Gokhale. From 1920 onwards, however, with the coming of Gandhi, there was a quantitative as well as a qualitative change. Politics ceased to be largely an urban or middle-class phenomenon; a diversion for the weekend, or for the Christmas week. Gandhi toured the country from one end to the other by train, by car, by boat, by bullock-cart, and even on foot. He went deep into the interior to villages that had been off the beaten track of political leaders. He came to epitomize the spirit of nationalism. He felt at home in every part of India and in every segment of Indian society. A Gujarati by birth, he had fought for Sindhi and Bohra merchants and for Tamilian plantation workers in South Africa. His first major agrarian agitation after his return to India was in Bihar. It was the tragedy of the Punjab in the spring of 1919 which hastened his transition to a rebel against the British Raj. There was hardly a province of India to whose succour he did not go on one occasion or another: earthquake-hit Bihar, flood-stricken Orissa, riot-torn Bengal, the Harijans of Kerala all stirred him to his depths. His patriotism had no room for racial or communal exclusiveness. He equally respected all religions and all cultures, and was singularly free from the not uncommon arrogance of the highly educated Indian towards his less fortunate brethren. Of the religion of the tribals of Assam, Gandhi once said, 'What have I to take to them except to go in my nakedness to them? Rather than ask them to join my prayers, I would join their prayers.'

Gandhi's deep feeling for the rich cultural diversity of India and for her unity was shared by Nehru, and indeed found in him a superb spokesman. 'We must try to understand,' he said, 'what India is and how this nation has developed a composite personality, with its many facets and yet with an enduring unity.' Nehru's writings on this theme were like heady wine to India's youth in the 1930s and 1940s. His use of the modern idiom, as distinct from the homely and somewhat mystical phrases of the Mahatma, made him more easily intelligible to the outside world. It was the publication in England of Nehru's autobiography in 1936, which for the first time presented Gandhi's principles and politics in terms which the West could begin to understand. Gandhi had made Indian freedom a moral issue; Nehru made it a world issue. Nehru's ringing phrases echoed in several countries of Asia and Africa; even in Europe, they undermined the imperialist complacency by sowing the seeds of doubt in liberal and socialist circles.

India's foreign policy, of which Nehru was the chief architect, fulfilled one of Gandhi's cherished aspirations: that Indian freedom should be a prelude to the freedom of all Asia and Africa. It was only fitting that Gandhi should have been present at the first Asian Relations Conference at New Delhi in March 1947. During the following decade, India's moral weight was strongly exerted in favour of the liquidation of colonialism in Indonesia, Indo–China and in several other countries. Nehru held up before the newly liberated countries the policy of 'non-alignment', which contributed to the lessening of the area of international tension at a time when the two Superpowers had not learnt to talk to each other. His crusade at international conferences against racial discrimination and for bridging the economic gap between the developed and underdeveloped countries stemmed from deep conviction. Gandhi's incessant emphasis on the power of the human spirit and on the two-edged nature of violence as an instrument of political and social change, had conditioned Nehru against colonialism, racialism, and militarism. 'The policy of non-alignment pursued by India', he told a Columbia University audience in 1953, 'is a positive and vital policy that flows from our struggle for freedom and from the teachings of Mahatma Gandhi.' He did not diverge from this policy despite difficulties and setbacks, and was able to create, what may be called, a national consensus on foreign policy, in which the protection of national self-interest is allied to a strong desire for peace. This was confirmed in a remarkable manner in December 1971, when Prime Minister Indira Gandhi, in the very hour of the Indian victory in the war with Pakistan, declared a unilateral ceasefire. There was not a single dissenting voice.

III

Gandhi's vision of free India was part of a larger vision in which he saw the 'end of the exploitation of the poor by the rich, of the masses by the "classes", of the villages by the towns, of the weaker or so-called underdeveloped races by the stronger or more advanced ones'. Nehru cherished the same vision. It was common ground between them that political freedom was only a means to an end: the provision of a better life for the mass of India's population. They did not, however, quite agree on how to achieve it. While Nehru pinned his faith on science, modern technology, and industrialization, Gandhi talked of 'Village Swaraj', in which each village was to be largely self-sufficient for its vital requirements, growing its own food, and its own cotton for its cloth, and (if surplus land was available) cash crops. Every village was to have its own school, theatre, and public hall. Education was to be compulsory, there was to be no untouchability and, as far as possible, every activity was to be conducted on a cooperative basis.

Contrary to the general impression, Gandhi did not idealize poverty for its own sake. Indeed, he considered grinding poverty, such as prevailed in India, as degrading and dehumanizing, and wanted a substantial rise in the standard of living of the masses. At the same time, he abhorred the quest for an unending multiplication of wants which, in his view, was bound to lead to commercial and colonial exploitation and to wars. He had a deep distrust both of industrialism and of the modern state. 'Pandit Nehru wants industrialization,' he wrote, 'because he thinks that if it is socialized, it would be free from the evils of capitalism. My own view is that the evils are inherent in industrialization, and no amount of socialization can eradicate them.'

Gandhi's views on industrialization did not commend themselves to the Indian intelligentsia, and even to many of his colleagues in the Congress leadership. To many of his eminent contemporaries—scientists, economists, industrialists, radicals, socialists, communists—Gandhian economics seemed a throwback to primitiveness; to a utopian pre-industrial position which was untenable in the modern world. The arguments for and against industrialization figured in discussions and correspondence between Gandhi and Nehru. Nehru's *Autobiography* fairly stated their respective positions. The intellectual gulf on this issue was sometimes narrowed, but rarely bridged. The Mahatma's ideas seemed to Nehru too empirical, too amorphous and simplistic. 'The processes of history and economics', Nehru wrote, 'cannot be stopped for long.' Nehru was convinced that India had no alternative but to tread the path to progress, which Europe, America, and Japan had traversed. Indeed, to make up for two centuries of arrested economic development, India had to accelerate her march on that path. In June 1939, as the Chairman of the National Planning Committee of the Indian National Congress, Nehru wrote a comprehensive note in which he defined democratic planning as 'technical coordination by disinterested experts, of consumption, production, investment, trade and income distribution in accordance with the social objectives set by bodies representative of the majority'. The fundamental aim, he wrote, was to ensure an adequate standard of living for the Indian masses, and this required an increase in national wealth by five or six times. A minimum standard of living for everyone required not only increase in production, but more equitable distribution. He suggested targets to raise nourishment to 2800 calories, clothing to at least 30 yards, and housing standards to at least 100 sq. ft per head, and a health centre per thousand of the population. Agricultural production had to be increased, a 'balanced structure' of heavy, medium, and cottage industries established, unemployment diminished, and illiteracy liquidated. All this was to be part of a national plan.

Believing that industrialization on a large scale was the answer to India's development problem, Nehru was not attracted by what he considered the Mahatma's rural utopia. 'I do not understand', he wrote to Gandhi in 1945, 'why a village should necessarily embody truth and non-violence. A village, normally speaking, is backward intellectually and culturally, and no progress can be made from a backward environment.'

In an essay on 'Gandhian Economic Thought', written more than thirty years ago, J.J. Anjaria had attempted a critique of the Gandhian model of rural development and indicated the several question-marks that remained. Was it possible to ensure substantial self-sufficiency on the part of each village and, if so, at what cost? Was khadi not dependent for its survival on the patronage of the cities rather than that of the villages? How was a village or even a group of villages to be insulated from the rest of the world for consumption and capital goods? How were the problems of costing, pricing, currency, and external trade to be resolved? Decentralization of economic and political power was an admirable principle, but if it was conceded (as Gandhi had done) that some basic industries were necessary, and would have to be run by the state, the nationalized sector under the Gandhian scheme might not be as insignificant as had been assumed.

IV

Gandhi died six months after the attainment of Independence, and did not have the time to perfect his economic model, or to try it out in the post-colonial period, on any substantial scale. Nevertheless, Gandhi's model, as expounded in his writings, contains valuable insights that remain valid today. He recognized certain unique features of the Indian situation. One of these is the predominance of the self-employed producer, agriculturist, or artisan engaged in producing for his basic requirements and not for the pursuit of wealth for its own sake. The mass of the small producers in India are thus a social category fundamentally different from either the medieval serfs or the modern proletariat, which formed the basic argument for the model of a classless society. Nor does the small self-employed producer, working and living within the constraints of community life, fit into the individual-based capitalist model loved by the liberal–rationalist school. This school is thought to have tended to identify economic development with the disintegration of the small peasant and artisan economy and the growth of large-scale enterprises based on modern technology. Gandhi saw the difficulties, and dangers, of indiscriminate industrialization in underdeveloped countries if millions of small producers forming the bulk of the society were to be alienated from the means of production.

Few people would disagree today that after the attainment of Independence, India could no more have opted out of industrialization than she could have effected unilateral disarmament. 'We cannot stop the river of change', Nehru had written in his autobiography, 'or cut ourselves adrift from it, and psychologically, we, who have eaten the apple of Eden cannot forget the taste and go back to primitiveness.' India has charted her course for planned economic development on Nehru's model of harnessing science and technology for that purpose. There have been significant gains all along the entire economic spectrum during these fifty years, but the progress has not been as smooth or as rapid or as evenly spread as was desired or planned.

The problems that have arisen in recent years were not absent from Nehru's mind. He was not daunted by the prospect of setbacks. 'Only the dead have no problems', he once said, 'the living have problems and they grow by fighting with them. It is a sign of the growth of this nation that not only do we solve problems, but create new problems to solve.'

As indicated earlier in this essay, while the strategy of the struggle against British imperialism had been largely Gandhi's, Nehru, through his radical views, had helped to stiffen it. It seems that in the post-Independence period, the process might have been reversed; into the framework of the economic progress originally set up by Nehru and adopted by the country since 1947, some Gandhian insights could have been usefully incorporated. For one thing, the focus, as the Mahatma had always said, could have been more and more on the village. There could have been greater emphasis on voluntary work, less dependence on the machinery of the state, and more on cooperative effort generated by the people themselves. Greater austerity all round, a reorientation of higher education and research to the needs of the village: all these stand out in the Gandhian model. Gandhi gave a great deal of thought to the problems of the village, especially after he had settled down at Sevagram in central India. 'How to turn waste into wealth,' was his summing up to Lord Farringdon of the work of the All India Village Industries Association. Of the four hundred adults of Sevagram, the Mahatma said 'They could put ten thousand rupees into their pockets if only they would work as I ask them. But they won't. They lack cooperation; they do not know the art of intelligent labour. They refuse to learn anything new.' Among the things that the villagers could do, but failed to do was to keep their villages clean. Gandhi attributed this to the fear of most Indians of touching their own dirt and, therefore, of cleaning it. He exhorted everyone to be his own scavenger, to join in a campaign to keep village tanks and wells and streets clean, and to remove the cause for Lionel Curtis's reproach that Indian villages were dung-heaps.

Nutrition was another problem to which he gave much thought. He realized with something of a shock that, apart from their poverty, the food habits of people in the villages were responsible for their undernourishment. The deficiency in vitamins was inexcusable when green leaves were available for the picking. Gandhi appealed to Indian scientists to pursue research into Indian diets in the context of Indian conditions:

It is for you to make these experiments. Don't say off-hand that Bengalis need half a pound of rice every day and must digest half a pound. Devise a scientifically perfect diet for them. Determine the quality of starch required for an average human constitution. I would not be satisfied until I have been able to add some milk and milk fat and greens to the diet of our common village folk. I want chemists who would starve in order to find an ideal diet for their poor countrymen. Unfortunately, our doctors have never approached the question from the humanitarian standpoint, at any rate from the poor man's standpoint.

As a 'practised cook', he wrote on the modes of cooking which did not destroy the nutritive value of foods. He stressed the superiority of hand-ground wheat and hand-polished rice to their factory equivalents. 'The textile mills', he wrote, 'had brought unemployment in their wake, but rice and flour mills have also brought in undernourishment and disease.'

Gandhi believed that 'Revivification of India's villages is a necessity of our existence. We must mentally go back to the villages and treat them as our pattern, instead of putting the city life before them for imitation'. The cities, he said, were capable of taking care of themselves. 'It is the villages we have to turn to. We have to disabuse them of their prejudices, their superstitions, their narrow outlook, and we can do so in no other manner than that of staying amongst them and sharing their joys and sorrows and spreading education and intelligent information among them.'

Gandhi was all for the gospel of work. 'To a people famishing and idle', he said, 'the only acceptable form in which God can dare appear is work and promise of food as wages.' If he had the good fortune, he said, to come face to face with one like the Buddha, he should not hesitate to ask him why he did not teach the gospel of work in preference to one of contemplation. In one of the meetings of the All India Village Industries Association, Gandhi spoke on socialism for the poor and the life in an ideal village. He suggested that those who could not afford milk, could get along with separated milk without fat, which retained considerable nutritive value. Those who could not afford fruit could make do with tamarind, sour lime, and tomatoes as fruit. He dwelt on model houses built of thatch, mud, and palm leaf matting. He wondered whether the number of cattle in villages could be reduced. Why was it necessary, he asked, for every household in a village to keep a bullock-cart? Could not the villagers under a cooperative scheme do with fewer carts? Why could they not run a cooperative animal shed? Why could they not have a marketing cooperative for the sale of grain and crops? Was it not possible for all the village land to be cultivated on a cooperative basis, and the produce distributed among those who had worked to produce it? Was it not possible to devise inexpensive warm clothing for the villagers so that they did not have to huddle together for warmth along with their family and animals in the same room?

Living in a village, constantly thinking about the problems of the village, Gandhi was seeking solutions to these problems within the human and material resources available there. This is an approach that could be profitably pursued even today. The 'gobar gas plant', of which we have heard so much, is an example of this approach; if Gandhi had been alive, he would have been one of its most enthusiastic supporters. On the contrary, he would have found it difficult to endorse the orientation of a system of higher education of whose products a sizeable number are tempted to go abroad to man the public health system of Great Britain and the high-technology industry of the United States and Canada rather than find gainful employment in rural India which needs them most.

V

It is a curious fact that in the debate on the legacy of Gandhi and Nehru in the post-1947 period, the focus has been mainly on their differing approaches to economic problems. There was, however, a whole range of other basic issues on which they were in agreement: in their commitment to the freedom and unity of India, to a pluralist polity, and to peaceful methods for the resolution of differences between groups, communities, and nations. Both of them denounced religious and linguistic fanaticism, caste exclusiveness, and untouchability; they would have been horrified by the eruptions of casteism, corruption, and criminalization in Indian politics which we see today. Both of them regarded politics as one of the avenues of service to society, and not as a means of acquiring personal gains and pursuit of power. Both eschewed populist rhetoric. They did not pander to the masses; their speeches and writings were a healthy mixture of exhortations and warnings. Gandhi had always insisted that Swaraj meant not only the end of British rule, but the attainment by the Indian people of 'self-rule', by which he meant self-discipline. This discipline was, however, to be inculcated among the people by the leaders themselves setting an example. Finally, both Gandhi and Nehru subscribed to non-violence as the ideal method of settling disputes within and between nations. In October 1960, in his address to the United Nations General Assembly, Nehru harked back to the teachings of the Mahatma. He said that the basic problem was that of comprehending the tremendous potentialities for prosperity and destruction of the industrial and military revolutions of the nuclear age. He pleaded for right means even for attaining right ends. 'That was the lesson,' he said, 'which our great leader Gandhi taught us. Though we in India have failed in many ways in following his advice, something of his message still clings to our minds and hearts.'

EIGHTEEN

Three Disciples

In 1994 India celebrated the birth centenaries of three of Gandhi's closest disciples. It may appear that there was little in common between Mahadev Desai, the small-town lawyer from Gujarat, Mirabehn, the daughter of a British Admiral, and J.C. Kumarappa, the US-trained economist from southern India; yet all of them were drawn to Gandhi and devoted their lives to the causes he championed.

Notwithstanding their vastly different background, intellectual equipment and individual temperaments, they found fulfilment at Gandhi's feet. The story of their association with the Mahatma is fascinating for the insights it offers not only into their own personalities, but also into the character of the man who won their whole-hearted allegiance. It is unlikely that such a relationship could have been established and nurtured without the guru–*shishya* tradition which has existed in India from time immemorial.

Gandhi was aware of this tradition, and has referred to it in his autobiography while narrating his own spiritual odyssey. He tells us about his own search for a guru: the nearest he got to one was when he met Rajchandra, the poet–jeweller–saint of Bombay. But even Rajchandra did not quite measure up to Gandhi's image of the ideal guru, and the throne in his heart, as he put it, remained vacant.[1]

Little did Gandhi know in those early years that a day would come when he himself would not only assume the role of a guru, but radically transform the ancient guru–*shishya* concept. While leading the struggle against racial discrimination in South Africa, he set up two little settlements at Phoenix and Tolstoy Farm for his close followers. Among those who joined him were a few Europeans: Henry Polak, Albert West, and Hermann Kallenbach. Their regard for Gandhi was only just short of idolatry but they did not accompany him to India.

One of the reasons for Gandhi's failure to find a guru after his own heart was that the idea of total obedience on the part of the disciple did not appeal to him. Moreover, the traditional guru–disciple relationship was primarily for spiritual growth, but Gandhi's religious quest did not end in a cave in the Himalayas. The ashrams he set up in South Africa and India were not only a haven for those who aspired to spiritual bliss through prayer and meditation, but imparted instruction in public service through truthful and non-violent means. Indeed, his ashrams were schools for training soldiers of satyagraha.

On his return to India in 1915, after twenty years in South Africa, Gandhi had to assemble a new team of co-workers. This he did while he was still on the periphery of nationalist politics, during the years of the First World War when he was seen more as a religious and social reformer than as a political leader. Among those who joined him was a twenty-five-year-old law graduate from Surat, Mahadev Desai. He had tried his hand at various jobs, as a translator in the Oriental Translator's Office, as an inspector of the cooperative societies, and as secretary to Jamnadas Mehta, a Bombay politician, besides making a half-hearted attempt at legal practice in the district courts of Ahmedabad. Well-read both in English and Gujarati literature, and wielding a smooth pen, Mahadev Desai caught Gandhi's perceptive eye, and the latter persuaded him to accompany him to Champaran in 1917. The Champaran Satyagraha, which triggered off Gandhi's thirty-year non-violent war against the British Raj, was one of the skirmishes which preceded the great non-cooperation battle of 1919–22.

Gandhi's deep involvement in nationalist politics profoundly altered his life as well as even at times Mahadev Desai's. Hitherto, Desai had been helping Gandhi, who was not yet much in the limelight, with his correspondence, travelled with him, and made his bed or cooked his meals. From 1919 onwards, as the dominant figure in Indian politics and the idol of millions, Gandhi bore the almost impossible burden of leading the Indian National Congress against the British Raj. What was to be Mahadev Desai's role in the changed situation? Desai's own instinct was to remain by Gandhi's side and serve him with his pen. He was a voracious reader, and wrote fluently, almost effortlessly, both in English and Gujarati. Gandhi sent him to Allahabad to help Motilal Nehru edit his newspaper, the *Independent*, the arrest of whose editor, George Joseph, was imminent. Desai left Gandhi reluctantly; one of the reasons for this was that ever since he had joined Gandhi he had been keeping a day to day diary of Gandhi's activities. Gandhi was aware of Desai's intense interest in his diary, but was not flattered by this. He was not looking for a Boswell; diaries and journals struck him as Western fads that tended to fuel egotism. 'My general routine', Gandhi had told the Hunter Committee in January 1920 'is to destroy as many documents as possible after I have dealt with them, and to retain only the most important which may be useful in future.'[2] He saw no sense in a record being kept of everything he did or said. Luckily, we have a letter written by Gandhi to Desai in August 1921, in which he examines the arguments for and against keeping a diary. Incidentally, in this letter he also analyses the character of his secretary, who had been with him for four years, with remarkable perspicacity. 'You have too little initiative', Gandhi wrote to him, 'and therefore whenever you get someone to whom you can look up, what little you have deserts you. Because too much reading has dulled your originality. You want to be an assistant.' He exhorted Desai to take his cue from Maganlal Gandhi, the manager of Sabarmati Ashram, who though a loyal colleague since the South African days, had never surrendered his judgement. As for Desai's diary, Gandhi wrote:

If I always keep someone with me merely in order that a record of my activities may be kept, I myself would come to behave unnaturally. It is one thing that someone may remain by my side in the usual course of things and keep notes unobtrusively, but quite another, that a person should keep notes of everything of set purpose. However, I do want you always to be with me. Since your grasp is so good and you are so well-equipped, I would like you to understand about my life and work. I have a great many ideas, but they find expression as occasions arise. There are subtleties sometimes which no one follows. The tempting thought does not leave me, therefore, that if I had a man like you by my side, he could in course of time take up my work ...[3]

Mercifully, the diary survived the early doubts and objections of the Mahatma, and Desai was able to leave a unique record of the twenty-five years he spent with him. Desai's first entry was dated 13 November 1917; the last, 14 August 1942, just a day before his death. The diary mirrors Desai's total identification with Gandhi. He readily accepts the Mahatma's changing priorities, whether it was a satyagraha struggle against the British, a crusade against untouchability, a campaign for village sanitation, for primary education, or for a non-violent world order. Unlike other eminent diarists such as Pepys and Boswell, Desai writes little about himself; the diary is all about Gandhi's thoughts, conversations, and activities. There are fascinating vignettes of Gandhi in his ashram, Gandhi on tour, Gandhi in jail, Gandhi with political and religious leaders, and high British officials, Gandhi jesting with a child, or in anguish over the sins and sorrows of his countrymen. There are lively snatches of dialogue rounded off with a penetrating remark; precious nuggets of information and insights. In March 1918, a year before he plunged into politics, Gandhi confides to Desai that he had resolved to transform both Indo–British and Hindu–Muslim relations through satyagraha.[4] We see Gandhi off his guard, thinking aloud. There is no rancour or malice, but there is candour, when he describes Malaviya as a spent force, doubts Annie Besant's political judgement, or expresses his horror at Maulana Shaukat Ali's defence of stoning to death as punishment for adultery. Among the most scintillating pages of Desai's diary are those pertaining to 1932 when Vallabhbhai Patel and Desai were Gandhi's fellow-prisoners in Yeravda jail.

Some of the material in the diaries was being continually drawn upon by Desai for his articles in *Young India, Harijan,* and *Navajivan.* As the de facto editor of these journals, even when the Mahatma's name appeared as the editor, Desai bore a heavy burden. When he was travelling he had little leisure during the day, and after the Mahatma and other members of the party had gone to sleep, he shut himself up in the toilet of the third-class carriage of the railway train to work away at the copy for the weekly journals. He had also to ensure that the manuscript was mailed from wayside stations in time to meet the publishing deadlines in Ahmedabad.

Gandhi's weekly papers, as he once said, were not newspapers, but 'views papers',[5] and the views were of one man: Gandhi. Desai had to understand and project these views in complicated and ever-varying situations. Gandhi enforced a strict code of journalism; the slightest inaccuracy or exaggeration elicited his instant reproof. It is remarkable that Desai should have been able to write so much, so well, and so fast, week after week, in the midst of constant interruptions. He was a born journalist, with a gift for a happy turn of phrase. 'How to turn waste into wealth?' was how he reported a conversation between a visiting British peer and Gandhi on village industries. He tells us about the Japanese monk in the ashram who 'worked like a horse and lived like a hermit'. It was, however, in his account of Gandhi's dialogues with his visitors that Desai was at his best, using them to illumine the Mahatma's ideas. There are some excellent examples of Desai's reportage in the letters and articles he sent from England where he had gone with Gandhi in 1931 for the Round Table Conference. He quotes the Dean of Canterbury:

Many have asked me whether I was going to convert Mr. Gandhi to Christianity … 'To convert him'! I have said to them indignantly: 'His is one of the most Christ-like lives that I have yet come across.'[6]

Then there was the meeting with Charlie Chaplin. Gandhi had never heard of him because, as Desai explained, 'for several years Gandhiji's life has been such as to allow him no time to see or hear or read anything that does not come to him in the ordinary course of work that he had cut out for himself'. We are told that Gandhi readily agreed to meet Chaplin when he was told that this great actor had sprung from the people and had made millions laugh. Questioned on his attitude to machinery, Gandhi explained to Chaplin the gravity of the chronic unemployment or under-employment of the millions in India's villages. 'But suppose', Chaplin asked, 'you had in India the independence of Russia, and you could find other work for your unemployed, and ensure equitable distribution of wealth, you would not then despise machinery? You would then subscribe to shorter hours of work and more leisure for the workers?' 'Certainly', replied Gandhi.[7]

Mahadev Desai's aim, indeed the sole purpose of his life, was to lighten Gandhi's burden and to interpret and disseminate his ideas. Some of his articles were scrutinized by Gandhi himself, but in course of time, his style came so much to resemble Gandhi's that it became difficult to distinguish the writings of the disciple from that of the master. Some of Desai's articles were published in books, such as *Gandhiji in India's Villages*, *With Gandhiji in Ceylon*, the *Nation's Voice*, and *The Epic of Travancore*. He wrote the history of the Ahmedabad textile workers strike, and the Bardoli Satyagraha, and dashed off, at Gandhi's instance, short biographies of Abul Kalam Azad, Abdul Ghaffar Khan, and Dr Khan Sahib. In the early 1930s when he was in jail, he wrote *The Gospel of Selfless Action or The Gita According to Gandhi*, though it was published after his death. He had started with the modest aim of translating Gandhi's book on the Gita from Gujarati into English. However, his 50,000-word introduction turned out to be an original commentary on the Gita, in which, by stressing the catholicity and universality of Gandhi's religious thought, Desai sought to appeal to India's youth and the intelligentsia as well as to the Western reader. By drawing parallels from the Bible and the Quran, he sought to show how 'in the deepest things of life, the Hindu and the Muslim and the Christian, and the Indian and the European, in fact all who have cared and endeavoured to read the truth of things, are so spiritually kin!'[8]

Desai had long since shed the passivity that Gandhi had noticed in the early years. He had grown into a shrewd observer of the political scene, a supremely efficient aide to Gandhi, and a brilliant journalist. Gandhi also occasionally entrusted him with special assignments. He had sent him to Allahabad to help the Nehrus run their newspaper, the *Independent*, and later to C.R. Das in Calcutta in the 1920s. In 1928 he deputed him to assist Vallabhbhai Patel in collating material for presentation to the enquiry committee on the agrarian problem in Bardoli appointed in the wake of the satyagraha struggle.

Desai was one of that select band of disciples, mostly centred in the Ashram, who completely identified themselves with Gandhi. His complete faith in the Mahatma's judgement spared him the dilemmas and heartaches that the Nehrus, C.R. Das, Abul Kalam Azad, C. Rajagopalachari, and other political leaders experienced. When Gandhi abruptly called off civil disobedience and switched over to the spinning wheel or went on a fast, Desai did not waste his time in arguing with him. Instead, he concentrated on grasping the nuances of Gandhi's decision and explaining them to the country. It was not an easy task to interpret satyagraha, which the Mahatma sought to apply to individual, social, and political problems; it was neither a well-defined doctrine nor a precise technique; it was, as Gandhi said, 'a science in the making'. Moreover, his ideas were developed not in the study, but in the course of social and political struggles waged by him. Not infrequently, his insights came to him as he tried to grope his way out of complex situations. This was why Desai was so keyed up to record every syllable that the Mahatma uttered. There were occasions when Desai did not have a piece of paper with him; undaunted, he jotted his notes on the palm of his hand, on his nails, or even on the back of a currency note, and transferred them later to his diary.

The diary is a monument to Desai's devotion to Gandhi as well as to his prodigious industry. When all the volumes of his diary have been translated into English, and become accessible to the public, he will be recognized as one of the greatest diarists of all time who left for posterity, a faithful record of the thoughts and actions of one of the most remarkable men of this century. Desai has often been compared with Boswell, but the comparison is true only up to a point. Boswell's *Journal* and *Life of Johnson* are justly famous, but as Lytton Strachey put it, Boswell was 'an idler, a lecher, a drunkard and a snob'.[9] Mahadev Desai, on the other hand, schooled in the Gandhian code of satyagraha, was an ascetic, a scholar, and a supremely efficient aide, who was dedicated not only to Gandhi, but to the causes for which Gandhi lived and died. Desai's greatest service to his own generation was, however, in the words of Verrier Elwin:

to make Gandhi real to the millions ... The punctual, vivid, intimate stories that appeared week after week in *Young India* and the *Harijan*, displayed to readers all over the world a personality so lovable that love was inevitably aroused in response.[10]

II

Mahadev Desai's decision to opt for a monastic life in Gandhi's ashram was not surprising; a few idealistic young men and women in India have done so in every generation. Madeleine Slade, who came to Sabarmati Ashram eight years later, had no such tradition; she came by a somewhat circuitous and unexpected route. Daughter of an admiral of the British Navy, she had had an upper middle-class upbringing, but her life took a curious turn at the age of fifteen when she first heard a piece by Beethoven, Sonata Opus 31 No. 2. Her whole being was stirred by it; she played it over and over again. As she recalled later, it was something beyond music that she had found; it was as if she were in communion with the spirit of Beethoven.[11] She wept at the thought that she had been born a hundred years too late to meet the great musician. She travelled to Germany and Austria on a pilgrimage to Beethoven's birthplace and his grave. She arranged concerts of Beethoven music in England. She learnt French so that she could read Romain Rolland's book *Jean-Christophe*, which she was told was partly based on Beethoven's life. She even visited Switzerland to see Romain Rolland. In the course of conversation, Romain Rolland mentioned a book he had recently written on Gandhi. When she looked blank, he asked her: 'You have not heard of him?'. 'No', she replied. 'He is,' said Romain Rolland, 'another Christ.'[12] Madeleine Slade was in Paris when the book was published. She bought a copy, started reading it, and could not stop until she had finished it. She felt a peremptory call to go out to India to sit at Gandhi's feet; it seemed to her that his work, based on truth and non-violence, though focused on India, was meant for the whole of humanity. Her parents, sensing the nature of her inspiration, did not object, even though, moving as they did in the highest circles in English society, it would be extremely embarrassing for them for their daughter to go and join the entourage of the arch-rebel against the British Empire.

Madeleine Slade resisted her first impulse to leave for India at once, and decided to train herself for a year so as to fit herself for life in Gandhi's ashram. She turned a vegetarian and a teetotaller, learnt hand-spinning, practised sitting cross-legged, engaged an Indian teacher to learn Urdu, ordered khadi from India to make frocks for herself, and subscribed to Gandhi's weekly journal, *Young India*. While she was in the midst of these hectic preparations, she read in the newspapers that Gandhi had undertaken a 21-day fast for Hindu–Muslim unity, and that it was not certain whether, at the age of fifty-five, he would be able to survive the ordeal. For Madeleine these were agonizing weeks. Was she going to be cheated by fate again? She had been born too late to meet Beethoven; would she now be deprived of the opportunity of meeting Gandhi? There was nothing she could do except pray. Gandhi survived. She wrote to him about her plans. He replied that she was welcome to India, but she must bear in mind that life in his ashram was not all 'rosy'; not only was it strenuous, but the Indian climate might be trying for her. 'I mention these things', Gandhi added, 'not to frighten you, but merely to warn you.'[13]

Thus forewarned and forearmed, Madeleine Slade landed in Bombay on 16 November 1925. The following day, when her train steamed into Ahmedabad station, she was received by Vallabhbhai Patel and Mahadev Desai and immediately driven to Sabarmati Ashram. She has described her first meeting with the Mahatma:

I entered [the room]. A slight, brown figure rose up and came towards me. I was conscious of nothing but a sense of light. I fell on my knees. Hands gently raised me up, and a voice said 'You shall be my daughter'.[14]

Madeleine soon discovered as Gandhi had warned her, that life in the ashram was not wholly idyllic. Its inmates were a heterogeneous lot consisting of men, women, and children of all ages who generated all kinds of tensions that jarred on her. The ashram diet did not agree with her; she had bouts of diarrhoea and dysentery. A bad attack of malaria laid her low: it was to recur every year for the next twenty-five years. Nothing could, however, deter her from her resolve to become a good disciple of the Mahatma. She had her hair chopped off and took a vow of *brahmacharya* (celibacy), even though Gandhi advised her not to be in a hurry to embark on the ascetic mode of life. He was even against her abandoning her Western clothes; there was, he told her, no need for her to make a sharp break with her cultural traditions. He gave her a new name, Mira, but it was an Indian, not a Hindu name. There was, of course, no question of converting her to Hinduism; he wanted her to become a model Christian.

As it was, there were inevitable strains in Madeleine's adjustment to her new life. She never met her parents again. Her father died in 1926 barely a year after her arrival in India; her mother passed away five years later. Even though Gandhi offered to arrange for her to visit England, she did not go. Hard as the process of adjustment must have been, there were compensations too. The ashram was astir with activity; there was an endless stream of visitors, and she had an opportunity of watching Gandhi in action in the ashram, in public meetings, and Congress party meetings. She was fascinated by the response he evoked from the people. The railway stations were thronged by surging crowds shouting 'Gandhi

Ki Jai', while he stood at the carriage window with folded hands but a stern demeanour indicating that he disliked excessive display of emotion.

Mirabehn, as Madeleine Slade came to be known, was good at secretarial work and could have settled down as a competent assistant to Mahadev Desai. She did indeed assist him in translating Gandhi's autobiography from Gujarati into English. Left to herself, she would have preferred personal service to the Mahatma: looking after his food, warding off unwanted visitors, and ensuring that his hours of work and rest were not unduly disturbed. Gandhi, however, wanted her to travel to see the country, to move among the people, and to grow in body and mind. He found time to write to her when she was not with him. His letters, three hundred and eighty-six of which were published by her after Gandhi's death, indicate a parental concern for her health, her studies, her spinning, her spiritual seeking and, above all, her peace of mind.

Despite her alien background, it was not long before Mirabehn began to feel mentally attuned to her adopted country. She dipped into the Upanishads and the Hindu epics; the effect on her, she tells us in her autobiography, was 'profound'.

For here I discovered various things that seemed to be part of my inmost self, part of something I had known long before and since lost. Here there was no nightmare of the unanswerable, but instead a vast illumination of the Unknown making its contemplation not a horror, but an infinite inspiration. While reading the Upanishads and a few extracts from the Vedas, I heard the same notes as in the music of Beethoven.[15]

Evidently she had imbibed the Hindu belief in reincarnation. In a letter to Gandhi, written in May 1932, she expressed her joy at reading in the *Ramayana* about

the forests, the hermits, the animals, the birds, the peasants, the fields, the villages, the towns. Though over 5000 years have gone by, it is all there in the heart still of this blessed land ... All the while it stirs in me a feeling of a long past association— it seems all something I have known and loved since time immemorial. Past births seem almost to stare me in the face sometimes.[16]

These periods of ecstasy did not last. There were also moments when she was bored, frustrated, or simply restless. Gandhi was ever ready to advise her and to help her over the stiles, but with the proviso that the final decision must be hers. 'Dive deep into yourself', he wrote to her, 'and find out, if you can, where you are, and act accordingly, irrespective of what I would like you to do. Or put it another way, I would like you to do what your inner spirit tells you to do.' On another occasion, he wrote to her,

'You will, therefore, reject all I have said in this [letter] that does not appeal to your heart or head. You must retain your individuality at all costs ... I do not want you to impute infallibility to me.' Gandhi was conscious of Mira's affection and reverence for him, but he wanted to divert these sentiments from his person to the causes that he espoused. He disliked blind adoration and excessive display of emotion. He also did not subscribe to the traditional equation in Hindu thought between the guru and the disciple in which the infallibility of the former and unquestioned obedience of the latter are taken for granted. Here was an instance of Gandhi's ingenuity in effecting a creative transmutation of a centuries-old concept to suit modern needs. This transmutation was all the more necessary because his ashrams were conceived not as a refuge from the turmoil of the world, but as laboratories for application of non-violence to individual, social, and political problems. Gandhi's insistence on the intellectual and moral autonomy of each individual helped to preserve Mirabehn's spirit of independence which had been part of her Western inheritance. An example of this came early when she went to an ashram in Rajasthan to learn Hindi in 1927 and discovered that some of the inmates, including a few sadhus, were addicted to drugs. She immediately reported her finding to Gandhi, who instructed her to leave the ashram at once, and to tell its manager and inmates why she was leaving.[17] Nine years later, she found life in Maganwadi Ashram at Wardha, where Gandhi and his entourage had come to stay, an ordeal, because one of the inmates was a somnambulist and when he walked in his sleep, another inmate, always got up and tried to catch him.' It was too much for her nerves and she sought an escape in long walks in the course of which she was shocked by the filth and lack of sanitation she noticed in village lanes. She broached the subject with Gandhi, who agreed that something must be done, and offered to take up the task himself. This started a chain of events that culminated in the development of a complex of institutions in Sevagram for rejuvenating rural India.[18] Mirabehn herself designed the cottage in Sevagram where Gandhi went to live in 1936.

One of the severest tests for Gandhi's principle of respecting the moral autonomy and independence of his disciples came in 1939, when Mirabehn met Prithvi Singh Azad, a revolutionary, who on Gandhi's advice, had renounced violence and surrendered himself to the government. Gandhi's correspondence with the Viceroy resulted in Prithvi Singh's release, and he came to live in Sevagram under the Mahatma's guidance. He took lessons in spinning from Mirabehn, and she agreed to read and revise the English translation of his autobiography. As she read the adventurous story of Azad's life, she was filled with deep admiration for him. It occurred to her that he could be an ideal comrade for her for the service of India, and then, in her own words,

this feeling grew so pressing that I spoke to Bapu about it. Bapu looked at me with unexpected seriousness and said, 'if you feel like that it means to my mind that you should marry'. And added, as if thinking aloud, 'perhaps marriage has been the unspoken word in your life'. I was taken aback and felt speechless. Bapu saw my astonishment. [Bapu said] 'Your former resolve not to marry should not stand in the way. As far as I am concerned, you are absolved from it.'[19]

What Mirabehn did not know was that, many years earlier, Prithvi Singh had resolved that he would not marry until India became independent, and also that he would not marry a foreign girl. He was not flattered by Mirabehn's claim that she had been his wife in a previous birth. 'She maintains', Gandhi wrote to Prithvi Singh, 'that she had a relation with you in the past, which will be maintained in the future. She feels very bad that in this birth you have become forgetful of your past life but she is happy. She is treating the affair as a spiritual problem and she is in penance.'[20]

Prithvi Singh did not have the courage to tell Mirabehn and the Mahatma that he could not accept her suit. He left Sevagram on the pretext that he wanted to see his brother in Burma. It was thus a one-sided romance. It is remarkable, however, that despite the supreme value that Gandhi attached to the ideal of celibacy, he gave his consent to Mirabehn marrying Prithvi Singh. It is no less remarkable that Mirabehn's account of this episode in her autobiography, written in the evening of her life, does not show any trace of bitterness. It is also to Prithvi Singh's credit that he came to recognize the spiritual quality of her love for him even though he was unable to reciprocate it.

Gandhi knew that Mirabehn was not cut out for politics, but he also knew that her presence in his entourage was a symbol of the future friendship between India and Britain which he dreamt of achieving one day through his non-violent struggle. Mirabehn took little interest in Congress politics, but when Gandhi launched his civil disobedience campaigns she courted imprisonment and bore witness to the terrible conditions under which prisoners were kept in women's jails. In 1931, she accompanied Gandhi to England for the Round Table Conference. Three years later, she sought Gandhi's permission to visit England in order to counter the false propaganda against Gandhi and the Congress in Western countries. Her initiative came as a pleasant surprise to Gandhi, and he readily agreed. But the 'friends of India', mostly in Agatha Harrison's India Conciliation Group in Britain, who kept a watching brief on behalf of the Indian nationalist cause, shook their heads and doubted her qualifications for a political role. Mirabehn was, however, confident and told them not to worry because Gandhi had fully briefed her. She called on the Secretary of State for India, Sir Samuel Hoare, who did not object to a lecture tour by her in the British Isles. She attended meetings of the Independent Labour Party and a Pacifists' Conference and delivered lectures in the provinces. She sought out British politicians: Lord Halifax, Lloyd George and Churchill. Lloyd George, who had met Gandhi in 1931, told her, 'I had always known Gandhi was a saint, but I had never realized till I met him that he was a statesman.' Churchill told her, 'Of course, I strongly oppose Mr. Gandhi from the political point of view, but I have the greatest admiration for his work for the moral and social uplift of his people.'[21]

Gandhi had told Mirabehn that she was free to stay in England as long as she wished. When she suggested a fortnight's visit to USA he instantly cabled his consent. She had a hectic but rewarding fortnight there, and addressed university students, churches of various denominations, businessmen, and all sorts of other groups interested in colonial and international affairs. She noticed that while in England the spotlight was on Gandhi's politics; in the USA it was on his personality.

Mirabehn's most important political assignment came eight years later when she took Gandhi's first draft of the 'Quit India' proposal from Wardha to a meeting of the Congress Working Committee in Allahabad in June 1942 in which there was a sharp difference of opinion among members. A month later, she went as Gandhi's emissary to the Viceroy. The Viceroy did not see her, but his private secretary, Laithwaite did. She explained to Laithwaite the logic behind Gandhi's call to the British to quit India; what he was doing was 'out of the depth of his love for England and his sole purpose was to save India from going helplessly into the hands of Japan'. Laithwaite was attentive and polite, while Mirabehn spoke out her mind freely and even bluntly, but government policies are rarely susceptible to moral appeals, least of all in wartime. Her mission thus proved abortive, but by sending an Englishwoman to explain his stand to the Viceroy for his final confrontation with the British Empire, Gandhi had made his point; it was part of the strategy of non-violence.

Mirabehn had come to India at the age of thirty-three. 'You shall be my daughter', Gandhi had told her at their first meeting, and so it was

till the end of his life. He lavished his affection upon her, but he was not
an over-indulgent parent. He wanted her to grow; to realize her moral
and spiritual potential. She discovered, as other disciples of Gandhi did,
that life with him was no picnic; it called for ceaseless effort, introspection, and self-discipline. She tended to see in Gandhi a father figure, but
he wanted to help her, sometimes by scolding her, to sublimate her personal attachment to some form of public service. He wanted to rid her
of her feeling of dependence upon him. In one of his letters he told her:
'You have left your home, your people, and that people prize most, not
to serve me personally, but to serve the causes I stand for.' When Mirabehn
realized that the spinning wheel and other programmes in the ashram
did not offer a suitable outlet for her energies, that her real interest, since
childhood, had been in birds, animals, trees, and fields, she decided, with
Gandhi's approval, to go to the Himalayas. It was in her beloved 'Pashulok'
(the abode of animals) near Rishikesh, where she was experimenting with
cultivation, cattle-breeding and afforestation, that she heard the shocking
news of Gandhi's assassination in 1948. She spent another eleven years in
India in the service of the hill people before returning to Europe. Her last,
and perhaps her greatest, service to Gandhi and India, was her autobiography, *The Spirit's Pilgrimage*. Several disciples and contemporaries of the
Mahatma have published their reminiscences of life with him, but none
has left a narrative so simple, so direct, so intimate, and yet so objective, as
Mirabehn's.

III

It would have been difficult to think of a more unlikely candidate for the
discipleship of Gandhi in 1929 than J.C. Kumarappa. He was thirty-seven-
years-old, a graduate in business administration from Syracuse University, a chartered accountant, and a Fellow of the Society of Incorporated
Accountants and Auditors in England. For nearly ten years he had been
practising as an auditor in Bombay, and had built up a lucrative practice.
He had an affluent and Westernized mode of life, and was popular among
the local Europeans, some of whom were his clients. He had never evinced
the slightest interest in politics. Even though he lived in Bombay, he had
never cared to catch a glimpse of Gandhi, much less to meet him. However, in 1929, circumstances conspired to bring Kumarappa face to face
with the Mahatma. In the preceding year, he had presented a dissertation
on 'Public Finance and Indian Poverty' for his Master's Degree in Economics to Columbia University, and was thinking of getting it published

in India. A friend advised him to show the dissertation to Gandhi. With a formidable array of facts and figures, Kumarappa had exposed the financial jugglery of the British Treasury and the British War Office in unjustly heaping the costs of imperial wars on the Indian exchequer, and thus deepening India's poverty. Who would be a fitter person to appraise such a monograph than the pre-eminent leader of Indian nationalism? Kumarappa called at Mani Bhawan where Gandhi usually stayed when in Bombay. The Mahatma was busy in a meeting. Kumarappa left his monograph with Pyarelal, one of the secretaries, whom, because of his simple clothes, he mistook for a peon. A few days later, he received a letter inviting him to meet Gandhi at Ahmedabad.

Dressed, as was his wont, in a smart Western-style suit, Kumarappa arrived at the Sabarmati Ashram on the afternoon of 9 May 1929, and then, in his own words:

on the way I saw an old man seated under a tree on a newly-cleaned cow-dung floor, spinning. Having never seen a spinning-wheel before, I leaned on my walking stick, and, standing with arms akimbo, was watching as there were still ten minutes for the appointment. The old man after about five minutes opened his toothless lips and, with a smile on his face, inquired if I was Kumarappa. It suddenly dawned on me that my questioner may be no other than Mahatma Gandhi. So I in my turn asked him if he was Gandhiji, and when he nodded, I promptly sat down on the cow-dung floor, regardless of the well-kept crease of my silk trousers.[22]

Gandhi complimented Kumarappa on his dissertation, and offered to publish it in *Young India* in a series of articles. 'You are almost the first economist,' he said, 'I have come across, who thinks on the same lines as I do,' and then made a proposition to Kumarappa. Would he conduct a rural economic survey for him in Gujarat? When Kumarappa tried to excuse himself by pleading ignorance of Gujarati, the local language, Gandhi offered to provide him assistance from the faculty and students of Gujarat Vidyapith, the national university at Ahmedabad; and in fact he immediately arranged for Kumarappa to meet its Vice-Chancellor, Kakasaheb Kalelkar. Kalelkar was, however, so put off by Kumarappa's dandyish appearance and affected accent, that he did his best to discourage him. However, Gandhi intervened and Kumarappa was persuaded to conduct the survey. Many years later, Gandhi confided to Kumarappa how Kalelkar had underrated him, but 'when I first saw you, I felt here is a young man I must grab'. Gandhi had, indeed, an uncanny gift for spotting talented men and women whom he could harness to the national cause. Kumarappa was a prize acquisition for Gandhi, just as Jawaharlal Nehru,

Vallabhbhai Patel, Rajendra Prasad, and C. Rajagopalachari had been a decade earlier.

The economic survey of Matar Taluka, which Kumarappa undertook, covered fifty villages in Kaira district in Gujarat. Gandhi's direction on its methodology was that the 'Indian economy had to be built from the bottom by a method of securing rock-bottom facts and drawing from them, by the most rigid process of reasoning, scientific conclusions which no amount of juggling could controvert.' Two teachers of the Gujarat Vidyapith and a team of students accompanied Kumarappa on foot when he gathered facts and figures for three months from the villages. He took another eighteen months to digest the material, and to write his report. His findings seemed to confirm Gandhi's hunches about India's national economy: the low per capita income (7 pies or 1/26th of a rupee per day), the prodigious unemployment and under-employment of men as well as of bullocks, the antiquated methods of cultivation, the lack of effective help from the agricultural and irrigation departments, the need for making villages or groups of villages self-sufficient in foodgrains, fodder, and cotton, and the importance of basing the development process on local resources and the resourcefulness of the local population.

Kumarappa had blazed a trail that few economists were to follow. Whatever else the survey did or did not achieve, it converted him from an academic into a practical economist. His dissertation on public finance had acquainted him with the iniquity of British rule; the few months he spent in the Gujarat Vidyapith, with its accent on rural economics, and the economic survey brought home to him a full picture of the agricultural scene and the dire poverty of the people.

Meanwhile, events had moved to a climax in the political sphere. Gandhi, who had embarked on the Dandi March, sent for Kumarappa, and asked him if he could help Mahadev Desai in running the *Young India*. Kumarappa pleaded that he knew nothing about Gandhian philosophy, nor had any experience in journalism, and it would be more appropriate if he was given an assignment that fitted his expertise in audit and accounts. Gandhi then came out with an ingenious, and irresistible, argument. He told Kumarappa that in *Young India* the name of the writer was always published under each article. 'If you write any trash', he said, 'the public will say Mahatma Gandhi's paper publishes trash. But if you write anything that was appreciated, they would give all credit to this Kumarappa, who is writing in Gandhiji's paper.' Kumarappa was thus persuaded not only to write articles for *Young India*, but even to take over editorial charge when Mahadev Desai was arrested, and then again in the following year when, after the Gandhi–Irwin Pact, Desai accompanied Gandhi to England for the Round Table Conference.

Kumarappa's articles in *Young India* landed him in jail, facilitating his decision to finally cast in his lot with Gandhi. After his arrest and conviction for sedition, it was doubtful whether his British clients would patronize his audit firm any longer. It was hardly two years since he had first met Gandhi, and every step he had taken had involved him more deeply with the Mahatma. In March 1931, at the Karachi Congress, came public recognition of Kumarappa as an exponent of the nationalist view of India's economics and finance, when he was appointed the convener of a committee to carry out 'a scrutiny' of the financial transactions of the East India Company and the British Government of India and 'the so-called Public Debt of India'.[23] Three years later, he was appointed Secretary of the newly set-up All India Village Industries Association at Wardha under Gandhi's aegis. It was, as a Gandhian economist, that he was to occupy a unique position on the national scene.

Professor Malcolm Adiseshiah has pointed out that the term Gandhian economics is not felicitous. 'It is not economics which is Gandhian,' he says, 'but its application to our time and conditions as expounded by Gandhi.'[24] The fundamental problems of the Indian economy, as Gandhi saw them, were chronic unemployment and under-employment in the villages. 'The problem with us', he wrote, 'is not to find a leisure for the teeming millions inhabiting our country. The problem is how to utilize their idle hours which are equal to the working days of six months in the year.' The Mahatma's thinking had a pronounced rural bias, and the revival and revitalization of Indian villages was his constant concern. 'We must mentally go back to the villages and treat them as our pattern, instead of putting up the city life before them for imitation,' he said. Living in a village, in Sevagram, constantly faced with and thinking about village problems, Gandhi sought solutions in terms of the human and material resources of villages. He talked of 'village swaraj' (village self-government) which would ensure that each village was self-sufficient in terms of vital requirements, growing its own food and its own cotton for its cloth, with its own school, theatre, and public hall, and its own local officials supervised by a locally elected panchayat.

Though Gandhi had periodically written and spoken extensively on economic issues he never had the time to evolve a coherent theory or a blueprint for its implementation. This task was undertaken by Kumarappa; in numerous articles and pamphlets, for a period of over twenty years, he expounded and developed Gandhi's ideas. In his *Economy of Permanence*, written in jail in 1944, he sketched a complete picture of life in a community working towards non-violence and peace. If there was to be a plan for India, he wrote, it must centre round the farmer first, and then grow out for the whole country: self-sufficiency in food and clothing had to be one of the prime features in such a plan, and there must be provision for drinking water, housing, village panchayats, cooperative societies, and cultural centres in each village. 'Our spiritual and higher self', he wrote, 'must be related back to life so that the daily routine of mundane existence may be regulated in accordance with the dictates of our better self.' Fifteen years in Gandhi's proximity had turned the chartered accountant-turned economist towards spirituality as a leaven for social and economic change. In another little book, *The Practice and Precepts of Jesus*, written during the same jail term, Kumarappa linked the fight against economic exploitation to the highest religion. 'Where God's will prevails,' he asked, 'can there be social inequalities of high and low ... economic differences of rich and poor ... [and] one nation lording it over the other?'

Kumarappa's excursions into philosophy did not mean that he did not have his feet firmly planted on the ground. In Wardha, in Maganwadi, the headquarters of the All India Village Industries Association, he conducted research on specific problems of particular village industries. He tried to upgrade the tools and methods of manufacture of cottage industries, and established a museum to exhibit the results of research to ease human labour and to improve productivity. He was against the use of fossil fuels for village lighting, and had a hurricane lamp (*magan deep*) devised that dispensed with kerosene and could be lit with non-edible vegetable oils. Then there was the *magan choolah*, an inexpensive, locally made oven, designed to conserve greater heat than the conventional *choolah*. And the improved plough for owners of small holdings.

1936–9 were the halcyon years for Kumarappa's village economics. Gandhi's presence lent high prestige to the All India Village Industries Association, and to the complex of institutions of constructive work growing up at Sevagram. The installation of Congress ministries in the provinces opened up new vistas. Kumarappa was called upon to conduct surveys in the Central Provinces and the N.W.F.P. which could help in determining the pattern of economic development. Unfortunately, the Second World War, the resignation of the Congress ministries and civil disobedience put the clock back. While both Gandhi and Kumarappa were in jail, and the Congress organization was outlawed, the work on rural economics languished.

There was again a ray of hope with the return of the Congress ministries in 1946, but the communal tension, the disturbances, and the turmoil preceding and following the partition of the country hindered progress. Nor did the situation improve much after the attainment of Independence in 1947. The fact is that the Indian intelligentsia and most of the Congress leaders had always been sceptical about Gandhi's economic model; they did not think it practicable for a strong and viable nation-state that they wanted to build in India. The Communists and the Congress Socialists had been even more critical; they considered the Mahatma's emphasis on a decentralized economy misplaced: the real issue in their opinion was not that of decentralization of industry, but of public ownership of the means of production.

Kumarappa wrote hard-hitting articles in *Harijan* and *Gram Udyog Patrika* to sell Gandhian economics to the Nehru government and the Indian political élite. He came out with a 'pilot plan' to set up 'laboratory units' of a village or groups of villages in selected areas to experiment in development on Gandhian lines simultaneously in the areas of agriculture, animal husbandry, village industries, basic education, uplift of Harijans and women, village self-government, and communal harmony. The experience thus gained could, he felt, yield insights for economic revival of rural India through local human and material resources, rather than through doles handed out from the top. There were few takers for Kumarappa's ideas. The centralized planning, through Five Year Plans propounded by Nehru held the field; it has certainly brought about a sizeable expansion of agricultural and industrial production, but it has had its limitations too. The gap between the rich and the poor, the urban and the rural, the educated and the illiterate has widened; growing production has gone hand in hand with increasing unemployment and poverty.

The Gandhian model, which Kumarappa elaborated and advocated, aimed at a low-energy, low-capital, nature-friendly, and decentralized development. Some of its assumptions, such as self-sufficiency of the villages and restricted trade with the outside world, seem hardly practicable in the fast-changing world of today. Then there are the complex economic issues, such as inflation, balance of payments, external trade, and the underground economy, for which the Gandhian model may not have had adequate answers. Had Kumarappa been alive, he might well have argued that many of these problems would not have become so complex, but for the limitless greed and indiscipline of individuals and sections of society entrapped in consumerism, and that after all, Gandhi's economic prescriptions also postulated a moral framework.

IV

As we have seen, the lives of all the three disciples who are the subject of this essay were transformed by their contact with Gandhi. What was the secret of his influence? The term charisma is often used to describe it. Gandhi was certainly a charismatic leader, but his charisma was not of the type familiar to students of history. Great orators, such as Demosthenes and Savonarola, and powerful dictators and rulers, like Cromwell, Kemal Ataturk and Hitler, knew how to cast a spell over masses of men, to rouse their emotions to fever pitch, and to dull their critical faculties. Gandhi was no orator: he hardly ever raised his voice, he neither tried to flatter nor frighten his audience, and his appeal was as much to the head as to the heart. Even when he addressed huge crowds, it appeared as if he viewed them as a collection of individuals: each individual was to him an autonomous personality whose capacity to think and act had to be respected. It is not surprising that Gandhi himself failed to find his ideal guru; he could not bring himself to accept the traditional concept of the infallible guru and the unquestioning disciple. Mirabehn recalls Gandhi's opinion that the ancient Hindu ideal of the guru was too lofty because

no one in these degenerate days was competent to live up to this ideal. There may have been supreme and great sages in the past, and there might be some living in unknown caves in the Himalayas, but the ancient conception of the guru is no longer a practical one. So seek God, and look upon him as a guru.[25]

Gandhi reciprocated the affection of those who worked with him and for him, but he was, as we have seen, reluctant to impose his ideas on them. He did not want to mould his followers into a fixed pattern. He tried to discern the talents, the temperament, the aptitude and the limitations of each individual, and to make use of him or her for the country. He had the gift of evoking for a great cause the spirit of self-abnegation, and the result was exactly what Max Weber had said about charismatic leadership of a certain kind:

in order to do justice to their mission, the holders of charisma, the master as well as his disciples and followers, must stand outside the ties of this world outside the routine obligations of family life.

Mirabehn and Kumarappa never married. Mahadev Desai's wife and son lived with him in the ashram, but he hardly had any time to spend with them. To Gandhi, Desai was, at once a secretary and son, and Mirabehn was a daughter and a disciple. Kumarappa was more a colleague than a disciple of the Mahatma. He had a strong sceptical streak: he had begun his association with the Mahatma by questioning the need for vows for those joining his ashram. He was a stickler for discipline, and no respecter of persons; he once refused payment for feeding Gandhi's party from the earthquake relief fund when he was on tour for relief work in Bihar. He was not impressed by Nehru's ideas on centralized planning, fell out with him, and resigned from the National Planning Committee. He was sometimes too blunt and harsh in his judgements, and when the complaint was carried to Gandhi, he replied with a smile: 'Kumarappa comes from Madras; you must allow for the chillies in his blood.'[26]

It was not only the chillies in his blood, but the long association with Gandhi and deep convictions that made him a sharp critic of the post-1947 developments, as when he denounced outright the idea of India taking a share from German reparations after the Second World War,[27] or criticized the decision about the salary of the Governor-General and the large amounts sanctioned for the maintenance of what used to be the Viceroy's House, or when he deplored the erosion of the values of the Gandhian era.[28] His anguish was manifest when in February 1948 he was placing an urn containing the Mahatma's ashes in a pit in Sevagram Ashram. With tears in his eyes, he murmured: 'Instead of burying Gandhi deep in our hearts, we are burying him deep into the earth.'

NOTES AND REFERENCES

1. M.K. Gandhi, *An Autobiography* (Ahmedabad, 1945 rpt.), p. 113.
2. Mahadev Desai, *Day-To-Day with Gandhi*, vol. II, p. 109.
3. Gandhi to Mahadev Desai, 13 Aug. 1921, Gandhi Papers.
4. Mahadev Desai, *Day-To-Day with Gandhi*, vol. I (Varanasi, 1968), pp. 56–7.
5. *Harijan*, 24 Sept. 1938.
6. C. Rajagopalachari and J.C. Kumarappa (eds), *The Nation's Voice* (Ahmedabad, 1947), p. 216.
7. Ibid., p. 129.
8. Mahadev Desai, *The Gospel of Selfless Action or The Gita According to Gandhi* (Ahmedabad, 1946), p. 4.
9. Michael Holroyd and Paul Levy (eds) *The Shorter Strachey* (Oxford, 1980), p. 193.
10. Verrier Elwin, 'Mahadev', in D.G. Tendulkar and others (eds) *Gandhiji, His Life and Work* (Bombay, 1944), published on Gandhi's 75th birthday in 1944.
11. Mirabehn (Madeleine Slade), *The Spirit's Pilgrimage* (London, 1960), p. 31.

12. Ibid., p. 58.
13. Ibid., p. 63.
14. Ibid., p. 66.
15. Ibid., p. 170.
16. Ibid., p. 179.
17. Gandhi to Mirabehn, 3 June 1927, Gandhi Papers.
18. See B.R. Nanda, *In Gandhi's Footsteps, Life and Times of Jamnalal Bajaj* (Delhi, 1990), p. 215.
19. Mirabehn, *The Spirit's Pilgrimage*, p. 217.
20. Quoted in Nanda, *In Gandhi's Footsteps*, p. 265.
21. Mirabehn, *New and Old Gleanings* (Ahmedabad, 1949), p. 16.
22. Kumarappa Papers.
23. The report of the committee appears as Appendix E, in J.C. Kumarappa, *Public Finance and Our Poverty*, (Ahmedabad, 1930). The book carried a foreword by Gandhi.
24. Malcolm S. Adiseshiah, 'Gandhi and the Indian Economy', in *Gandhi Marg*, Jan.–March 1992.
25. Mirabehn, *The Spirit's Pilgrimage*, p. 75.
26. Chandra Shanker Shukla (ed.), *Incidents of Gandhi's Life* (Bombay, 1949), p. 142.
27. *Harijan*, 22 June 1947.
28. *Gram Udyog Patrika*, April 1949.

Jamnalal Bajaj

When Jamnalal Bajaj first met Gandhi in 1915, he was only twenty-six, but he had already established himself as a successful businessman, a progressive educationist, and a social reformer. On the surface he appeared to be one of the most favoured individuals—born in a waterless village in Rajasthan, he had been adopted by a rich Marwari family of Wardha in central India.

Jamnalal Bajaj had a natural aversion to politics. It was, therefore, fortunate that in those early years, after his return from South Africa, Gandhi seemed to Jamnalal, as to most other observers, a religious and social reformer rather than a political leader. By 1920 Jamnalal's bond with Gandhi had become so strong that he could not but follow him even into the political vortex. When Jamnalal gave his lack of fluency in English as an argument for turning down the chairmanship of the reception committee of the Nagpur Congress (December 1920), Gandhi laughed it away and advised him to deliver his address in Hindi. Gandhi did not equate wisdom with the mastery of the English language, nor did he set much store by book learning, once having advised his secretary, Mahadev Desai, 'to think more and read less'.

It could not have been easy for Jamnalal to cast in his lot with Gandhi in 1920. As a businessman in a small district town, he was immeasurably more vulnerable to official vindictiveness than the eminent lawyers of Allahabad and Calcutta. The great merchants and industrialists of India knew the risks of incurring the wrath of the British authorities and, with a rare unanimity, refrained from associating themselves with Gandhi's non-violent rebellion.

Jamnalal was one of the few members of his class, if not the only one, to take the plunge. He knew the price he might have to pay, and was prepared to pay it. It was not merely the jail terms that he, his wife and sons had to undergo during the civil disobedience campaigns; his whole life underwent a metamorphosis, becoming progressively simpler and more austere, so as to conform to the Gandhian model. Business and domestic concerns henceforth took a secondary place in it and his own family saw little of him, while he travelled around the country on the Mahatma's errands. Even while he was in Wardha, he had little time which he could call his own. His house became a *dharmshala*, a caravanserai, for visiting Congress leaders and constructive workers.

The epithet 'The merchant prince' that Gandhi conferred on him had long ceased to be applicable. Rammanohar Lohia, the socialist fire-brand, who knew Jamnalal well, noted that Jamnalal had reduced his standard of living to that of 'the lower middle class'.

'Whenever I wrote of wealthy men becoming trustees of their wealth for the common good,' Gandhi wrote after Jamnalal's death, 'I had Jamnalal in mind.' Gandhi further revealed that Jamnalal would have renounced everything if he had not prevented him from doing so. 'Although Jamnalal had great possessions', Mahadev Desai wrote, 'he had divested himself of the sense of proprietorship over them.' Jamnalal insisted that trade and industry could not be exempted from ethics. He aspired to imbibe the Gandhian ethic, and to liberate himself from the conventional code of conduct of the affluent Marwaris. In Wardha he preferred to walk to the railway station to receive his guests. Once while in Bombay when seeing off Gangadharrao Deshpande, a fellow-member of the Congress Working Committee, he could not get hold of a porter, and carried Deshpande's luggage to the train. 'I felt a little embarrassment at first', Jamnalal wrote in his diary that night, 'but later felt happy that I had performed this chore.' On another occasion, when travelling by train, he found that a passenger in his compartment persisted in chewing and spitting betel-nut. Jamnalal got up and swept the floor with his hands; the culprit felt ashamed and apologised.

Jamnalal also imbibed from the Mahatma the endearing trait of for-getting and forgiving wrongs done to him. When his cousin, Harikishen, who had harassed him for six long years with a tortuous civil suit, was on his deathbed, Jamnalal went to see him and asked if he could do anything for him. 'I have written a book to defame you', Harikishen replied. 'I want to publish it before I die and need five hundred rupees for it.' Jamnalal gave him the money. Then there was the case of Balasaheb Hudder, a Communist of Wardha who used to denounce Jamnalal as a capitalist. When Hudder was detained by the authorities, Jamnalal sent money to support his family.

Gandhi claimed that he had inducted Jamnalal into politics not for his money, but for his intelligence and integrity. When the Mahatma launched the Tilak Swaraj Fund in 1921, the single greatest fund-raising effort by the Indian National Congress in the pre-Independence period, it was a source of great satisfaction to him that the custodian of the Congress funds was not only a man of unimpeachable integrity but also the single largest donor to it. During the following two decades, when Jamnalal was the treasurer of the Congress, not a breath of scandal touched the management of its finances.

In the Congress Working Committee, Jamnalal rubbed shoulders with such veterans as C.R. Das, Lajpat Rai, Motilal Nehru, Jawaharlal Nehru, Vallabhbhai Patel, C. Rajagopalachari, Rajendra Prasad, and Subhas Chandra Bose. Curiously, Jamnalal's lack of formal education did not prevent him (as Mahadev Desai noted) from seeing more quickly than the others, 'the implications of intricately worded Congress resolutions'. His colleagues learnt to value his advice as that of a man of the world on public as well as on private affairs. On matters of high policy, however, Jamnalal took his cue from the Mahatma. He had boundless faith in Gandhi's political judgement, but this attitude was probably no more than the reflex action of a devoted disciple.

Whatever the reasons for Jamnalal's unquestioned allegiance to Gandhi, it spared him the tensions and heartaches from which some of his colleagues in the Working Committee suffered during the successive crises in the Congress party: in 1924 over the Swarajist rebellion, in 1928 over dominion status versus independence, in 1936 over the socialist challenge, in 1937 over the acceptance of office under the new Constitution, and in 1939–42 over the Congress policy during the Second World War. Jamnalal did not figure in the public controversies that made banner headlines in the national press, but thanks to his proximity to the Mahatma, his friendship with Jawaharlal Nehru, and his own lack of personal ambition, he could play a mediatory role behind the scenes, softening the acerbities between the colleagues, and thus helping to preserve the unity of the party.

It may seem odd that a man who stood so close to Gandhi, who managed the finances of the Congress, and was in its highest echelons longer than any other of his colleagues, scarcely figures today in the popular imagination or in the accounts of the freedom struggle. To this conspiracy of silence the greatest contribution was made by Jamnalal himself. He studiously shunned the limelight; he hated presiding or speaking at public meetings; he did not reel off press statements. These necessary chores of nationalist politics he left to his colleagues in the Congress Working Committee.

His chief mission in life was different. He believed that in Gandhi, India had the greatest national asset which needed to be sustained. If there was one thought that occupied his mind more than any other, it was how to lighten the Mahatma's burdens. He wanted to create conditions in which Gandhi would give his best to the country. When the Mahatma fell ill at Sevagram and needed rest, Jamnalal became the gatekeeper at his hut. This earned him the affectionate epithet of 'jailor' from Gandhi. After Jamnalal's death, the Mahatma described him as his *Kamadhenu*, the mythical cow which could fulfil all desires. 'As soon as I embarked on a new project', Gandhi wrote, 'he would take responsibility for it on himself and relieve me of most of my burdens. He was constantly on vigil. He looked after my work, my comforts, my health, and my finances.'

There was one important plank in Gandhi's programme with which Jamnalal identified himself more than any other of his colleagues: this was the 'constructive programme', comprising such activities as the promotion of khadi, village industries, national language, basic education, Hindu–Muslim unity, and eradication of untouchability. Ardent nationalists and radical politicians found it difficult to believe that such activities could ever add up to a political programme, or have a place in an anti-imperialist struggle; they pooh-poohed Gandhi's 'two-annas a day socialism'. However, from Gandhi's standpoint, the constructive programme was not only the best preparation for a non-violent mass struggle against foreign rule, but the best training for citizenship in independent India.

It is only natural that Gandhi's major civil disobedience campaigns should find pride of place in the accounts of India's struggle for freedom. It is also natural that the triangular contest of wills between British imperialism, Indian nationalism, and Muslim separatism should dominate the history of the last decade of British rule. The bitter controversies of those years have spilled into our history books; they weighed heavily on the minds of Gandhi and other Congress leaders when they assembled at Wardha for the meetings of the Congress Working Committee; they were an essential part of the last act of the drama of the struggle for Indian independence which unfolded in a blinding glare of publicity.

But away from the footlights, and almost off stage there were other scenes at Wardha and Sevagram that were no less significant: Gandhi in Sevagram patiently trying to reason the village barber out of caste prejudices; Mahadev Desai all keyed up to record every word uttered by the master; Jawaharlal Nehru and Abul Kalam Azad travelling in a bullock-cart to Sevagram; Vinoba Bhave cleaning village latrines during the day and discoursing on the Gita in the evening; J.C. Kumarappa expatiating on village industries and Gandhian economics; Srikrishnadas Jajoo puzzling over a minimum wage for the spinners on the charkha; Zakir Husain and Aryanayakam discussing the syllabus for basic education; Kakasaheb Kalelkar racking his brains to devise a uniform keyboard for a Hindi typewriter; Manohar Diwan organizing a centre for leprosy patients; and finally, Jamnalal Bajaj keeping a vigilant eye on all that was going on to see where he could lend his helping hand.

Gandhi called Jamnalal 'the fisher of men'. Jamnalal, whose perceptive eye had spotted the potential of Vinoba Bhave while he was still a young man, was always on the look-out for talented and public-spirited men, but he knew that men do not live by patriotism alone. He sought to free them from the anxieties and distractions of daily life; he sorted out their personal problems; he ironed out tensions inevitable in institutions. Rather than hold any office, he preferred to keep himself in the background. Nevertheless, he was the linchpin of the organizations for constructive work which came up in and around Wardha under the aegis of the Mahatma. He was (in Mahadev Desai's words) 'a living link between the outside world and Gandhiji'. The link was broken with Jamnalal's sudden death in February 1942.

Gandhi had nominated Jawaharlal Nehru as his political heir. Jamnalal Bajaj, exactly the same age as Nehru, would have inherited the non-political legacy of the Mahatma: the regeneration of rural India through voluntary workers. Fate, however, had willed otherwise.

TWENTY

Gandhi as a Trade Union Leader

M ost people think of Gandhi as a political leader or as a social
and religious reformer and may find it difficult to imagine
him in the role of a labour leader. However, the fact remains
that he led a labour strike at Ahmedabad in the spring of 1918 during the
First World War. He had not yet stepped on to the centre stage of Indian
politics, nor acquired the halo of a Mahatma. The strike attracted little
notice at the time, but had significant long-term results and implications
as an experiment in the application of Gandhian ideas to industrial relations.

As is well known, during the first four years after his return from
South Africa Gandhi studiously abstained from taking part in active
politics. It was not only because Gokhale, his political mentor, had advised
him to carefully study the situation in the motherland before taking the
plunge, but also because Gandhi felt that his code of satyagraha required
him to refrain from embarrassing Britain while she was engaged in a life-
and-death struggle with Germany. This self-denying ordinance did not,
however, deter him from taking up social and agrarian issues. In satyagraha,
he felt, he had a matchless weapon for resisting injustice and righting
wrongs. He responded to the call of the indigo cultivators of Champaran
and the peasants of Kaira, so when the dispute between the textile mill-
owners and workers in Ahmedabad came to a head, he could not help
being drawn into it. Some of the mill-owners, such as Ambalal Sarabhai,
were on very cordial terms with him, and the leader of the textile workers,
Anasuyabehn, was a disciple of his. Chatfield, the British Collector of
Ahmedabad, who was anxious to avoid labour trouble in wartime, urged
Gandhi to mediate and avert a showdown. The bone of contention was
the plague bonus, equivalent in some cases to 80 per cent of the wages,
which had been paid to dissuade the labour from fleeing the plague-ravaged
town. When the epidemic was over, the employers wanted to discontinue

the bonus. The workers resisted the move on the ground that the cost of living had more than doubled during the war, and the bonus had only partially offset the loss in purchasing power.

As was his wont, Gandhi made a close study of the facts, the cost of living and market conditions in Ahmedabad and Bombay, and came to the conclusion that even though the workers were demanding fifty to eighty per cent bonus, thirty-five per cent was the irreducible minimum which they deserved and must fight for. He was able to persuade both the parties to agree to arbitration by a tribunal consisting of three representatives of employers and three representatives of labour, with the British Collector as the umpire. The three labour representatives on the arbitration tribunal were to be Vallabhbhai Patel, Shankarlal Banker, and Gandhi himself. However, before this tribunal could commence its work, the mill-owners, taking advantage of a stray strike, declared the agreement void, backed out of arbitration, and threatened to dismiss workers who would not accept a twenty per cent bonus. Gandhi was shocked by the mill-owners' attitude and decided to champion the workers' cause. 'I am not particularly disposed to favour workers as workers', he wrote to the Secretary of the Mill-owners Association, 'I am on the side of justice and often this is to be found on their side. Hence the general belief that I am on their side.' His pleas to the mill-owners for fair play fell on deaf ears. They declared a lock-out. It was then that the workers decided to go on strike and Gandhi agreed to lead them.

Gandhi treated the strike as an experiment in satyagraha, and declared that it would be different from the usual pattern of labour strikes. The workers' morale was not to be boosted by working up their passions. There was to be no violence against the employers and even against the black legs. Nor was there to be any exaggeration of claims or any competition in invective. The striking workers were to depend upon their own resources; they were to use their enforced idleness in constructive activities, such as learning alternative trades and repairing houses and roads in workers' colonies.

Not the least interesting feature of this strike was that Gandhi's chief lieutenant in organizing the workers was Anasuyabehn, the sister of Ambalal Sarabhai, one of the leading mill-owners. She had broken off her studies in medicine in England and returned to her home town to work among the textile workers who adored her. Throughout the strike she arranged meetings at a fixed hour every day under a tree on the bank of the Sabarmati river which were addressed by Gandhi. Perfect discipline prevailed at these meetings; speeches were sober in content and style. The workers marched through the streets peacefully, singing and raising slogans such as 'Ek Tek' ('Keep your pledge'). The British authorities, apprehending an outbreak of violence, had taken precautions, but after two days were convinced that Gandhi had the situation well in hand, and withdrew the special police posted for the strike. A news bulletin, written by Gandhi and published by Anasuyabehn, appeared daily. It was Gandhi's way of communicating with the striking workers. He told them that there was no essential clash between the interests of capital and labour, that the ideal relationship between the mill-owner and his men was one of mutual regard in the spirit of Ruskin's *Unto This Last*. Such idealism did not seem to strike a chord in the mill-owners; they brought out their own news-sheets criticizing 'outsiders' like Gandhi who were interfering in the private domain of the employers.

Gandhi's problem was how to prick the conscience of the mill-owners, and at the same time to keep up the morale of the striking workers who were without employment and without wages. Seeking financial assistance from outside to keep the strike going was contrary to the spirit of satyagraha, and alternative employment was not practicable except for a few. After a few days Gandhi sensed that the workers' morale had begun to sag. The mill-owners tried to break the strike by luring back workers who were prepared to accept the 20 per cent bonus offer. It was at this moment, when the strike reached a critical stage, that Gandhi went on a fast—the first of his seventeen 'fasts unto death'.

The object of Gandhi's fast was to rally the workers, Nevertheless, it could not but affect the mill-owners, many of whom deeply respected him. It was this feeling that his fast was exercising an element of coercion on his opponents that led Gandhi, after three days' fasting, to agree to a compromise as a result of which the object of the strike was literally, but not really, fulfilled. The workers agreed to go back to work with the promise of thirty-five per cent wage increases for the first day, twenty per cent for the second day, and twenty-seven per cent from the third day until the final verdict on the quantum of bonus was given by an arbitrator. This looked like a face-saving formula, and a tactical defeat for Gandhi, but it contained the seeds of his ultimate victory. After all, the real issue on which the breach between the workers and the mill-owners had occurred had been the refusal of the latter to accept the principle of arbitration; on this issue they had now yielded. The arbitrator's award went in the workers' favour and the thirty-five per cent bonus was eventually won.

Gandhi broke his fast before a hushed gathering on 18 March 1918. He said the whole country had reason to be proud of the workers of

Ahmedabad for keeping the peace and striking without the least display of bitterness. The British Commissioner of Ahmedabad, who was present, congratulated everybody on the happy ending of the strike, and told the workers that so long as they followed 'Gandhi Sahib's advice', and did what he told them, they would do well and secure justice.

The strike received scant notice in the press; it was reported, if at all in the back pages. The *Bombay Chronicle* (28 February 1918) wondered why Gandhi had staked so much on a local issue 'from which he had little to gain and everything to lose'. *The Times* (London, 8 April 1918) ridiculed Gandhi's 'obsession with passive resistance' and his efforts to coerce the mill-owners of Ahmedabad through a hunger-strike into conceding a rise in wages to their employees.

What the contemporaries could not foresee was that the strike would prove a turning point in labour–employer relations in Ahmedabad, introducing the principle of arbitration into industrial relations for the first time. The Royal Commission on Labour (Whitley Commission) noted in 1929 that the only attempt to set up a machinery for regulating relations between employers and workers in India had been made at Ahmedabad with a permanent arbitration board consisting of one nominee each of the employers and labour associations, and that 'Mr M.K. Gandhi has represented labour on the board since the beginning'.

In 1920, two years after the strike, Gandhi had inaugurated the labour union of the employees which was to blossom into the Ahmedabad Textile Labour Association (TLA) and to bear the stamp of Gandhian ideas on employer–employee relations. The Association developed its own library, reading-rooms, schools, newspapers, and hospitals. Thus, the one intervention by Gandhi in an industrial dispute led to a great constructive edifice. Though other preoccupations prevented him from devoting much time to industrial relations in later years, he never ceased to take interest in the textile workers of Ahmedabad and their Association which he considered a good model for trade unions in India.

The story of the 1918 strike was first narrated by Mahadev Desai in a book published in 1929. Forty years later, S. Erikson, a Harvard psychoanalyst, was attracted to this episode which struck him as an example of Gandhi's method of 'taking up local grievances of high symbolic value as a way of mobilizing the Indian masses both spiritually and politically— a method that distinguishes Gandhi from the charismatic figures (Lenin and Woodrow Wilson) of the post-World War period'. The principal theme of Erikson's book *Gandhi's Truth* was, however, different: the exploration and analysis of Gandhi's intellectual and emotional processes; a profile of the 'Middle-aged Mahatma'.

We now have a comprehensive account of the strike by M.V. Kamath,[1] which not only traces the sequence of events immediately before and after the strike, but places them in a historical perspective. We get fascinating glimpses of the principal actors in the strike, Ambalal Sarabhai and his sister Anasuyabehn, who were pitted against each other, the local British officials who were not yet certain whether Gandhi was a friend or a foe, and the mill-workers who willingly submitted to Gandhi's severe discipline of a 'satyagrahic strike' to set a precedent of 'militant but non-violent trade unionism'. The textile industry of Ahmedabad was to be the real beneficiary in the coming decades of harmonious relations between employers and the employees. To socialist and communist critics the idea of cooperation between labour and capital was a negation of class struggle and therefore 'reactionary'. Gandhi, however, insisted that he did not regard capital as the enemy of labour and that it was perfectly possible to harmonize their interests. When the All India Trade Union Congress approached him for the affiliation of the Textile Labour Association, he replied that he was making 'a unique experiment in trade union movement' and that Ahmedabad was his laboratory for this purpose. 'My idea', he wrote, 'is that capital and labour should supplement and help each other. They should be a family living in unity and harmony.' He was opposed to labour strikes for political purposes. 'The labour world in India, as elsewhere', he wrote, 'is at the mercy of those who set up as advisers and guides.' Gandhi's views on industrial relations seemed novel and impracticable to many of his contemporaries in an age in which socialist ideas were in the ascendant. However, now that Indian industries will have to survive global competition as united entities, Gandhi's concept, closer to that of the Japanese, of instilling a sense of common purpose and interest into employers and workers, and resolving conflicts as and when they arise, may seem more relevant.

NOTES AND REFERENCES

1. M.V. Kamath and V.B. Kher, *The Story of Militant but Non-violent Trade Unionism—A Biographical and Historical Study* (Navajivan Trust, Ahmedabad, 1993).

TWENTY ONE

Pyarelal

Pyarelal was one of the bright, impressionable, young idealists who
fell under Gandhi's spell in 1919–20. He had his first glimpse of
the Mahatma at the Amritsar Congress when he was barely twenty.
The following year he walked out of Government College, Lahore, where
he was studying English literature for his Master's degree, and joined
Gandhi's entourage. He acted as a deputy to Mahadev Desai, and after
Desai's death, served as the Mahatma's private secretary. The term private
secretary in relation to Gandhi was a misnomer; as Desai once said, the
duties included, besides secretarial work, such chores as cooking, washing
of clothes, tending the sick, and editing journals. The ashram life, with
its exacting routine and austere discipline, was no picnic. Gandhi was a
hard task-master, as those who were close to him found; indeed, he was
hardest on himself. The slightest negligence could elicit a reproof. Despite
his total dedication to the Mahatma, Desai compared working with him
to sitting on the top of a volcano which could erupt at any time, and once
wrote in *Harijan* that 'to live with saints in heaven is bliss and glory, but
to live with a saint on earth is a very different story'. There is, however,
no doubt that Desai, Pyarelal, and others in Gandhi's entourage, felt
amply rewarded by the intellectual and moral elevation they experienced
in serving him and the causes to which he had devoted his life.

The essays in *Gandhiji's Mirror*[1] are a miscellaneous collection; some
of them seem to have been hurriedly written for a newspaper or a journal;
some are scholarly pieces; some were written during Gandhi's lifetime
and had been scrutinized by him. They provide pen-pictures not only of
national leaders such as Motilal and Jawaharlal Nehru, Vallabhbhai Patel,
C. Rajagopalachari, and Abdul Ghaffar Khan, but also of the close associates
of the Mahatma such as Mahadev Desai, J.C. Kumarappa, K.G. Mashruwala,
and Rajkumari Amrit Kaur. Two Englishmen, Henry Polak and C.F. Andrews,
who identified themselves with Gandhi's work in South Africa and India,

also figure in the book. There are two interesting vignettes of the Liberal leader Tej Bahadur Sapru and the Hindu Mahasabha leader Shyama Prasad Mookerjee whose political differences with Gandhi did not detract from their regard for him. Pyarelal's devoted sister, Sushila Nayar, to whose initiative we owe this book, has added valuable profiles of the Mahatma's own family, and a moving account of Mahadev Desai's death in the Aga Khan Palace.

Most of the pen-portraits are of men and women with whom Pyarelal came into close contact; here he is at his anecdotal best and doles out insightful revelations. For example, we learn, on the authority of Tej Behadur Sapru, who was closely involved in the negotiation of the Poona Pact in 1932, that B.R. Ambedkar, despite his later denials, had been overwhelmed by Gandhi's generosity during the negotiations and had willingly accepted the terms of the pact. We are told how, after Pandit Madan Mohan Malaviya had pleaded in the appeal of the accused in the Chauri Chaura tragedy before the Allahabad High Court, the Chief Justice rose from his seat and congratulated the venerable Pandit 'on arguing out this case in such a brilliant manner'. No less than 150 accused were saved from the gallows by the judgement of the High Court. As against this instance of British decency, must be set British vindictiveness in delaying for several months Gandhi's telegram from the Aga Khan Palace prison to Mahadev Desai's wife informing her that her husband had passed away.

There is an amusing story of how once, as the Mahatma's cashier, Pyarelal entrusted C.F. Andrews, friend of Gandhi and Tagore, with a ten rupee note to pay off the *tongawala*. In the evening Andrews returned and innocently announced that the ten rupee note had slipped out of his 'open pocket'. 'I shall never forget', Pyarelal writes, 'the trouncing which I got from Gandhiji when I reported this matter to him. "Could you not foresee," he thundered, "that he would give it away to the nearest beggar if he did not lose it; you might as well entrust a baby with a gold ring."'

One of the most perceptive pieces is on Vallabhbhai Patel. In Congress circles Patel had long enjoyed the reputation of being a Gandhi loyalist, who hardly ever aired his differences with the Mahatma. Gandhi himself treated him as a colleague rather than as a disciple. 'Brother Vallabhbhai' is how Gandhi began his letters to Patel. He was perhaps the only member of Gandhi's circle who could pull his leg. Pyarelal tells us about the 'standing joke' between them that neither was to precede the other into the next world. During his last days when the Mahatma was distraught by the bitterness and bloodshed in the country in the wake of the partition and said he wished God would take him away, Patel protested. 'So you want to get out of your commitment and leave me in the lurch!'

Much has been written on differences between Gandhi and Patel towards the end. Some critics have charged Patel with disloyalty. Pyarelal did not think so. He tells us that, after Patel assumed office, he was part of the administration, 'which had its own dynamics while Gandhi's role was that of a mentor and a monitor'. When confronted with a choice between personal loyalty and national security, Patel tended to opt for the latter. Patel doubted whether Gandhi's non-violence and unilateral generosity could work on the leaders of Pakistan. Pyarelal refutes the charge of communalism levelled against Patel. The fact is, Pyarelal says, Patel 'never bothered about abstract philosophy or formal religion; he was anti-humbug and those who used religion for ulterior purposes got short shrift from him.' We are told that when Patel was Home Minister in the Interim Government, one of his favourite officers was Qurban Ali Khan, Inspector-General of the Special Police Establishment who later rose high in the service of the Pakistan Government.

As for Patel's friendship with the princes and capitalists, Pyarelal reminds us that it was Patel who put an end to the princely order. The Indian capitalists knew full well that Patel was no friend of the capitalist system either. Like Gandhi, he made a distinction between men, and the system of which they were a part. His friendship with individual capitalists and princes was based on the assumption that 'they were not altogether devoid of patriotism and good sense and that they would play the game'.

Pyarelal's gallery of pen-portraits includes Rajkumari Amrit Kaur. Brought up in princely surroundings, she had studied at Oxford, but rather than settling down to a life of ease and comfort, she decided to join Gandhi's entourage. For a girl who aspired to be Gandhi's secretary she was put through a strange apprenticeship. She was enjoined to brush up her knowledge of Hindustani and even to compile an English-Hindustani dictionary. She was to prepare herself for a life of simplicity, self-denial and a gruelling routine. She had to learn spinning and scavenging and take her turn in the ashram kitchen. When ill, she was given a course of nature cure. She was occasionally drafted as Gandhi's secretary. He began his letters to her with 'My dear idiot'. That Gandhi occasionally used her for contacts with the Christian community and with British officials is not surprising; in a non-violent mode of struggle, the aim is to convert the enemy of today into a friend of tomorrow and for this purpose all lines of communication with him have to be maintained even when the battle is on.

During the Quit India movement Amrit Kaur was in solitary confinement for eight weeks in extremely unhygienic surroundings and had to subsist on food prescribed for ordinary criminals. Not surprisingly, she fell ill; the government relented, released her on grounds of health and placed her under "'ouse arrest'. After independence, she had a long stint in the

Nehru Cabinet as Health Minister, the first woman to hold a cabinet rank.

Not surprisingly, these pen-portraits of Gandhi's colleagues and disciples also illuminate his own personality and philosophy. The introductory essay by Pyarelal is an intimate sketch of what Erikson described as 'the Middle-aged Mahatma'; in 1920, Gandhi was at the height of his physical and intellectual powers and India's freedom was his overwhelming concern. His ashram was not merely a haven for those who sought moral and spiritual growth; it was also designed as a training school for 'satyagrahis' for the non-violent battles to come. It is significant that Gandhi chose all the 78 volunteers for the Dandi March in 1930 from his ashram in Ahmedabad. Pyarelal tells how, several years earlier, Gandhi used to take the ashramites for a stroll right up to the gate of the Sabarmati Central Prison, and remark with a laugh: 'This is our other ashram.' Pyarelal, whose flair for journalism had caught Gandhi's perceptive eye, received some valuable tips at an early stage:

Call for facts, do not speculate in the void; it is a waste of energy, a sign of mental weakness. Do not cite epigrams, distrust them; learn to think for yourself, thought is more precious than language and judgement most precious of all.

Though himself steeled in self-discipline, the Mahatma was deeply human. He deprecated the tea and coffee habit as being incompatible with simple living, but knowing that some members of his entourage had it, he would sometimes during railway journeys go out and fetch a tea tray from the railway stall for his companions while they slept.

These sketches contain a rich fare for the general reader who wants to get an intimate glimpse of the Mahatma's inner circle. Pyarelal's proximity to the subjects of these short biographies was his strength; it was also his weakness. These are not portraits 'with warts and all'; the warts have been omitted. Pyarelal may also have been following the Mahatma's style of conscious magnanimity while publicly assessing colleagues as well as critics. The fact that most of these pieces were published as obituaries might explain their adulatory tone; a critical assessment on such occasions may have seemed inopportune, if not indecent.

Gandhi once described Mahadev Desai's life, 'as an uninterrupted hymn of *bhakti*'. The same description would as well apply to Pyarelal, who spent twenty-seven years at the Master's feet, and the next thirty-four years in unremitting labours on a multi-volume biography.

NOTES AND REFERENCES

1. Pyarelal, *Gandhiji's Mirror*, (Delhi).

TWENTY TWO

'I Have Become a Villager'

Before setting out on the Dandi March in March 1930, Gandhi had declared that this was going to be his last battle and that he would not return to his ashram until Swaraj was won. After release from jail, the Mahatma visited Ahmedabad, but, in accordance with the vow he had taken, he did not stay in Sabarmati Ashram. He decided to dissolve the ashram, and offered the land and the buildings to the government an offer it did not accept. Gandhi then decided to turn over the ashram properties to the Harijan Sevak Sangh. It was at this time that Jamnalal Bajaj reiterated the offer he had made to the Mahatma eighteen years earlier to find the land, buildings and funds for the ashram if he agreed to come to Wardha. Vallabhbhai Patel was keen that Gandhi should transfer his ashram to Bardoli and not leave Gujarat. Gandhi had not quite made up his mind when he paid a visit to Wardha in September 1933. He stayed there for six weeks before leaving for his Harijan tour. He returned on 10 June 1934, and the first thing he did was to call on Vinoba Bhave, who had been managing a branch of Sabarmati Ashram in Wardha since 1921. The Mahatma attended a meeting of the Congress Working Committee at Wardha on 12 and 13 June, and soon afterwards resumed his travels to campaign against untouchability.

Meanwhile the political landscape was changing. The suspension of civil disobedience and the re-emergence of a parliamentary wing had created new tensions in the Congress. The nascent socialist group was very critical of the Congress leadership. Gandhi sensed that some of his adherents had tired of his methods and pretended to accept policies with which they really did not agree. His renewed emphasis on the spinning wheel as 'a lung of the nation' seemed misplaced to many people, as did his moral and religious approach to the problem of untouchability. It was, however, on the crucial issue of non-violence that he felt most deeply the differences between himself and the intelligentsia. After fifteen years of preaching and practising non-violence, it almost hurt him to see how little it was understood by those who professed to follow him. Mass civil disobedience had struck the imagination of most Congressmen, but this was only one aspect of his non-violent technique. There was another aspect, the constructive programme, which he now stressed and which struck his critics as irrelevant to the struggle against imperialism. It was this divergence in outlook that drove Gandhi to announce his retirement from politics when the Indian National Congress met at Bombay in October 1934.

The resolution of the Bombay Congress, which formally registered Gandhi's retirement, also authorized the formation, under his guidance, of the All India Village Industries Association to work 'unaffected by and independent of the political activities of the Congress', for the revival and encouragement of village industries and the moral and physical advancement of the village.

The formation of the All India Village Industries Association offered an opportunity that Jamnalal seized with both hands. He offered to house it in Wardha and to donate for it his large garden-house, with its twenty-acre orchard. Gandhi accepted the offer. The Association was established in December 1934, with Srikrishnadas Jajoo, Jamnalal's friend and collaborator since his youth, as president, and J.C. Kumarappa, a chartered accountant and Gandhian economist, as general secretary. The house in which the Association was based, and in which Gandhi and his party resided, was named Maganwadi, after Gandhi's favourite nephew, Maganlal Gandhi, who had been the first manager of Sabarmati Ashram and who had died a few years earlier.

From the beginning of 1935, Wardha became the centre of Gandhi's activities. The fact that he had recently shed direct responsibility for Congress work meant that he would tour less and spend more time at Wardha. There was enough to engage him in Wardha. The constructive work that Vinoba Bhave and Jamnalal Bajaj had been nurturing for a decade received fresh impetus. Gandhi visited some of the villages, addressed constructive workers, and encouraged them to work out the most effective methods of improving the conditions in which the villagers lived. Jamnalal's diary contains some fascinating vignettes of Gandhi at work. On 6 May 1936, there was a Khadi Yatra exhibition: 'After some songs Vinoba gave a fine and impressive talk. Then Bapu [Gandhi] spoke. Then we all plied the *charkha* and *takli* between 2.30 and 3 p.m. From 3 p.m. there was introduction of constructive workers. At 5.30 p.m. Vinoba gave his concluding talk. I also spoke. At night we had devotional songs by Tukdoji. We returned to Wardha after 1.30 a.m.' The following day Gandhi addressed the workers of Gram Seva Mandal.

Part of the building in Maganwadi was occupied by J.C. Kumarappa and the offices of the All India Village Industries Association; the rest accommodated Gandhi and his entourage which included many of his associates from Sabarmati, Kaka Kalelkar, Mirabehn (Miss Slade), Mahadev Desai, K.G. Mashruwala, Pyarelal, Sushila Nayar, and others. Mirabehn tells us about the Mahatma's dietetic experiments. He was so impressed by the nutritive value of soyabeans as a source of protein that they were served with every meal, until they disagreed with everybody including Gandhi. Some of the inmates were far from normal. As Mirabehn recalled in her autobiography:

A few of the old Sabarmati Ashramites were still there, but a strange medley of various kinds of cranky people had collected around Bapu. Since we were all cheek by jowl in one building, there was no peace and no escape. Even at night the disturbance went on. For one of the inmates was a somnambulist and when he walked in his sleep, another inmate who had St Vitus's dance, always got up and tried to catch him with the result that at the dead of night blood-curdling shrieks would rend the air. In spite of this, Bapu carried on with a prodigious amount of work.

Mirabehn found the atmosphere in Maganwadi suffocating, and sought escape from it by going for long solitary walks in the early mornings. In order to reach open country, she had to go through a village called Sindi. She was shocked to see that, while the little houses were clean and tidy within, the village lanes and surroundings were dirty. She mentioned this to Gandhi. 'If that is so,' the Mahatma said, 'we should do something about it. We have come here to help improve the villages.' It was decided that Mirabehn should try to improve the sanitation in Sindi with the help of two or three members of Maganwadi Ashram. These efforts did not meet with much success, and Gandhi was unhappy at the lack of response from the villagers. Suddenly one day he announced that he would go and live in Sindi all alone, taking such help as he needed from the village itself. The announcement caused consternation in Gandhi's entourage. He was in his sixty-sixth year; his workload was already heavy; his blood pressure fluctuated violently. His health and his life were national assets: were they to be jeopardized in response to a whim? How could he insulate himself from the many problems that claimed his attention even after his formal retirement from politics? Mirabehn came in for sharp criticism:

her meddling in the affairs of Sindi had created an unnecessary crisis. In a desperate effort to save the situation, she offered to go and live in Sindi if Gandhi abandoned the idea of going there.

Gandhi accepted the compromise, and Mirabehn went to Sindi to stay in a one-roomed cottage. She was unable to make much headway with the problem of sanitation, but she argued that Sindi was really a suburb of Wardha. If the idea was to understand and solve the problems of the villages, a better sample had to be chosen. Gandhi agreed to depute someone from Maganwadi Ashram to stay in Sindi if Mirabehn could find a more typical village in the neighbourhood. She walked day after day in all directions, and was dismayed by the hard, dusty, countryside and unresponsive, even hostile, attitude of the inhabitants of most of the villages. Her choice finally fell on Segaon, a village four miles to the east of Wardha, which seemed to be 'the least unsatisfactory'. Its greatest asset was that it had an orchard and a farm belonging to Jamnalal Bajaj. Mirabehn then spoke to Gandhi and Jamnalal, and was allowed to move to Segaon, and to live in a small hut made of wood, bamboo, and mud-plaster with a tiled roof.

Meanwhile Gandhi had a breakdown brought about by high blood pressure and went to Ahmedabad for a change. He sensed from Mirabehn's letters that she was not altogether happy in her new surroundings, and wrote to her that if she was unable to stay on in Segaon he would go and live there. Gandhi's proposal to move to Segaon raised a storm. Virtually everyone was opposed to it. Jawaharlal Nehru and Vallabhbhai Patel considered the proposal preposterous. The Mahatma's doctors shook their heads. His colleagues in the ashram failed to see what would be gained by moving from Maganwadi, which was a sort of a village, to another village a few miles away. Above all, Jamnalal Bajaj was wholly opposed to the proposal. There was nothing to recommend Segaon. It was not even connected by road with Wardha; it did not have a post-office; it was infested with snakes; it was situated in a low-lying area, inaccessible during the rains, and its stagnant pools of water made it seriously malarial. There were even stories of robberies and murders in the neighbourhood. These disqualifications notwithstanding, Gandhi's resolve to settle in Segaon was unshaken. On the morning of 30 April 1936, he walked from Wardha to Segaon to select a site for his cottage; on the way he met Roodmal, Jamnalal Bajaj's manager for agricultural operations. Gandhi told him that he was going to Segaon. 'Mahatmaji you have taken away Maganwadi from Jamnalal. Now you will also snatch Segaon from him', Roodmal remarked. 'What else do you expect from a man like me?' Gandhi quipped.

He spent the night in Segaon in an improvised shelter beneath some trees; the evening prayers were held in the village. The Mahatma's speech in Hindi was translated into Marathi:

I have come [Gandhi said] to your village to serve you. Mirabehn who lives amongst you came resolved to stay with you permanently. She may not be able to do so, not because she does not want to do so, but because she is not physically very strong. I thought I should complete the work which Mirabehn may not be able to do .... However, I would not want to inflict myself on those who view me with suspicion or fear. The fear arises from my dedication to fight against untouchability .... I can only try to persuade you to shed [your] ideas.

Gandhi told the villagers that, besides working against untouchability, he would help to clean the residential areas and revive dead or dying village handicrafts. They welcomed him, but an old Patel stood up and said: 'We are happy that you are coming here, but we do not accept what you say about Harijans.' Gandhi laughed and said: 'Gradually you will understand the truth of what I have told you.' That very day there was a quarrel the Segaon village. A man with a bleeding head was brought to the Mahatma; somebody had struck him with a *lathi*. 'Do not take this to the police', Gandhi said. 'Both sides will suffer; whoever has hit the man is guilty. Try to settle your quarrels within the village by mutual accommodation and understanding.'

A week later, Gandhi left for Nandi Hills in Mysore. He left instructions for the construction of his cottage, which Mirabehn was to supervise with the help of two volunteers from Maganwadi Ashram, one of them was Balwant Singh, the only person in Gandhi's group who had a real farmer's background; the other was Munnalal Shah, a lawyer, who had given up legal practice and cast in his lot with Gandhi.

The construction of the cottage, which was to be ready by the middle of June when Gandhi was scheduled to return to Wardha, was a race against time. The walls were to be of solid mud: if the rains came before the roof was laid, they would collapse. As ill-luck would have it, Mirabehn, who was acting as architect as well as engineer, fell ill; poor Balwant Singh and Munnalal had to nurse her besides attending to the building operations. Gandhi was back in Wardha on 14 June; he sent a note to Mirabehn that, weather permitting, he would be in Sevagram at 7.30 next morning. The following day it was raining heavily, but undaunted by it, Gandhi walked into his cottage at Sevagram 'drenched to the skin and laughing heartily'.

Segaon was nearly four miles from Wardha. There was another village in Maharashtra called Shegaon on the Nagpur–Bombay railway line; to avoid confusion, the government decided, with Gandhi's concurrence, to change the name of Segaon to Sevagram.

When Gandhi started living in Sevagram, it was his intention to live all by himself. At first his was the only hut, and had a large room measuring 29 feet by 14 feet, with a 7-feet veranda running all around it. Gandhi yielded to the entreaties of Munnalal and Balwant Singh, who had built the cottage, that they may stay with him and cook for him. Later, however, others came along. 'However radical he may be', Gandhi's secretary Mahadev Desai wrote, 'he is conservative in his tastes and attachment to friends and co-workers. Old co-workers gravitate towards him and he gravitates towards them.' By the end of July 1936, Kasturba, Manu Gandhi, Dr Khan Sahib (the Congress leader of the North West Frontier Province) and Tukdoji Maharaj, a melodious singer of devotional songs, were lodged in Gandhi's one-roomed cottage. The quiet and privacy he had dreamt of in a village seemed to elude him. 'This has become', he wrote to Mirabehn on 20 July 1936, 'a confused household instead of a hermitage it was expected to be. Such has been my fate; I must find my hermitage from within.'

Early in 1937 Gandhi was persuaded to move into a smaller cottage which Mirabehn had originally built for herself. It came to be known as *Bapu Kutir*, and has been preserved to this day, as it was during Gandhi's lifetime. During the first few weeks Gandhi seemed to savour the solitude of Sevagram.

The cottage here [he wrote on 12 July 1936 to Rajkumari Amrit Kaur] is a picture. I have just now a young sadhu [Tukdoji Maharaj]. He is a great *bhajani*, a singer of *bhajans* of his own composition. He will be with me for a month. I occupy one corner, he occupies another; the third is occupied by Munnalal, a co-worker. All round is open and beautiful. Fresh breeze blowing throughout the day. It is quite cool. Perfect walks all over.

Rajkumari Amrit Kaur was so fascinated by this account that she joined Gandhi in Sevagram, and her bed was added to the seven or eight others that had been squeezed into the one-roomed cottage.

'Whatever it may be to others', Gandhi wrote on 12 August 1936 to a correspondent, 'Segaon is to me an inexhaustible source of joy.' Life in Sevagram was, however, no bed of roses for Gandhi or those who joined him there. He had moved in when the monsoon had already broken, so those who came to meet him had to pick their way along muddy tracks. Then soon everyone seemed to be falling ill. Mirabehn was down with typhoid. Balwant Singh had an attack of malaria. Dysentery and cholera were endemic in the village. Amrit Kaur was so run down that Gandhi packed her off to Simla for recuperation. Gandhi himself had a virulent attack of malaria. Dr Mahodaya, a local doctor, felt that it was necessary to remove Gandhi to the civil hospital. Gandhi was reluctant, but yielded when the doctor's advice was backed by Jamnalal Bajaj. 'I have just learnt by telephone', Jawaharlal Nehru wrote to Agatha Harrison on 3 September 1936, 'that Gandhiji is seriously ill with malaria. I have no particulars yet. Malaria by itself is not uncommon or dangerous. But in his state of health it is a disconcerting business. He has been removed from his village to the hospital at Wardha. I am afraid, I do not appreciate his living in village huts.'

There was no road from Wardha to Sevagram; just a cart track that raised clouds of dust and became unusable during the rains. Jamnalal Bajaj improvised a curious vehicle, which he called 'Oxford', for journeys between Wardha and Sevagram; it consisted of the rear portion of an old Ford motor-car pulled by a pair of oxen. This was the vehicle which was used by Nehru, Patel, Rajagopalachari, and others; it was, however, a fair-weather vehicle. On several occasions the ordinary bullock-cart had to be used. There is an interesting entry in Jamnalal's diary of 21 July 1937: 'Maulana [Azad] and I went to Segaon in a bullock-cart. It had rained heavily and a drizzle continued. On the way, one of the wheels of the bullock-cart came off; it delayed our arrival there; we had only a brief discussion with Bapu.'

There was no electricity in Sevagram and kerosene lamps were used; Gandhi tried to reduce dependence upon kerosene by promoting the use of non-edible oils, which were locally available for lighting lamps. Whether he liked it or not, it was impossible to keep Sevagram insulated from the rest of the world. The District Board built a road in due course to connect it with Wardha and a post office was also opened.

Unlike Gandhi's previous ashrams at Phoenix, Tolstoy Farm and Sabarmati, the one at Sevagram was the least planned. His original idea of living all by himself in Sevagram proved impracticable; he had not the heart to turn away those who had given their lives to work with him. A number of individuals who were originally lodged in Maganwadi moved over to Sevagram; it was only to be expected that Kasturba, Mahadev Desai, Pyarelal, and his doctor sister, Sushila Nayar, should follow him. Others however joined him too, and included K.G. Mashruwala, the ideologue of Gandhian philosophy and president of the Gandhi Seva Sangh; Rajkumari Amrit Kaur, who was eager to serve the Mahatma as secretary; E.W. Aryanayakam, the Cambridge-trained educationist and his talented wife, Ashadevi; Maurice Friedman, a Polish engineer, who had become a convert to the Gandhian conception of a handicraft civilization based on non-violence; Parchure Shastri, a Sanskrit scholar, a victim of leprosy, who was housed next to the Mahatma's hut so that he could personally attend on him; the eccentric Professor Bhansali, who had roamed in forests naked and with sealed lips, subsisting on neem leaves; and a Japanese monk, who 'worked like a horse and lived like a hermit', merrily beating his drum morning and evening. It was a motley crowd which led Vallabhbhai Patel to describe Sevagram as a 'menagerie'. Gandhi did not mind the description. 'I have collected about myself a crowd of invalids. I have even likened it to a lunatic asylum, by no means an inappropriate comparison ... But luckily lunatics are unaware of their lunacy. And I regard myself as sane.'

With the increase in activities in Sevagram, the ashram could not but expand. So heavy was the incidence of illness in the village, and so poor the medical aid, that a dispensary became indispensable. The need for milk led to the organization of a small dairy. Some of the organizations for constructive work that Gandhi wanted to personally supervise, such as 'Nai Talimi Sangh', manned by the Aryanayakams, shifted their headquarters to Sevagram.

The sprawling colony in and around Sevagram, however, never acquired the organization and discipline of Gandhi's earlier ashrams. There was no attempt to enforce a daily regimen and a strenuous timetable in Sevagram. All that Gandhi expected from the ashramites was that they would exemplify the principle of non-violence in their daily lives through selfless service. Their loyalty to Gandhi and his ideals, despite their diverse backgrounds and idiosyncrasies, gave to most of them a sense of purpose. They cooked their own food, washed their own clothes, and cleaned their own latrines, besides performing the duties assigned to them.

Gandhi had wanted to settle in a 'typical' Indian village. Sevagram, however, turned out to be an uncommonly backward village, and almost impervious to progressive impulses from outside. Some of the psychological resistance he encountered in Sevagram may have been due to adverse political influence from his political opponents in nearby Nagpur. The real bane of this village was, however, the stranglehold of untouchability on its inhabitants. The majority of its population consisted of Harijans who were not only denied access to temples, but could not avail themselves of the services of the local priests, tailors, and barbers; they were forbidden to draw water from the wells, to send their children to schools, and even to use certain roads. Gandhi used every weapon in his non-violent armoury to make a dent in this tyrannical system. He engaged Govind, a Harijan boy, to cook for him. He refused to have his hair cut by the village barber so long as he denied his services to Harijans. Despite high-caste opposition, he caused a private well in Sevagram, owned by Jamnalal, to be opened to Harijans. He argued patiently with the leaders of orthodoxy who professed to revere him, but were reluctant to shake off their prejudices. 'Everything is permissible', said the village headman to Gandhi, 'to a Mahatma like you, but not to fellows like us.'

To Gandhi untouchability was not merely a religious issue, a question of the interpretation of scriptures; it had a direct bearing on the village economy. The occupation of the *bhangi*, the scavenger, was the most despised; he was kept at arm's length even by many Harijans who had their own social hierarchy of ritual purity. This irrational prejudice made it difficult to improve sanitation, and fight disease in the village, it also operated against the use of human and animal excreta as manure.

Gandhi's preoccupation with these problems jarred on some of his colleagues. They wondered why he should fritter away his energies on such apparent trivialities, when momentous political issues were crying for his attention. Mahadev Desai tells us about a conversation Jawaharlal Nehru had with Gandhi on 3 October 1936 when he visited Sevagram along with Vallabhbhai Patel. He compared Gandhi's insistence on personally nursing patients to the effort of King Canute to hold back the tide. 'That is why', Gandhi quipped, 'we have made you King Canute so that you may do it better than the others.' Gandhi was referring to the fact that Nehru had been elected Congress President for the year.

'But is there no better way?' Nehru asked. 'Must you do all these things yourself?' 'Who else is there to do it?' Gandhi replied. 'If you go to the village nearby, you will find that out of 600 people there, 300 are ill. Are they all to go to the hospital? We have to learn to treat ourselves. How are we to teach these poor villagers except by personal example?'

'Why am I in Sevagram?' Gandhi asked in an article in December 1936, and answered: 'Because I believe that my message will have a better chance of penetrating the masses of India, and, maybe, through them, the world.' If one village could be rid of poverty, ignorance, and disease, it might serve as a model to the rest of the country.

It was an uphill task; performance fell woefully short of expectations. 'It is no use', Gandhi told Bharatan Kumarappa in 1939, 'expecting startling results as those of the Five-Year Plans in Soviet Russia ... Our acid test is ... Have we organized any single village according to our programme? Have we introduced food reform there? Are their roads and their lanes clean and perfect? Have we revived any industries? Have we tackled the problem of drink and vice? If we could do this even in one village, I should think we had achieved a great deal. From individuals you may get a response, but I should not call it making headway. Making headway is touching one whole village.'

Sevagram caused a heavy overdraft on the patience and perseverance of the reformers. 'What about the work', Mahadev Desai asked nearly three and a half years after the Mahatma's arrival in Sevagram, 'which made Gandhiji take the irrevocable decision to come and settle down in a village which was chosen because it was the most difficult to tackle?' 'I confess', Desai wrote, 'the answer cannot be given in a resounding affirmative. All we have been able to do is to give a fair number of employment on a meagre wage. We have given a bad blow to untouchability; we have introduced a few spinning wheels in the village and interested the children in our work and "basic" system of education, and we have given medical aid to many of them. But there is a hiatus between the villagers and us. There is no living link between us.' Gandhi wanted to bridge this hiatus: he wanted his co-workers to overcome the fears and suspicions of the villagers by 'gently insinuating themselves into their affections'. He sensed two main hurdles in his way, the passivity and inertia of the long-suffering population of the villages, and the dearth of earnest and selfless workers to dedicate themselves to the service of the villages. There was in fact a resistance, conscious or unconscious, from the urban educated classes to essential reforms that would raise the masses from the depth of poverty.

TWENTY THREE

Gandhi and the Jews

Gandhi's extraordinary capacity for making friends with all kinds and conditions of men was first revealed in South Africa. In those days of his youth, even when he was the unquestioned leader of his compatriots in that country, he had not yet become a world celebrity, and those who knew him were less liable to be awed and over-whelmed by his personality.

Looking back on his South African days, Gandhi is reported to have remarked, 'I was surrounded by Jews'. In reality there were only a handful of Jews around him; what was important was not the number of his Jewish friends, but the quality of his relationship with them. There were two Britons, Henry Polak and L.W. Ritch, both lawyer–journalists; there was the German architect, Hermann Kallenbach; there was the stenographer and secretary, Sonia Schlesin of Russian origin, besides William M. Vogl, the draper, and Gabriel Isaacs, the jeweller. What was it that attracted these European Jews settled in South Africa to the strange Hindu lawyer–politician–saint?

Most of them were trying to grow out of their inherited traditions and beliefs and to seek wider horizons. They had begun to question the values of the competitive materialism of Western civilization; they dabbled in theosophy and frequented vegetarian restaurants; they read and admired Tolstoy's radical views on religion and society. Two of them, Henry Polak and Hermann Kallenbach, came closest to Gandhi.

Henry Polak was educated in Britain and Switzerland, and came to South Africa at the age of twenty-two as subeditor of *Transvaal Gazette*. He met Gandhi in 1904; a year later, he married and joined Gandhi's household in Johannesburg. His wife, Millie Polak, has left a delightful pen-portrait of Gandhi in his late thirties in a book entitled *Mr. Gandhi The Man*. There is nothing in this book to indicate that the Polaks were practising

Jews; Millie herself was a Christian, and both she and her husband were fully attuned to Gandhi's religious eclecticism and cosmopolitanism. She relates that after dinner, if there were no strangers present, Gandhi used to recite a couple of verses from the *Bhagavad Gita*, after which Polak read the English equivalent from Edwin Arnold's *The Song Celestial*. 'When guests were present', Millie Polak writes, 'philosophies of different countries would be compared and many varieties of religious and mystic experiences dwelt upon. One never-ending theme was the different civilizations of East and West.'

Polak was thirteen years younger than Gandhi, but he became more of a friend than a disciple. It was Polak who lent to Gandhi Ruskin's *Unto This Last*, the book that overnight changed the style of Gandhi's life. Polak had begun his legal career as an articled clerk with Gandhi, and more than repaid his debt to him by appearing in courts on behalf of Gandhi's adherents during the satyagraha struggle. He visited India twice, in 1909 and in 1911, to brief Gandhi's mentor and friend Gokhale who was collecting funds and rousing Indian opinion on the heroic battle the Indian settlers were waging in South Africa. Polak made a deep impression on Gokhale and other Indian leaders who for the first time got an inkling of Gandhi's personality and politics from a man who, though a European, understood and shared his thought and principles. Polak was in the thick of the last phase of the satyagraha campaign in 1913, addressed rallies in important towns in South Africa, and was imprisoned. He was Gandhi's most efficient confidant and colleague in the South African struggle. He did not accompany him to India, but returned to England. Notwithstanding his affection for Gandhi, he disagreed with him when he applied the weapon of satyagraha in the encounter with the British Raj.

Hermann Kallenbach was as close to Gandhi as Polak, perhaps closer, but he was more a disciple than a friend. The Gandhi–Kallenbach correspondence, which recently became available and from which the author[1] quotes copiously, provides fascinating glimpses of their relationship. In a letter written in June 1909, Gandhi wonders whether their strong mutual attachment dated from their relationship in some previous life. A few months later he tells Kallenbach: 'Your portrait (the only one) stands on my mantelpiece in my bedroom.' Gandhi is generous in giving advice to Kallenbach on his diet, on the value of fasting, and on the need for economy and austerity. As Margaret Chatterjee suggests, Kallenbach's Tolstoyan background might have predisposed him to a simple life, but what Gandhi was enforcing was asceticism of the horse-hair-shirt variety! Kallenbach does not seem to have chafed under this tyranny of love. He was a tower of strength to Gandhi; it was on land provided by him near Johannesburg that the Tolstoy Farm for housing the satyagrahi prisoners' families came up. In July 1914, when Gandhi set sail for England en route to India, Kallenbach accompanied him. If the world war had not broken out, and if Kallenbach had not been interned as a German national in a detention camp in England for the duration of the war, he would in all probability have stood staunchly at Gandhi's side in India. He returned to South Africa after the war, but life was never the same for him again. As he wrote to Gandhi:

I feel very lonely, very alone at Johannesburg, like an abandoned dog. You have spoiled my life by giving and showing me real friendship, affection and love and I am vainly seeking for it. You told me I shall never be satisfied to return to the old life, and indeed I am not only not satisfied, I am unhappy ...

Kallenbach was not destined to be Gandhi's lieutenant, but he was able to visit him twice in India.

The third Jewish associate of Gandhi, who looms large in his autobiography, was Sonia Schlesin. She held a diploma in shorthand and proved a very competent aide to Gandhi. She was born a Jew, but was 'not one of those who went to the synagogue to pray'. What was true of Sonia Schlesin was also true of Polak and Kallenbach; they had already distanced themselves from Judaic doctrine and rituals before they gravitated to Gandhi and his liberal and essentially ethico–religious code. Polak, Kallenbach, and Schlesin were no more typical Jews than Gandhi was a typical Hindu. The fact is that Gandhi's relationship with his Jewish friends had little to do with their being Jews; it rested on allegiance to moral values and common causes. It is significant that though some of his Jewish friends were Gandhi's right-hand men in the Indians' struggle against racial discrimination in South Africa, the Jewish community as a whole kept away from the struggle. The Jews, being white, were not subject to the racial bar, though they had their own disabilities in South Africa. They were a small minority; they were vulnerable because of anti-Semitism prevalent in certain sections of the European community, and they did not want to incur the displeasure of the government. Gandhi himself took care not to seek their support and thus add to their vulnerability.

While delineating Gandhi's relationship with his Jewish friends, Margaret Chatterjee ranges widely, and discursively, over Gandhi's formative years in South Africa, the interaction between various racial and religious groups, the evolution of Gandhi's ideas and the struggle of the Indian immigrants for elementary civic rights. She then passes on to the Jewish ordeal in Europe, in the 1930s under the Nazi tyranny, and finally to the emergence of Israel. She arraigns Gandhi on two counts. The first is that he did not know enough about Judaism and tended to see it 'through Christian spectacles'. The second is Gandhi's inability to fully comprehend the Jewish predicament on the eve of the Second World War and to sympathize with Zionism.

Gandhi may not have had as deep a knowledge of Judaism as he had of Hinduism or Christianity, but this gap in his education was largely because his closest Jewish friends had distanced themselves from traditional Judaism. Two Jewish businessmen, William Mc Vogl and Gabriel Isaacs, in Johannesburg, whom Gandhi came to know well, took him to the synagogue and gave him an opportunity of partaking of a Seder meal, but they did not have the intellectual equipment to instruct him in the nuances of the Judaic doctrine and belief. Curiously, neither William M. Vogl nor Gabriel Isaacs finds a mention in Gandhi's autobiography.

As for Gandhi's refusal to support Zionism, it was certainly not from lack of sympathy with the Jews. The pages of *Indian Opinion* bear ample testimony to Gandhi's awareness of the persecution which the Jews had suffered in Europe over the centuries. He had noticed and publicly deplored the prevalence of anti-Semitism in South Africa. In India, even though the Jews were a tiny minority (20,000 in a population of 300 million) and did not figure much in satyagraha campaigns, Gandhi described on the eve of his arrest in March 1922 'Hindu–Muslim, Parsi, Christian and Jewish unity as the four pillars of Swaraj'. Sixteen years later, when asked by a Jewish delegation whether Jews should participate in the nationalist movement in India, he exhorted them to keep clear of it as they were such a small minority that they ran the risk of being 'crushed between the three mighty conflicting forces of British imperialism, Congress nationalism and Muslim separatism'. In the years preceding the Second World War, Gandhi whole-heartedly approved of Nehru's efforts to find asylum for German Jewish refugees in India. One of them, Margaret Spiegel, who had joined Gandhi's ashram, expressed a wish to embrace Hinduism. Gandhi dissuaded her. 'If Judaism does not satisfy you', he wrote to her, 'no other faith will give you any satisfaction.' He also assured her that her Semitic origin would be least resented in India.

There is not the slightest doubt about Gandhi's deep feeling for the Jews' ordeal in Europe in the 1930s. The Congress party's policy of un-qualified denunciation of Nazism and Fascism was forcefully articulated by Jawaharlal Nehru with Gandhi's full support; indeed what could be a stronger condemnation of Nazism than Gandhi's comment in *Harijan* (26 November 1938):

The German persecution of the Jews seems to have no parallel in history. But tyrants of old never went so mad as Hitler seems to have gone. And he is doing it with religious zeal. For he is propounding a new religion of exclusive and militant nationalism in the name of which any inhumanity becomes an act of humanity to be rewarded here and hereafter ... If there ever could be a justifiable war in the name of and for humanity, a war against Germany, to prevent the wanton persecution of a whole race, would be completely justified.

Gandhi added, however, that he did not believe in any war, and commended his own weapon of non-violent resistance to the Jews for use against the Nazis. Margaret Chatterjee asks why Gandhi 'singled out the Jews for martyrdom'. The fact is that he gave the same advice to the Abyssinians against the Italians, to the Chinese against the Japanese, to the Czechs against the Germans, and to his own countrymen.

After the fall of France in 1940, and in the face of a threat from Japan in 1942, when the majority of Gandhi's colleagues in the Congress Working Committee favoured cooperation with the British for armed resistance to the Axis Powers, Gandhi, rather than abandon his principle of non-violence, decided to distance himself from politics.

The policy of the Indian National Congress on the future of Palestine may have been influenced by its distrust of the motives of the British government, which ruled over Palestine under a mandate from the League of Nations. Further, the Congress, as a political party, could not but take into account Muslim opinion in India. It is, however, doubtful whether Gandhi's own views were affected by such calculations. He was neither pro-Arab nor pro-Jew; he tended to see the problem only from a moral and humanitarian perspective. In commending coexistence and cooperation to the Arabs and Jews, he was not saying anything different from what the Balfour Declaration of 1917 itself had postulated while envisaging the establishment of a national home in Palestine for the Jewish people in which 'nothing shall be done which may prejudice the civil and religious rights of existing non-Jewish communities in Palestine'. Five years later, Winston Churchill, Colonial Secretary in the British Cabinet, stated that the British government did not contemplate 'the disappearance or the subordination of the Arab population, language or culture in Palestine'. During the inter-war years there were some Zionists, such as Arthur Ruppin and Judah Leon Magnes, who advocated cooperation between Arabs and Jews in Palestine.

In recommending non-violence to Jews rather than to Arabs, Gandhi was not guilty of what Margaret Chatterjee calls 'double standards'. Evidently he had more hopes of getting a response to such a call from the Jews than from the Arabs. Gandhi was aware that in recommending non-violence to the Jews he was making heavy demands on human nature. In December 1938 he wrote in *Harijan*. 'How do I expect the Jews to accept my prescription when I know that India, where I am working, where I call myself a self-appointed general, has not accepted it *in toto*.' Gandhi's dilemma was the dilemma of a prophet who was also a political leader, who felt he must speak out the truth despite the yawning gap between his vision and the contemporary realities; he knew his idealism was the realism of tomorrow.

NOTES AND REFERENCES

1. Margaret Chatterjee, *Gandhi and His Jewish Friends* (London, 1992).

TWENTY FOUR

Gandhi and the West

When Gandhi left South Africa in 1914 after 20 years' struggle against racialism, General Smuts wrote to a high British official, 'The saint has left our shores, I sincerely hope for ever.' The reputation of a subversive saint followed Gandhi to India. As the leader of the nationalist movement he became the bête noire of the British ruling class. British politicians, civil servants, and journalists tended to see Gandhi as an astute politician determined to dismantle the British Empire.

As late as February 1947, Lord Wavell, the last but one Viceroy, told King George VI that Gandhi was 'a most inveterate enemy of the British'. The guardians of the British Raj were unable to accept Gandhi's claim that he was fighting not against Britain or the British people, but against British imperialism, nor did they appreciate, what was most important from Gandhi's point of view, the non-violent basis of his struggle.

As Gandhi had clashed head-on with the British Empire, he could hardly be popular in countries of Europe which had empires of their own, such as France, Belgium, Holland, Portugal, or others like Germany and Italy which were hungering for colonies. A few exceptional individuals, such as Romain Rolland, Albert Einstein, and C.F. Andrews were quick to recognize Gandhi's stature, but the prevalent image of Gandhi in Europe and America in the inter-war years was largely that of an eccentric saint or a wily politician.

This was not surprising because the news from India to the West was filtered through the British-owned Reuter news agency. An English Quaker, John S. Hoyland, noted in 1931 that satyagraha was 'looked upon in the West as ridiculous and undignified. Working class audience, when told about it, characterized it as grown-up sulks. More educated audiences regard it with cold disfavour. It is too exotic, too unconventional, in a word too Christian for us.' In Britain most of the newspapers ridiculed and belittled Gandhi when he visited England in the winter of 1931 to attend the Round Table Conference. His most important speech at the opening of the Conference was not reported. The press revelled in the prospect that the Conference would fail and Gandhi with it. Pope Pius XI twice refused Gandhi's request to call on him when he stopped over in Rome in December 1931 on his way back from London to Bombay.

In the United States there were admirers of Gandhi such as John Haynes Holmes, who told his community church congregation in New York in 1921 that Gandhi was the greatest man in the world: greater than Lenin and Woodrow Wilson. 'When I think of Gandhi, I think of Jesus Christ', he added. On the whole, however, the American press followed the British line when it came to the appraisal of the Mahatma and the Indian nationalist movement. Gandhi was aware how important it was for his struggle to receive the support of world opinion; he also knew how heavy the odds were against him. 'When I see so much misrepresentation of things in general in [the] American and European press', he wrote in 1922, at the height of the non-cooperation movement, 'I despair of the message of the struggle ever reaching the Western world, but my abiding faith in the Unseen keeps my hope for ever. Truth must penetrate the deepest darkness.'

It was in the last years of his life, with the imminence of Indian independence, that the West began to see Gandhi in less lurid colours. In 1944, Einstein, the greatest scientist of the day, paid a memorable tribute to Gandhi: 'A leader of his people, unsupported by any outward authority; a politician whose success depends not upon craft or mastery of technical devices, but simply on the convincing power of his personality—a man of wisdom and humility ... who has confronted the brutality of Europe with the dignity of the simple human being.'

After Gandhi's death, some of the barriers to understanding him, which had existed in his lifetime, disappeared. Colonialism was dead or dying; racialism was under siege in its last bastion in South Africa. The life and thought of Gandhi could now be seen without imperialist and racialist blinkers. Non-violent resistance acquired respectability when it was used by the Norwegians during the Second World War, by the people of Czechoslovakia in 1968 and then again in 1989, and the Poles under the leadership of Lech Walesa. The African National Congress was unable to adhere to non-violence after the Sharpeville massacre, but Nelson Mandela consciously adopted a policy of national conciliation in the spirit of Gandhi in the transition to a multiracial democratic system. Other African leaders, such as Kenneth Kaunda in Zambia and Kwame Nkrumah in

Ghana, acknowledged their debt to Gandhi in conducting their struggle against colonialism.

In the United States, Martin Luther King blazed a trail with non-violent resistance to racial discrimination. King and his colleagues named the Education Fund which supported the civil rights movement 'as the Gandhi Society for Human Rights'. When the appropriateness of this appellation was questioned by a Church magazine, King replied, 'It is ironic yet inescapably true that the greatest Christian of the modern world was a man who never embraced Christianity.' The ideas of Martin Luther King and Gandhi became a source of inspiration to the 'Green' parties which arose in Germany, Australia, Brazil, Canada, Ireland, Japan, United States, and elsewhere. Their object is to draw attention to the environmental devastation caused by the piling up of lethal weapons and unbridled industrialism.

There is also a growing recognition of the worsening plight of the poor of the world, which was one of Gandhi's major concerns. In 1981, a remarkable manifesto was issued by 53 Nobel Prize recipients to awaken mankind to the suffering caused by the 'global holocaust' of hunger and underdevelopment. Calling upon all established authorities, national and international, to enact laws and carry out the policies that would end this holocaust, they appealed to the Gandhian legacy of non-violent action:

Although the powerful of this earth bear the greatest responsibility, they are not alone. If the helpless take their fate into their own hands, if increasing numbers refuse to obey any law other than the fundamental human right, which is the right to life, if the weak organize themselves and use ... non-violent actions exemplified by Gandhi ... it is certain that an end could be put to this catastrophe in our time.

Thirteen years later, Gandhi's crusade for inter-faith and international understanding received recognition when the UNESCO linked the observance of 1994 as the 'Year of Tolerance' with the celebration of Gandhi's 125th birth anniversary and commissioned a book on non-violence. That very year I was pleasantly surprised to receive 64 thought-provoking articles by distinguished writers from 43 countries for a commemorative volume, *Gandhi: 125 Years*, which I edited for the Indian Council for Cultural Relations.

At about the same time a Harvard scholar, Howard Gardner, wrote a book entitled *Creating Minds* in which he profiled 'seven geniuses of the modern era'—Einstein, Freud, T.S. Eliot, Stravinsky, Martha Graham,

Picasso—and Gandhi. He argued that these men not merely solved existing problems, but identified new ones.

I felt embarrassed when some foreign visitors, focusing on our celebration of the 50th year of independence, asked me: 'What is Gandhi's legacy for present-day India? Why do we hardly hear him mentioned?' I was reminded of Rabindranath Tagore's remark: 'The West will accept Gandhi before the East. For the West has gone though the cycle of dependence on force and other things for life and has become disillusioned ... The East hasn't yet gone through materialism and hence has not become disillusioned.'

The West may not yet have accepted Gandhi, but there are scores, indeed hundreds of thinking men and women in Europe and America, who are earnestly exploring and experimenting with Gandhian alternatives to help mankind out of its predicament. Nothing on that scale seems to be happening in our country, where Gandhi is universally honoured, but little understood, much less followed. One can only hope that Ivan Illich's prophecy that India may have to re-import Gandhi via the West will not come true.

TWENTY FIVE

Churchill's 'Half-naked Faqir'

Sarojini Naidu, poetess, orator, the first woman president of the Indian National Congress, and long-time member of the Congress Working Committee, was an incorrigible humorist in Gandhi's entourage. One of her oft-quoted (and misquoted) remarks was, 'It costs a lot of money to keep Gandhi in poverty.' I can well imagine Gandhi roaring with laughter when he first heard these words. Little did Sarojini Naidu know that her joke would be taken seriously and used to cast doubts on Gandhi's lifestyle.

In a recent book on the history of India's freedom movement, Patrick French, a British writer, refers to 'the giant entourage' that accompanied Gandhi during his travels, and quotes Jinnah's remark that he (Jinnah) spent less than Gandhi on his tours despite travelling first-class as he had to buy only one ticket. Jinnah travelled in style from one metropolitan town to another for his political or professional engagements; Gandhi's travels in third class were essentially part of his mass contact campaigns across the country in which he was accompanied not only by his secretary, but by other political and social workers. These journeys were an ordeal, not only for him but for the railway administration. The four or five hours' sleep which public engagements left him were often disturbed by the uncontrollable enthusiasm of the crowds that thronged railway stations at all hours of the day and night, and insisted on having his *darshan*. The railways sometimes found it convenient to accommodate him and his party in a separate third-class carriage, which, to avoid a mêlée, could be detached at a wayside station short of the destination.

Though Gandhi started travelling third-class after his return to India in 1915, it was part of the process that began in South Africa of simplifying his lifestyle. In his twenties and thirties two conflicting trends struggled in him for expression. One was the pull of convention, the desire to live up to the standard of an English-trained barrister, and the other was an inner urge towards the reduction of wants that had been inspired by the ideal of *aparigraha* (non-possession) in the Bhagavad Gita. The trend towards simplicity received a tremendous impetus in 1904 when he read Ruskin's *Unto This Last*, and opted for community life in a farm at Phoenix, a few miles from Durban. He enjoyed the change from a barrister's life to that of a peasant's life. When his public and professional work made it imperative for him to stay in Durban, and later in Johannesburg, he introduced as much austerity as he could in his household in the urban setting. He walked twelve miles a day to and back from his office in Johannesburg. His legal practice had reached a peak of £5000 a year, a lot of money then, but the struggle on behalf of his countrymen against the racist regime in South Africa left him less and less time for professional engagements. The game of making money ceased to attract him; indeed he sank all his savings in the cause to which he had committed himself. Joseph Doke, his first biographer, wrote in 1909:

Money, I think, has no charm for him. His compatriots are angry; they say he will take nothing. The money we gave him when he went as our deputy to England, he brought back to us again. The presents we gave him in Natal he handed over to our public funds. He is poor because he will be poor.

On return to India in 1915 he set up an ashram at Ahmedabad for himself and his fellow-workers who had returned with him from South Africa. Among the vows which the inmates of the ashram took were vows of truth, non-violence, and 'non-stealing', which meant that they would use minimal resources from the ashram to meet their personal needs. There were no servants there. All the inmates, including the Mahatma, were expected to share in the daily chores, such as chopping vegetables and cleaning of utensils. The emphasis was not on doctrine or ritual, but on the daily conduct of each individual. Both by precept and example, Gandhi brought home the strict moral code of the ashram to its inmates. Once there was a theft of a box belonging to his wife, Kasturba. He made this theft the subject of his talk after the evening prayers. It was evident, he said, that the thieves believed that the ashram had things worth stealing, and the members of the ashram had failed to imbue the people of the locality, including the potential thieves, with its spirit. As for Kasturba's box, what astonished him was that she possessed one. When she explained that it contained her grandchildren's clothes, he told her that it was for her children and grandchildren to mind their own clothes.

On another occasion, it came to light that a sum of four rupees given

to Kasturba by an elderly relative had not been promptly deposited by
her with the manager of the ashram, in accordance with the ashram rules.
Gandhi expressed his dismay at this incident; private possession of wealth
was inconsistent with the principles of the ashram. He took the extraordinary step of recounting the incident in his weekly paper, *Navajivan*, in
an article entitled 'My Shame and Sorrow'. It seemed Gandhi was making
a mountain out of a molehill; the amount involved was petty, and it was
probably no more than a lapse of memory on Kasturba's part in not
immediately passing on the four rupees to the ashram manager. Perhaps
the Mahatma did this deliberately to set a high standard for his disciples,
and to make it clear that no one, not even his wife, could flout the rules of
the ashram with impunity.

Gandhi's second ashram in India grew up at Segaon, a small village
near Wardha, in one of the hottest regions of the country. 'I am going to
become a villager,' he wrote on 6 July 1936 to Henry Polak, his friend and
associate of South African days. 'The place where I am writing this has a
population of about 600—no roads, no post office, no shop.' It had no
electricity either.

Louis Fischer has left a pen-picture of Gandhi at work in his thatched
mud hut in Segaon:

When I entered Gandhi's room six men in white were sitting on the floor of his
room. A woman in black saree was pulling the rope of a fan. There was only one
decoration in the room, a glass-covered black and white print of Jesus Christ, on
which were printed the words 'He is our Peace'. There was a board behind his
back and a pillow between the board and his back.

Life in Segaon was no picnic for Gandhi and his co-workers. The
monsoon had already broken; those who came to meet him picked their
way along muddy tracks, and everyone seemed to be falling ill with malaria
or typhoid or dysentery. Gandhi himself had a severe attack of malaria.
The local physician, who was treating him, panicked; he said it was imperative to move him to the civil hospital at Wardha. Gandhi was reluctant, but yielded when the doctor's advice was backed by the entreaties
of Jamnalal Bajaj. Later he regretted that he had allowed himself to be
talked into entering the hospital. He felt he had no right to go to a hospital, a facility beyond the reach of the villagers of Segaon. His illness gave
him a fresh insight into the health problems of rural India:

I rarely have fever. The last attack I had was twelve years ago and I had treated
myself. There is all the greater reason for me if I have another attack of malaria
or another ailment, not to stir out of Segaon in search of health.

My malaria has quickened my resolve to study the problem of making Segaon malaria-proof. All round me the fields are water-logged.

If I am to make my approach to village life, I must persevere in my resolve not to desert it in the hour of danger to life or limb.

There was no road from Wardha to Segaon (which came to be renamed as Sevagram), only a dusty cart track which became unusable during the rains. At first the Mahatma was not enthusiastic about a road connection with Wardha; he said he wanted the national leaders, who came to see him, to understand the problems of those who lived in villages. There was no electricity and kerosene oil was used. He tried to reduce the dependence on kerosene by suggesting the use of locally available non-edible oils for lighting lamps.

The changes that Gandhi periodically introduced in his lifestyle were partly a response to his inner urge for austerity, but they also satisfied another urge in him: to identify himself with 'the least, lowliest and the lost'. He used a stone instead of a soap for his bath, wrote his letters on little bits of paper with little stumps of pencil which he could hardly hold between his fingers; he shaved with a crude country razor, and ate his frugal meal with a wooden spoon from a prisoner's bowl. Winston Churchill called him a 'half-naked faqir'. He did not know he was paying Gandhi a compliment. The Mahatma's asceticism, however, sat lightly on him. In 1931, on his way to London, he told the customs officials at Marseilles: 'I am a poor mendicant. My earthly possessions consist of six spinning wheels, prison dishes, a can of goat's milk, six home-spun loin-cloths, and my reputation which cannot be worth much.'

TWENTY SIX

C.F. Andrews and Gandhi

'One of the greatest and best Englishmen,' was how Gandhi described C.F. Andrews. 'I have not known,' the Mahatma wrote, 'a better man or a better Christian.'[1] Rabindranath Tagore, with whom Andrews lived and worked for many years, affirmed that in no man had he seen 'such triumph of Christianity';[2] and Jawaharlal Nehru noted in his autobiography: 'India does not possess a more devoted friend than Charlie Andrews, whose abounding love and spirit of service and overflowing friendliness it is a joy to have.'[3]

It would have been a remarkable achievement for any man to have enjoyed the confidence and friendship of Gokhale, Gandhi, Tagore, and Nehru, and the affection of hundreds of thousands of Indians in this country and in far-off British colonies. It was all the more remarkable that the recipient was an Englishman during the very years when the Indian struggle for independence came to a head and relations between India and England were under unprecedented strain.

This achievement was not without its price. In his early years some of his colleagues and most of his countrymen in India considered Andrews at best a crank and at worst an apostate and a traitor. His correspondence was censored, and St Stephen's College, with which he was associated, acquired a taint of sedition. His name was struck off the list of nominees for Fellowship of Punjab University by the Lieutenant-Governor himself. His shapeless clothes and bare feet were a subject of amused comment by fellow-European passengers. Once while travelling to Kenya with Srinivasa Sastri, he noted 'an atmosphere of veiled hostility pervading the ship'. 'I have been', wrote Andrews, 'a marked man and an object of intense dislike ... It is the penalty that has to be paid and I must not grumble.' In 1921, when Andrews accused the government, with reference to the events at Chandpur in Bengal, of siding more and more 'with vested interests, with the capitalists, with the rich, with the powerful, against the poor and the oppressed', a British MP demanded in the House of Commons that 'this so-called gentleman' should be sent to England to be tried for sedition. Curiously, while Andrews was in Santiniketan, especially in the early years, a whispering campaign was started against him and he was labelled a British spy.

Such misunderstanding and misrepresentation may be taken as the inevitable lot of a man who sets out to be a reconciler between contending races and nations. Sixty years after Andrews's death it should be possible to assess his place in history more objectively. He emerges, not only as Mahatma Gandhi described him, as a great Englishman and a great Christian, but as a pioneer builder of bridges between embattled races and nations without which the future of mankind would be bleak indeed.

II

There was hardly any inkling until the age of thirty-three, when Andrews arrived in India, of the role that he was destined to play in this country. There were, however, influences that had shaped his formative years and fitted him for that role. His home background could not have been less favourable to sympathy with the Indian people. His father John Edwin Andrews was a true-blue Tory and an ardent admirer of the British Raj; one of the books which was compulsory reading for his children was *Deeds that Won the Empire*. These deeds included the successful waging of Opium Wars in China and the suppression of the Mutiny in India in 1857.

Charlie was a shy, thoughtful, and serious child, excelling in his studies and winning prizes in his school. The dominant influence in his childhood was that of his mother. 'It is because of this unchanging motherly influence,' Andrews wrote later, 'that the mother in me has grown so strong. My life seems only able to blossom into flower when I can pour out my affection upon others, as my mother did upon us.' A serious illness kept him out of vigorous outdoor games, but he learnt to amuse himself by writing articles and acquired a fluency that made him the editor of the school chronicle, and a prolific writer of letters, articles, and books. Elected to the Open Classical Scholarship at Pembroke College, Cambridge, he braced himself, as he put it, 'in the keen and biting air of Cambridge in an age of intellectual inquiry'. What marked him off from most of his contemporaries was not merely academic brilliance, but a deep religious sensitivity. His parents were devout church-goers and some of the earliest memories of young Charlie were those of choir practices he had attended and the sermons he had heard. He was barely nineteen when his father suggested that he might find his vocation in the ministry of their Church: the Catholic Apostolic Church. Andrews did not, however, feel the call, and for weeks felt torn by the conflict between duty to his father and duty to his conscience. His anguish was brought to an end by a remarkable experience which may best be described in his own words:

... as I knelt to pray before retiring to rest, the strong conviction of sin and impurity came upon me without warning, with such overpowering strength that every shred of false convention was torn aside and I knew myself as I really was. The sudden agony that followed ... broke in upon me like a lightning flash, leaving at first nothing but black darkness behind it. I buried my head in my hands and knelt there with God in an anguish of spirit that blotted out everything else and left me groping for the light ... At last a new wonderful sense of peace and forgiveness came stealing into my life at its very centre, and the tears rushed out, bringing infinite relief.[4]

The following morning he rose refreshed at half-past five and went to the Church where he felt 'the flood of God's abounding love was poured upon me like the great ocean, wave upon wave, while I knelt with bowed head to receive it'. Such an experience, which was the precursor of many others, may seem pure fantasy to some, but those who have read or heard about Christian, Hindu, and Buddhist mysticism, would at once recognize the deep springs from which Andrews drew his spiritual sustenance. Immediately, the effect of this experience was to enable him to face estrangement from his family rather than pretend an allegiance which he did not feel to his parents' Church. He needed a broader intellectual basis for his beliefs, and a closer connection between his beliefs and daily life; these he found in the teachings of Bishop Westcott of Durham and his Cambridge disciple, Charles Gore, who sought to apply the criteria of scientific inquiry to the Bible, and make the teachings of Christianity relevant to the social and economic problems of the day. 'Remember, Andrews', Bishop Westcott exhorted him, 'nothing that is truly human can be left outside the Christian faith without disturbing the very reason for its existence'.

Bishop Westcott gave a practical edge to Andrews's religion. In 1897 Andrews was ordained priest at Sandhurst Cathedral. In the course of the following two years he came face to face with poverty and degradation, drunkenness and delinquency in the slums of London. In 1899 he was elected to a Fellowship at Pembroke College, Cambridge, but was unable to settle down as a teacher of theology. Thanks to Bishop Westcott, his interest in India had been aroused, and he decided to join the Cambridge Brotherhood in Delhi and to teach at St Stephen's College.

III

Andrews arrived in India on 20 March 1904. This day he was to observe later as his 'Indian birthday'; it marked his entry into a new world of experience, and made him, as he put it, 'one of the twice-born'. One of his Cambridge contemporaries, Hibbert Ware, was the principal of St Stephen's College, but the man who was to become his most intimate friend in India was the vice-principal, Susil Kumar Rudra. 'I owe to Susil Rudra,' Andrews wrote many years later, 'what I owe to no one else in the world, the friendship which has made India from the first not a strange land, but a familiar country.'

Fortunately for Andrews, his first impressions of the country and her people were not filtered through the prism of the British Establishment in India. It is curious that most foreign missionaries assumed the superiority of their race and nation as much as the superiority of their religion; their faith in God ran parallel to their faith in the Raj. As a rule, the missionaries saw the West robed in light, and the East clothed in darkness and were pessimistic about India, a land which seemed to them overburdened with its past and afflicted by woes that only British rule could alleviate. No wonder then that most of them were upholders of constituted authority and accepted the assumptions of the ruling race in a dependency.

Shocks were in store for Andrews. In 1906, while he was the officiating Chaplain at Sanawar School for the sons and daughters of British soldiers in the Simla Hills, he invited his friend Susil Rudra to spend a few days with him. This so aroused the hostility of an English colleague that Andrews realized it would not be possible for him to put up Rudra again. While this painful incident was still weighing on his mind, he happened to see a letter in the *Civil & Military Gazette*, couched in the most contemptuous language, about educated Indians and Indian nationalists. Immediately he wrote a letter of protest to the Editor and signed it: 'C.F. Andrews, Military Chaplain, Sanawar.' The publication of this letter put him out of court with English official and non-official circles in the Punjab, but it opened to him new vistas of friendship with Indian patriots. Among those who were to extend their hand of friendship to him included Gokhale, Lajpat Rai, Ramananda Chatterjee, and Tej Bahadur Sapru.

Andrews's central thought at this time was the racial barrier that divided the European from the Indian, and even the coloured Christian

234 *In Search of Gandhi*

from the white Christian. There was a separate hostel for Christian students in St Stephen's College, and not even non-Anglicans, had a voice in its management. There were not only separate benches in parks and separate compartments in trains for Europeans, but there were even separate burial grounds for Europeans and Indians. 'The one great need', Andrews told a Christian Conference in November 1906, 'is sincere and whole-hearted personal friendships within the Christian body between men of different races.'[5] He would not hear of a European succeeding Hibbert Ware as principal, and instead threw all his weight in favour of his friend S.K. Rudra who thus became the first Indian principal of St Stephen's College. The idea seemed revolutionary at the time; the Bishop of Lahore warned that discipline in St Stephen's College was likely to deteriorate if it was headed by an Indian.

Andrews felt it was not enough to build bridges between Christians in India; he wanted a closer understanding between Christians and non-Christians. In a pamphlet entitled *India in Transition*, published in 1910, he argued that if Christianity was to succeed in India, 'it must not come forward as an antagonist and a rival to the great religious strivings of the past. It must come as a helper and fulfiller, a peacemaker and a friend. There must no longer be the desire to capture converts from Hinduism, but to come to her aid in the needful time of trouble, and to help her in the fulfilment of duties she has long neglected.'[6] Soon after he had come to Delhi, Andrews had made friends with the saintly Maulvi Zaka Ullah, the scholarly Maulvi Nazir Ahmed, and the gentle Hakim Ajmal Khan. He was deeply moved by the mystical outpourings of Swami Ram Tirath, and fascinated by the simplicity, energy, humour, and educational methods of Mahatma Munshiram, better known as Swami Shraddhananda. An English missionary fraternizing with an Arya Samaj leader was an unusual phenomenon. In 1913 Andrews spent a few weeks at Gurukul Kangri in Hardwar and paid a great tribute to Munshiram and his work. 'Here in Gurukula', he wrote in the *Modern Review* 'was the new India, the sacred stream of young Indian life nearest to its pure unsullied source.'

A few months earlier, in June 1912, Andrews had in the course of a visit to England met Rabindranath Tagore, who had not yet won the Nobel Prize, and was still on the threshold of world renown. They instantly became friends. Tagore liked the spontaneity and sincerity of the young English missionary, and Andrews was thrilled by his initiation under Tagore's guidance into the mysteries of Indian religion and philosophy. Andrews did not find it easy to return to the old grooves and thought of settling down at Santiniketan where, untrammelled by dogma or allegiance to any institution, he could interpret Eastern thought to the West, and Christianity to the East. By a strange coincidence, just at the time when he was at the crossroads of his career, he was to meet the man who was to provide him with the framework for his work during the next twenty-five years.

IV

In the closing months of 1913, the Indian struggle in South Africa under Gandhi's leadership reached a critical stage. Gokhale summoned the last reserves of his failing health and toured India to collect funds and educate public opinion on the heroic resistance of the Indian minority in South Africa. He was in constant touch with the Viceroy, Lord Hardinge, who scandalized the South African government and the British Cabinet by publicly drawing attention to the atrocities committed against the Indian satyagrahis. General Smuts and his colleagues were embarrassed and hinted at the possibilities of a compromise; they appointed an Enquiry Commission, but Gandhi refused to have anything to do with it. Lord Hardinge deputed Sir Benjamin Robertson, a senior British member of the I.C.S. to South Africa and at the same time urged Gokhale to use his moderating influence on Gandhi.

Andrews had nurtured great admiration and respect for Gokhale ever since he had met him at the Calcutta Congress in 1906. In his very first letter to Gokhale, he had written: 'If at any time there is any way you can suggest in which I can help the national cause, you know how glad I shall be to do so if it is within my power.'[7] The opportunity came in 1913. In response to Gokhale's appeal, Andrews not only brought out all his capital (£300) for the Indians in South Africa, but offered to go there. 'Your wire', Gokhale told Andrews, 'was like a gift of God. We need you in South Africa.' Accompanied by his friend W.W. Pearson, Andrews sailed for Natal in December and landed at Durban on 1 January 1914. He had never seen Gandhi. He was introduced to a slight ascetical figure dressed in a white dhoti and kurta such as the indentured labourers in Natal wore. With a sudden upsurge of emotion Andrews bent down and touched Gandhi's feet. This spontaneous gesture horrified the local European community. The editor of a Durban newspaper came to see him to expostulate in person: 'Really you know Mr. Andrews, really you know, we don't *do* that sort of thing in Natal, we don't do it, Mr. Andrews. I consider the action most unfortunate, *most* unfortunate.' 'They boil over with indignation', wrote Andrews to Tagore, 'that *I an Englishman*, mind you, should have touched the feet of an Asiatic. When I remind them that Christ, St. Paul and St. John were Asiatics, they grow restive and say that things were altogether different then.'[8]

Andrews's role in the negotiations was commended by Gandhi, who in a cable to Gokhale described the final settlement as the joint work of Andrews and himself. Andrews's contribution was certainly more, much more substantial than that of Sir Benjamin Robertson, the representative of the Viceroy, who proved more of a liability than an asset to the Indians.

The negotiations were long and difficult. General Smuts had his own difficulties; he had to carry his colleagues and party with him on the explosive issue of race, and it was not easy to make Gandhi budge from a position once he had taken it. 'You know', Andrews confided to Gokhale, 'how every point becomes with Gandhi a matter of principle to live or die for and it was extremely difficult to separate the chaff from the grain and to lay down what was worth fighting for and what was not.'[9] The strain on Andrews must have been immense; while these negotiations dragged on, his mother fell seriously ill and died in England.

Andrews's South African adventure, besides rewarding him with Gandhi's friendship, was a highly educative experience for him. 'South Africa will be a shock to your Christianity,' Gokhale had warned him. The issue of the 'white race domination', as he called it, had been weighing on Andrews's mind since the first few weeks of his stay in India, but in South Africa he saw it in its most blatant form. It seemed to him, however, that the situation in South Africa was only the exaggerated symptom of a widespread malady. He became convinced that deep-seated racial hatreds could only be purged by religious insight. That is why he devoted a good deal of his time and energy during the following two decades to the problems of Indians living abroad. He visited Fiji, Uganda, Kenya, Zanzibar, Guiana, South Africa, Canada; indeed every country where Indian immigrant communities were struggling for survival. To him it was not simply a question of doing away with the needless humiliations and hardships suffered by a few hundred thousand Indians in British colonies, but a test of professed principles of the British Empire and indeed of Christianity. If the Indian subjects of the British Empire could not enjoy even elementary civic rights, 'did the Empire make any sense?' he asked. How could the Western nations profess Christianity and still treat Asiatics and Africans as if they were members of a subhuman species? Andrews's compassion was not, however, reserved for the Indian immigrants overseas. While he fought for the rights of Indian immigrants in Africa, he had the foresight to advise them not to concentrate too much on money-making, but to identify themselves with the aspirations of the African majority, and indeed to view every problem from the Africans' point of view. If the Indians in the former British colonies in Africa had heeded Andrews's advice, it is likely that they would have been spared much of the uncertainty and hardship they suffered in later years.

Andrews would not countenance racial discrimination even if, for once, it discriminated in favour of the Indians. In the winter of 1929–30, while touring the United States, he opposed the Copeland Bill which proposed to admit Indians to the United States on an equal footing with the Europeans on the score of their Aryan blood. 'I am against it,' Andrews wrote to Jehangir Petit; 'it is racial in principle, and it would not help non-Aryan Southern India. I am trying instead for a quota system into which racial distinctions do not enter.'[10] No one would doubt the soundness of Andrews's view today, but many Indians in America were furious at what they described as Andrews's 'idealistic humbug', and went to the length of questioning his sincerity, and accusing him of taking his cue from the British Embassy in Washington.[11]

V

It is significant that Andrews had taken no interest in English politics until the age of thirty-three, and even in India in his early years as a Christian missionary and a teacher, his principal preoccupation was with the promotion of better ties between the races, rather than with direct participation in public affairs. There were moments, however, when he felt the fundamental contradiction in his own position in India as a Christian and as an Englishman. 'While I have meditated,' he wrote, 'I have said to myself again and again in silence: How can you, an Englishman who love your own freedom and independence as an Englishman refuse to allow the same freedom and the very same independence to every Indian?' It was not the political, but the moral and spiritual side of the issue of Indian independence that attracted him. No one knew better than Andrews himself that he was not cut out for the role of a politician. He was happiest when he was at his desk at Santiniketan answering letters, drafting memoranda, teaching children, or watching them scamper in or out of his room. 'All my life through', he wrote in 1920, 'I have been a scholar and a thinker and a reader of books—eager indeed at every turn to put thought to the test of action, but constitutionally unwilling and unable to take a lead in such action except on very rare occasions. Whenever such occasions have arisen, I have instinctively shrunk back as quickly as possible, because I have felt the political life to be something apart from my own.'[12]

Andrews's correspondence with Gokhale during the years 1906–7 shows that, while his sympathy lay unmistakably with the nationalist cause, he was not eager to enter the fray. When Lajpat Rai was deported in 1907, Andrews wrote to Lord Minto, the Viceroy, warning him of the effects of this action on Indian opinion. Lord Minto's successor, Lord Hardinge, was more receptive to Andrews; he heard him preach at Simla, and was glad to get his frank and uninhibited views on public questions. When the war broke out in 1914 Andrews pleaded for the grant of the King's Commission to Indians. 'There is nothing in the world that Indian students of the noblest type feel more bitterly', he wrote to Lord Hardinge, 'than this refusal to recognize their manhood.'[13] Here again Andrews was not overtly taking part in politics, but fighting against racial discrimination. His visit to South Africa had also been part of the same campaign.

It was only with the emergence of Mahatma Gandhi in Indian politics that Andrews's real identification with the nationalist struggle begins. Unlike other British friends of India, such as A.O. Hume, William Wedderburn, Henry Cotton, and Annie Besant, Andrews did not hold any office or preside over the Indian National Congress. He preferred to remain in the background, as a friend, philosopher, and constructive critic, eager to interpret, to be useful, and to undertake such assignments as were entrusted to him. In 1919 the news of the Jallianwala Bagh tragedy and the imposition of martial law drew him to the Punjab, but he was taken off the train at Amritsar, put under military arrest, and sent back to Delhi from where he returned to Santiniketan and was with Rabindranath Tagore when he renounced his knighthood. A few months later, Andrews was able to enter Punjab and collect information for the Malaviya Committee which was to be placed before the Hunter Commission of Inquiry. What he saw and heard about the Punjab tragedy left him aghast. 'It was a massacre, a butchery ...', he wrote to Mahadev Desai, 'I feel that if only I could take each single Englishman and show him out of my own eyes what I have seen, he would feel the same as I.'[14] The events of 1919 sharpened the lines of racial cleavage. The British persuaded themselves to believe that they had narrowly escaped the horrors of another mutiny; the Indians were equally convinced that they were innocent victims of an insensitive and draconian regime. A Cambridge-educated English missionary hobnobbing with Indian politicians was an outrageous spectacle to his compatriots. Once he was refused entry to a Christian church: 'This House of God', they told him, 'is not for rebels.'[15]

Andrews urged Sir Edward Maclagan, the new Lieutenant-Governor to apply the soothing balm to Punjab. To the people of the province he counselled patience and forgiveness. Addressing a public meeting in Lahore's Bradlaugh Hall on 15 November 1919, he urged the people 'not to dwell upon vengeance, not to linger in the dark night of hate but to come out in the glorious sunshine, of God's love'. The root of the mischief, he perceived, was in the unnatural relationship between the rulers and ruled, and this relationship had to be transformed if goodwill was to be restored between the two countries. Andrews revealed his startling deduction from the Punjab tragedy in a letter to the Editor of the *Indian Daily News*: 'Sir,— Having witnessed with my own eyes the humiliation of Indians, I can see no possible recovery of self-respect except by claiming an independence from British domination not less than that of Egypt. This requires absolute unity of moral purpose for its fulfilment, not compromise or concession.'[16] He elaborated his ideas in a series of articles. 'I am aware', he wrote, 'that the idea of complete Indian independence is still regarded with suspicion even by very many Indians themselves. The outlook is too adventurous for them; it takes their breath away,—just as a boy who is a weak swimmer stands shivering on the brink before making the final plunge.'[17]

Jawaharlal Nehru recalls in his autobiography that when he read Andrews's essay: 'Indian independence—The Immediate Need', he felt not only that it made out an unanswerable case for independence, but mirrored the inmost recesses of the hearts of the Indian people. 'The deep urge that moved us and our half-formed desires', writes Nehru, 'seemed to take clear shape in his simple and earnest language ... It was wonderful that C.F. Andrews, a foreigner and one belonging to the dominant race in India, should echo that cry of our inmost being.'[18]

As the non-cooperation movement gathered momentum, Andrews watched it with mingled hope and anxiety. He was glad to see the signs of a new political awakening, but he was disturbed by what seemed to him a subtle suggestion of violence in the bonfires of foreign cloth. Indeed, the whole atmosphere seemed to him charged with 'a wild political excitement' rather than with that deep moral conviction he had witnessed in Gandhi's following in South Africa in 1914. The Chauri Chaura tragedy in 1922 confirmed his worst fears and his heart went out to the Mahatma when he called off civil disobedience. Andrews understood what many of Gandhi's colleagues and virtually all his opponents could not quite understand, that Gandhi was in dead earnest about non-violence and would not be diverted from it for immediate political gains. Later, while he was in England, Andrews was told by the Archbishop of Canterbury that Gandhi had been arrested by the British government in March 1922 because he had given up non-violent resistance and taken to violence. 'If you forsake

Christianity', Andrews replied to the Archbishop, 'Gandhi will forsake non-violence.'[19]

It did not require a major satyagraha campaign to stir Andrews into action. There were any number of causes that demanded his attention: the fight against opium and drug traffic, relief to victims of riots, famines, or earthquakes, mediation on behalf of workers in tea plantations, jute factories, and railway workshops. Once he had visitors from Rajasthan who told him about forced labour (*begar*) prevalent in some Rajasthan states. He could not sleep that night: he had another cause to champion. Exploitation in any form was repugnant to him whether it was *begar* in the Simla hills or the employment of ten-year-old boys down the manholes of Calcutta to clean the sewers.

It is indeed remarkable that the politics and economics of this man of faith were ahead of those of many professed radicals. Detecting in Jawaharlal Nehru's writings a welcome awareness of the importance of the economic factor in nationalist politics, Andrews wrote to him suggesting concentration on definite economic objectives such as de-linking the rupee from sterling, immediate Indian control over land revenue and railway policy, currency, customs, and banking. 'I always wonder,' Andrews added, 'whether in the face of the utter misery of our *ryot*s in India, who are sinking lower and lower into debt and misery; the first and foremost thing to lay united stress upon, is that economic freedom, which will help all religious communities alike and draw them closer together, rather than this abstract political freedom which seems at once to divide us all up into separate compartments, making us disunited and eager to get the loaves and fishes.'[20]

Despite his clear perception of India's political goals and methods, Andrews's participation in the nationalist struggle was indirect and behind the scenes, through letters, articles, books, and meetings with officials and non-officials in India and England. Despite the continual touring and endless assignments he took upon himself, it is amazing that he should have written twenty-five books, edited another five, besides numerous essays and articles on topical subjects. The two major themes in his writings are Christianity and India. Even the recitation of the titles of his books would indicate the versatility of his interests. His first book was *The Relationship of Christianity and the Conflict between Labour and Capital* published in 1896, and one of his last books in collaboration with Girija Mookerjee, was *The Rise and Growth of the Congress in India* (1938). In between came, *The Renaissance in India* (1912), *The Opium Evil in India* (1926), *Zaka Ullah of Delhi* (1929), *India and the Simon Report* (1930),

India and Britain—A Moral Challenge (1935), *Thoughts from Tagore* (1928), *Mahatma Gandhi's Ideas* (1929), *India and the Pacific* (1932), *What I Owe to Christ* (1932), and others. Andrews's great opportunity came in 1931 when the Mahatma went to England for the Round Table Conference. He acted not only as the 'door keeper-in-chief' at Kingsley Hall where Gandhi stayed, but arranged for him to meet some of the best minds in England. The Round Table Conference proved a failure, but Andrews's efforts did not go entirely in vain. As he wrote at the time: 'Gandhi's unique personality gripped the best English minds, and his originality of thought set those whom he met thinking as they had never done before. They were not always in agreement with him; but they all immensely respected the greatness of soul which they found in him ... England is a very small country and impressions like these go round fast indeed. No serious-minded man or woman could any longer take the view, which had been widely held before, that Mahatma Gandhi was an impossible fanatic after all.'

By the early thirties Andrews had lived down much of the ridicule and suspicion in England, and earned the respect, if not the agreement, of influential men in Whitehall and Fleet Street. This influence, which was later skilfully exercised by his friends and disciples such as Agatha Harrison and Horace Alexander to an increasing degree, enabled him to bestir the British ministers and thus to hasten the decision-making process that enabled Gandhi to end his fasts in 1932 and 1933. Andrews did not always agree on the merits of the fasts, but he knew how deeply the Mahatma felt on those issues and how important it was to save his life and let India breathe again.

VI

It is tempting to think of C.F. Andrews as a noble, self-effacing person, a great humanitarian rushing to trouble-spots hit by famines, earthquakes, riots, or strikes; virtually functioning, if one may say so, as a one-man Red Cross squad. Admirable as this work was, Andrews's place in history really lies in his having the foresight to see, at the turn of the century, what few Europeans could see: that India was astir, that the racial gulf had to be bridged, and Indo-British relations built on a basis of equality and friendship in the interest of both countries. He drew his dynamic not from books and manifestoes, but from deep spiritual springs which were continually renewed by observation, introspection, and meditation. This 'God's Own Fool', as Edwin Montagu once graphically described him, could see farther and deeper than the 'experts' on India who had turned grey in the service of the Empire. By 1914 Andrews had outgrown the framework of the English Establishment in India of which, as a Christian missionary and educationist, he was expected to be a part. His encounter with Gandhi did not come a day too soon; Gandhi provided the goal and defined the method which Andrews's Christian conscience could endorse.

If Andrews needed a Gandhi, Gandhi also needed an Andrews. The basic assumption of satyagraha was that it was possible through self-suffering to change the heart of the adversary, and that the enemy of today could be the friend of tomorrow. In the nationalist context, the inference was that the British could be persuaded, through non-violent resistance, to voluntarily shed their imperial burden. This assumption seemed fantastic to most Indians and almost all Britons eighty years ago, but it was something for Gandhi's following that they saw at least one Englishman who shared this idealism. One swallow does not make a summer; one Andrews did not change the basic alignments of contending forces in India between imperialism and nationalism. For many years Andrews was no more than a symbol, but such a symbol was an asset to a mass movement; particularly one which posed the issues on the moral plane and needed to sterilize anger and hatred as much as possible in its adherents. On his part, Andrews, deeply rooted in English culture and Christianity, never ceased to believe in or work for an Indo–British accord. From his deathbed in Calcutta in 1940 he reaffirmed his conviction that Britain's best instincts and best interests would soon drive her to a settlement with nationalist India. It was not until seven years later that the British political élite was reconciled to this conclusion. Meanwhile, for two decades C.F. Andrews had performed the historic function of serving, if I may quote Gandhi again, as a 'living link' between India and Britain.

NOTES AND REFERENCES

1. *Visva-Bharati News*, vol. VIII, no. 12, 1940, p. 90.
2. Ibid., vol. VIII, no. 10, p. 76.
3. Jawaharlal Nehru, *An Autobiography* (London, 1936), p. 375.
4. Benarsidas Chaturvedi and Marjorie Sykes, *Charles Freer Andrews, A Narrative* (London, 1949), p. 12.
5. Ibid., p. 66.
6. Ibid., p. 63.
7. C.F. Andrews to Gokhale, 24 Jan. 1906, Gokhale Papers.
8. C.F. Andrews to Tagore, 6 Jan. 1914, quoted in Benarsidas Chaturvedi and Marjorie Sykes, op.cit., p. 98.

9. C.F. Andrews to Gokhale, 30 Jan. 1914, Gokhale Papers.

10. Benarsidas Chaturvedi and Marjorie Sykes, op.cit., n. 4, p. 245.

11. Ibid., p. 247.

12. C.F. Andrews, *The claim for Independence within or without the British Empire* (Madras, n.d.), pp. 13–14.

13. C.F. Andrews to Lord Hardinge, 10 Dec. 1914, Hardinge Papers.

14. C.F. Andrews to Mahadev Desai, 6 Oct. 1919, Gandhi Papers.

15. Benarsidas Chaturvedi and Marjorie Sykes, op.cit., p. 137.

16. Ibid., p. 155.

17. C.F. Andrews, *see* n. 12, p. 6.

18. Jawaharlal Nehru, *see* n. 3, p. 66.

19. Mahadev Desai, *Diary* (Hindi), (Varanasi, 1966), p. 136.

20. C.F. Andrews to Jawaharlal Nehru, 13 Nov. 1933, Nehru Papers.

TWENTY SEVEN

The Film Gandhi

The award of eight Oscars to *Gandhi* marks the triumph of Richard Attenborough's twenty years' odyssey 'in search of Gandhi'. Film juries have their own criteria for distinguishing the numerous skills which go into the making of a great film. There is, however, an impression in the film world that the award is a tribute as much to the technical excellence of the film, as to its great 'theme'; that Gandhi's charisma influenced the judges no less than the achievement of Attenborough and his team.

'A film that staggers the mind and feeds the soul,' wrote the film critic of *New York Post*. If hard-headed critics can be swept off their feet, it is not difficult to understand why the ordinary film-goer has succumbed to the charm of *Gandhi*. Curiously, the very elements in the film that jar on historians and biographers have contributed to its popularity. The selection of a few episodes in Gandhi's life, the tampering with chronology, the telescoping of events, the injection of just a little fiction into the hard facts of history, the simplification of complex issues, have all helped to narrow the focus and to heighten the emotional impact. Some of the inaccuracies could have been eliminated without reducing the impact of the film, but there is no doubt that in its total effect the film succeeds in providing vivid glimpses of Gandhi's role in South Africa and India, his vision, his deep humanism, his 'combination of infinite love and infinite patience', his total commitment to public causes, his humour and his serenity in the most adverse circumstances. The twenty years that elapsed between the conception of the project and its execution also seem to have worked in its favour. Most of the viewers of the film today were not even born in 1948 when Gandhi was assassinated. They have grown up in the midst of economic discontent, social upheaval, and political cynicism in a world plagued with numerous 'small wars' and haunted by the nightmare of a nuclear holocaust. This generation can hardly believe that, not long ago, within the living memory of their parents, there was a man who successfully defied the mightiest Empire of the time without hatred and without violence.

The interest in Gandhi which Attenborough's film has triggered in the West is a heartening phenomenon. It is, however, not for the first time that the significance of the Mahatma's message has been discovered. Prescient observers saw his world mission even in those early years when he was still emerging as the dominant figure in Indian politics. The French savant, Romain Rolland, in his famous essay on Gandhi wrote in 1924: 'The Apostle of India is the Apostle of the world ... He is one of us. The battle that the Mahatma began fighting four years ago is our battle.' Fourteen years later, as the world was trembling on the brink of the Second World War, John Middleton Murry described Gandhi 'as the greatest Christian teacher in the modern world', and declared that he saw 'absolutely no hope for western civilization except the kindling of a vast and consuming flame of Christian love. The choice appears to be between that or a mass murder on a scale at which the imagination sickens.'

Gandhi instigated, if he did not initiate, three momentous revolutions of the twentieth century: the revolutions against racialism, against colonialism, and against violence. He lived long enough to see a measure of success achieved by the first two revolutions, but the third, the revolution against violence, which was nearest to his heart, has yet scarcely got underway. Gandhi knew that it was no easy task to change the minds and hearts of men. In his own campaigns of non-violent resistance in South Africa and India, he had continually to reckon with scepticism, ridicule, and opposition not only from his opponents, but sometimes from some of his close adherents, who discounted his politics as romantic and argued that force would only yield to force.

Gandhi discarded violence not only because an unarmed people had little prospect in waging an armed rebellion, but because he regarded violence as a clumsy weapon, which created more problems than it solved, and left a trail of bitterness in which real reconciliation was impossible. His emphasis on non-violence jarred alike on his British and Indian critics. To the former, it was a camouflage; to the latter it was sentimentalism. Those who questioned the efficacy of non-violent resistance were too prone to apply to it yardsticks pertinent to violent warfare. Satyagraha did not aim at destroying the enemy, but at setting in motion forces that could lead to his conversion; with such a strategy it was perfectly possible to lose all the battles and still win the war. Indeed, victory or defeat do not adequately describe the true object of a satyagraha struggle: a peace honourable to both parties. Gandhi's battles were waged on the moral, or what is the same thing, the psychological plane. 'I have found Englishmen', he wrote, 'amenable to reason and persuasion, and as they always wish to appear just, it is easier to shame them than others into doing the right thing.' The process of conversion at which Gandhi aimed was two fold; Indians no less than the British needed a change of heart.

Gandhi's ideas were the very antithesis of Marx and Freud. He questioned the almost universal belief that the essence of civilization consisted in the endless multiplication of wants. He foresaw the dangers of runaway technology and indiscriminate industrialization, and warned against the hazards to the environment long before ecological concern became a fashion. He deeply distrusted the ever-growing apparatus of the modern state, 'a soulless machine' as he termed it. He was no defender of the status quo in politics or economics, but he believed in the possibility of resolving social conflicts through non-violent techniques. He believed the construction of a just society was fundamentally the construction of a new type of human being: 'You cannot plant a thorn tree and expect it to bear mangoes', he said. He had an unshakeable faith in the spirit of man and in the power of love: 'The hardest fibre must melt in the fire of love. If it does not melt, it is because the fire is not strong enough.'

Gandhi had no illusions about the built-in resistance to his ideas in the modern world. He once said that satyagraha was at the same stage of development as electricity in the days of Edison.

Stanley Jones, an American missionary, asked Gandhi in 1924 to give a message to the Western world on how to live a Christian life. Gandhi thought for a moment and answered: 'Such a message cannot be given by word of mouth, it can only be lived. All I can do is to try to live it—that will be my message.'

Nearly sixty years later, a vivid recreation of that remarkable life came to millions of people in the world through the cinematograph. One can only hope that the curiosity the film has kindled will not prove to be a passing phenomenon; that it would provoke a serious interest in the life, thought, and methods of the only humane revolutionary of our age. The film *Gandhi*, as a British paper aptly put it, is not the last word on Gandhi; it may well be the first.

TWENTY EIGHT

Gandhi and Non-violence

Gandhi was the greatest exponent of the doctrine of ahimsa or non-violence in modern times, but he was not its author. Ahimsa has been part of the Indian religious tradition for centuries: Hindu, Jain, and Buddhist. It was Gandhi's genius that transformed, what had been an individual ethic, into a tool of social and political action. This he did in the course of his twenty-year long struggle against racialism in South Africa. Since 1894 he had been pleading with the colonial regime for the removal of iniquitous curbs and disabilities from which Indian immigrants in Natal and Transvaal suffered. He made little headway. In 1906 an exceptionally humiliating law was enacted for registration of Indians in the Transvaal; Gandhi found he had reached a dead end. The colonial government in Pretoria, supported by the dominant European community, was adamant; the Government of India was indifferent, and the imperial government in London reluctant to intervene. A stage was reached in Gandhi's agitation when something more than reasoning and persuasion were demanded. It was at this critical juncture that he stumbled upon a new technique of fighting social and political injustice. He called it satyagraha (holding on to truth). Its principles were to gradually evolve in the ensuing years; its author was a man for whom theory was the handmaiden of action. Of one thing Gandhi had no doubt; it was to be a method without hatred and without violence. During the next eight years he used this method with a measure of success until 1914 when he reached an agreement with the South African government and left for India. It was as the author and sole practitioner of satyagraha that he entered the Indian political scene in 1919–20, which he was to dominate for the next three decades.

If the Indian National Congress had not accepted his basic tenet of non-violence in 1920, he would have had nothing to do with its struggle for liberation from British rule. 'I would like to repeat to the world, times without number', Gandhi said in 1931, 'that I will not purchase my country's freedom at the cost of non-violence.' Nine years later, in the midst of the Second World War, when he was asked what he would do if India became independent during his lifetime, he replied: 'If India became free in my lifetime and I have still energy left in me ... I would take my due share, though outside the official world, in building up the nation strictly on non-violent lines.' We must remember that Gandhi applied his method of non-violent resistance not only against foreign rule, but against social evils such as racial discrimination and untouchability. Indeed, he claimed that non-violence lay at the root of every one of his activities, and his mission in life was not merely the freedom of India but the brotherhood of man. His satyagraha was designed not only for India, but for the whole world; it could transform relations between individuals, as well as between communities and nations. In the early 1920s, when he had just emerged as the stoutest champion of nationalism in Asia, Gandhi unequivocally subscribed to the ideal of a world federation. 'The better mind of the world desires today', he told the Belgaum Congress in 1924, 'not absolutely independent states warring against each other but a federation of friendly interdependent states.' In the late 1930s, when the forces of violence were gathering momentum in Europe, he re-affirmed his faith in non-violence. Through the pages of his weekly paper, *Harijan*, he expounded his approach to political tyranny and military aggression. He advised weaker nations to defend themselves by offering non-violent resistance to the aggressor. A non-violent Abyssinian, he argued, needed no arms and no succour from the League of Nations; if every Abyssinian man, woman, and child refused cooperation with the Italians, willing or forced, the latter would have to walk to victory over the dead bodies of their victims and to occupy their country without the people. The motive power of Nazi and Fascist aggression was the desire to carve out new empires, and behind it all was a ruthless competition to annex new sources of raw materials and fresh markets. In Gandhi's opinion, wars were thus rooted in the overweening greed of men as also in the purblind tribalism that placed nationalism above humanity. In the ultimate analysis, to shake off militarism, it was necessary to end the competitive greed and fear and hatred which fed it.

Gandhi's pleas for renunciation of violence and for non-violent resistance to aggressors fell on deaf ears; they were dismissed as the outpourings of a visionary. The Second World War lasted six years and took a heavy toll of human lives, but the Allied victory did not usher in the era of peace for which the world had longed. Gandhi was shocked by the use of the atom bomb by the United States of America against Japan: he described it 'as the most diabolical use of science'. When Jawaharlal Nehru came to see him in 1945, Gandhi closely questioned him about the atom bomb: its manufacture, its capacity to kill and poison, and its toll on Japanese cities. Nehru recalled later that Gandhi listened to him silently, and then, 'with deep human compassion loading his gentle eyes, remarked that this wanton destruction had confirmed his faith in God and non-violence, and that now he [Gandhi] realized the full significance of the holy mission for which God had created him and armed him with the mantra of non-violence'. According to Nehru as Gandhi uttered these words he 'had a look of revelation about his eyes' and he resolved then and there to make it his mission to fight and outlaw the bomb. Gandhi was assassinated in January 1948. The following year, when Nehru visited the United States, he related his conversation with Gandhi to Albert Einstein. With a twinkle in his eyes, the great scientist took a pad and pencil and wrote down a number of dates on one side, and events on the other, to indicate the parallel evolution of the nuclear bomb and Gandhi's non-violent technique of satyagraha respectively, almost from decade to decade since the beginning of the twentieth century. It turned out that, by a strange coincidence, while Einstein and his fellow scientists were engaged in researches that made the fission of the atom possible, Gandhi was embarking on his experiments in peaceful, non-violent resistance in South Africa and India; indeed, the 'Quit India' struggle almost coincided with the American project for the making of the atomic bomb.

II

Gandhi's great achievement was to evolve and practise a non-violent method for conflict-resolution at the beginning of the twentieth century, which proved to be the most violent century in the annals of mankind. In the first half of the century, which almost synchronized with Gandhi's entire public life, there were two devastating world wars with a colossal loss of life. In the second half we were spared the catastrophe of a third world war, but the 'cold war' between two rival ideological-cum-military blocs brought the world to the verge of an atomic holocaust: only a 'balance of terror' between them kept the peace. However, their rivalry led to localized conflicts, instigated or fanned by the Superpowers, largely in Third World countries. In 1995, the then Secretary-General of the United Nations estimated that between 1945 and 1994 there had been 127 conflicts with 22 million casualties in comparison to 88 conflicts during the first half of the century. Gandhi offered a non-violent alternative to this recurring cycle of hatred and violence. Beginning his public life in the hostile environment of South Africa, he discovered that in an imperfect and changing world, conflicts of interests within and between countries were inevitable. His technique of satyagraha sought reconciliation through dialogue and compromise, but if justice was denied, it provided for a confrontation, but it had to be a non-violent confrontation. *Webster's Third New International Dictionary* aptly sums up this technique as one of 'achieving social and political reform by means of tolerance and active goodwill coupled with firmness in one's cause expressed through non-violence, passive resistance and non-cooperation.'

Gandhi rejected the common belief that force yields only to force. The principle of 'an eye for an eye', he said, 'would end up with the whole world becoming blind'. He conceded that in our present state human beings are 'partly men and partly beasts', but he believed that man's nature is not essentially evil. He did not divide mankind into two opposite categories of good and bad; there were only evil acts, and even in the wickedest of men, there was a better side, a latent spark. Gandhi's critics, however, tended to dismiss his views as the impractical idealism of a visionary which had no relevance for the modern world. In February 1938 Frances Gunther, the wife of John Gunther the American journalist, and author of the best-seller *Inside Asia Today*, wrote to Jawaharlal Nehru that she told Lord Linlithgow, the then Viceroy of India, that Gandhi had brought Indians up from the tenth to the nineteenth century but it was Nehru's task to carry them from the nineteenth to the twentieth. She was not alone in thinking that Gandhi's ideas were antediluvian and suited to a pre-industrial, and pre-modern society. Most intellectuals not only in the West but in India would have endorsed her verdict. It does not seem to have occurred to them that Gandhi may have been thinking ahead of his time.

III

It was only in the latter half of the twentieth century that Gandhi's methods came to be invoked across the globe, in Asia, Africa, America, and Europe. In South Africa, the African National Congress carried on non-violent agitation and passive resistance for nearly forty years. Chief Albert Luthuli, the president of the ANC and a Nobel Peace Prize laureate, belonged to the Zulu warrior tribe, but was inspired by Gandhi's writings and became a champion of non-violence. The ANC was, however, unable to sustain its non-violent struggle in the face of ruthless oppression by the apartheid regime. After the massacre of Sharpeville and until the release of Nelson Mandela, the major liberation movement in South Africa took to guerilla warfare. However, the armed struggle would have been much more difficult and prolonged had not students, industrial workers, religious leaders, youth, and women's organizations joined in non-violent resistance to the racist regime on such issues as rent, consumer embargoes, and bus boycotts. Thus the liberators of the blacks in South Africa were not only the guerilla fighters, but hundreds of thousands of men, women, and children, shop assistants, and workers living in shanty towns who consciously or unconsciously adopted methods which Gandhi would have approved.

In the United States Gandhi's teachings and example inspired Martin Luther King Jr., a Baptist minister, who was able, in the words of an American writer,[1] to 'meld the image of Gandhi and the image of the Negro preacher, and to use biblical symbols that bypassed cerebral centres and exploded in the well of the Negro psyche'. King championed the non-violent method as a practical alternative not only to armed conflicts within a country but between countries. 'The choice', he wrote in his *Stride Towards Freedom* (1958), 'is no longer between violence and non-violence. It is either non-violence or non-existence.'

The last two decades of the twentieth century witnessed some spectacular demonstrations of 'peoples' power' to non-violently resist colonial rule, foreign domination, racial discrimination, and tyrannical regimes. In the Czech Republic and Poland, the Baltic States, the Philippines, and several other countries, unarmed men and women collectively dared to defy the might of the modern state. In Poland, Lech Walesa, the leader of the 'Solidarity' movement, acknowledged that he derived his insights from his study of Gandhi's campaigns. He skilfully alternated disciplined and peaceful strikes with negotiations. He was one of the first to be clapped into prison from where he sent out earnest appeals to his countrymen to refrain from violence. His struggle had its vicissitudes, but by 1989 Poland became the first country in eastern Europe to free itself from Soviet domination.

In Czechoslovakia a massive non-violent protest in 1968 fizzled out, but twenty one years later, on 17 November 1989, a spontaneous upsurge against Soviet occupation turned into the largest demonstration in the history of the country. Hundreds of demonstrators were injured when the security forces charged the crowd. Over a hundred thousand marchers gathered in Wenceslas Square in Prague, sat down on the road, and sang nursery rhymes. They held candles and waved flags. Their leader Vaclav Havel, speaking in virtually the Gandhian idiom, exhorted them to refrain from violence. A 'Civic Forum' emerged, which incorporated all opposition groups and avowed its commitment to non-violence. Havel paid a tribute to the students of Czechoslovakia who had thrown themselves into 'the non-violent struggle for giving this revolution a beautiful, peaceful, dignified, gentle, and I would say, loving face, which is admired by the whole world'. This was, he declared, 'a rebellion of truth against lies, of purities against impurities, of the human heart against violence'. The Prague demonstration had a chain reaction across the country. Protests and participants grew daily. Thousands of strike committees were formed. Peaceful crowds, holding nothing but candles and flowers, were beaten up by truncheon-wielding police. In the words of Mary E. King, the author of *Gandhi and Martin Luther King Jr.* (UNESCO, 1999), the people of Czechoslovakia enacted 'the power of Truth, as Gandhi had defined it, as Havel interpreted it'. On 7 December the Prime Minister of the Communist government resigned. On 10 December a government of 'national understanding' was announced. By the end of the December 1989, the Soviet-dominated regime had surrendered and the Federal Assembly had elected Havel, as the president of Czechoslovakia.

Another striking victory of non-violence was witnessed in Philippines as a result of which the despotic and corrupt regime of President Ferdinand Marcos was overthrown. Marcos threw into the prison one of the protagonists of democracy and his chief rival, Senator Beniquo Acquino. In prison Acquino pored over the Bible and the writings of Gandhi and was converted to the creed of non-violence. When he returned home after three years of self-exile, he was assassinated. His death galvanized the country and paved the way for a non-violent struggle. The crisis came in 1986 in the wake of a fraudulent election conducted by the Ferdinand Marcos's government, which enraged the people. On 22 February, two army generals with their troops defected. This was followed by an amazing scene. Three million men, women and children, many of them praying, poured into the streets to protect the defecting soldiers from the advancing tanks and troops sent by Marcos. The atmosphere became so electric that some of Marcos's soldiers joined the rebellious troops. This confrontation between the armed forces and unarmed people lasted for 77 hours till the Marcos regime crumbled.

IV

Gandhi's ideas have fuelled not only struggles against foreign domination and tyrannical rule, but also crusades against the piling up of nuclear weapons and the havoc being wrought by developed countries through wanton and wasteful use of the resources of the planet. Petra Kelly, a leader of the Green Peace movement in Germany who was influenced by the ideas of Martin Luther King and Gandhi, denounced methods of production which depended upon a ceaseless supply of raw materials and were leading to the exhaustion of natural resources and threatening ecological devastation. Speaking almost in the Gandhian idiom, she said, 'We cannot solve any political problem, without also addressing spiritual ones.'

Despite these examples of non-violent struggles over the past two decades, which have highlighted the power potential of the oppressed, it must be admitted that Gandhi's ideas and methods are still appreciated by only a small enlightened minority in the world. Gandhi himself had no illusions about their ready acceptance. He did not claim finality for his views, which he regarded within a broad ethical framework as aids for bettering the lives of his fellow men; they could be altered if they did not work. Though he expounded his philosophy of life in hundreds of articles and letters, he never tried to build it into a system. Nevertheless, the truth is that more than fifty years after his death, his deepest concerns have become the concerns of thinking men and institutions working for a peaceful and humane world.

NOTES AND REFERENCES

1. Lerone Bennet Jr., *What Manner of Man* (Chicago, 1964), p. 72.

TWENTY NINE

Towards Understanding Gandhi

'I am not built for academic writings', Gandhi wrote, 'action is my domain.' He was constantly trying to understand the world around him, but he was not content with interpreting it: he wanted to transform it. His 'mission' was to 'convert every Indian whether he is a Hindu, Muslim or any other, even Englishman, and finally the world to non-violence for regulating mutual relations'. His ideas grew out of his experience; they were, as he was wont to say, experiments with truth; theory was usually the handmaiden of practice. When he spoke or wrote, he did not make a conscious effort to be consistent with what he had said earlier. Indeed, one can discern the evolution of some of his ideas: he was, as he loved to put it, growing from 'truth to truth'. The vast corpus of Gandhian thought, recording as it does the day-to-day and indeed hour-to-hour response of the Mahatma to men and events over half a century, lacks the architectural symmetry of the philosophic edifices built in the privacy of the study by Marx, Weber, and Freud.

That Gandhi's ideas did not fit into neat categories was not the only barrier between him and his contemporaries. To the British, indeed to most Europeans, he remained an enigma till the end. Not only were they unable to appreciate the cultural context of his ideas, he touched them on a tender spot: their racial prejudice and the vested interests of the Empire. A few exceptional individuals, such as Romain Rolland, Albert Einstein, and C.F. Andrews, expressed their admiration of Gandhi but the common image of the Mahatma in Europe and America oscillated between that of a whimsical saint and a wily politician. Stanley Jones has recorded how in the 1930s, Gandhi was 'a semi-joke with the people of the West'. An English Quaker, John S. Hoyland, noted in 1931 that satyagraha was 'looked upon in the West ... as ridiculous and undignified. Working class audiences when told about it characterized it as "grown-up sulks". More educated audiences regard it with cold disfavour. It is too exotic, too unconventional, in a word, too Christian for us.'

It was not only the British who were baffled by the Mahatma's ideas. J.B. Kripalani recalls that when Gandhi returned from South Africa in 1915 he struck him 'rather as an eccentric specimen of an England-returned-educated Indian'. Of the Indian leaders of the time, none was closer to Gandhi than Gokhale, but even he laughed at many of the opinions expressed in *Hind Swaraj* and told Gandhi, 'After you have stayed in India your views will correct themselves.'

Edwin Montagu, the Secretary of State for India, who visited India in 1917, described Gandhi as a 'pure visionary'. The verdict would have been endorsed by most Indian leaders of the day. Gandhi's criticisms of industrialism and Western civilization grated on their ears. His outlook on life, shaped by his own unique personality and experience in the crucible of the South African struggle, was at variance with that of India's English-educated class, which since the days of Raja Rammohun Roy, had sought to remake itself in the Western image. That Western education was the open sesame to the path of 'modernization', that India must tread and, however slowly, achieve English constitutional evolution; that India's economic salvation lay in industrialization on the European model were all self-evident propositions to the educated élite.

If the government had not banned *Hind Swaraj* in 1910, it is likely that it would have been ignored or laughed out of court in India. It was not only Gandhi's religious idiom that jarred on the educated élite; his views on education, machinery, and a village-based civilization seemed to them strange and outlandish. His strictures on parliamentary democracy could not but appear as perverse to those whose El Dorado was Westminster. Scepticism about Gandhi's philosophy of life continued long after he became a dominant figure in Indian politics. In 1921 Rabindranath Tagore deplored the 'Chinese Wall' being built by the non-cooperation movement between India and the West, and termed it 'spiritual suicide'. Soon afterwards, a former Congress president, C. Sankaran Nair, published a book with the startling title, *Gandhi and Anarchy*. Gandhi was thus accused of undermining the foundations of society not only by British officials but by his own countrymen. Some of his closest colleagues in the Indian National Congress, even as they followed his lead in politics, felt that he was harking back to a pre-industrial and pre-modern society. In his autobiography (1936) Jawaharlal Nehru voiced some of these doubts, and quoted Verrier Elwin's description of Gandhi as 'a medieval Catholic saint'. 'We cannot stop the river of change', Nehru wrote, 'or cut ourselves adrift from it, and psychologically, we who have eaten the apple of Eden cannot forget the taste and go back to primitiveness.' Throughout the 1930s, Gandhi was the chosen target of Indian radicals. Members of the Congress Socialist Party and the Communist Party of India talked of the inevitability of class war, and questioned the efficacy of non-violence in solving India's social and political problems. They denounced Gandhi as the evangelist of a reactionary philosophy. Among his sharpest critics were M.N. Roy and Jayaprakash Narayan.

II

Perhaps one of the principal barriers between Gandhi and his critics was his religious idiom. 'The fullest life', he wrote, 'is impossible without an immovable belief in a Living Law in obedience to which the whole universe moves.' Again, 'We are all tarred with the same brush and are the children of the same Creator and as such divine powers within us are infinite.' Self-realization was, he affirmed, his goal and indeed the ultimate goal of all human endeavour. He perceived an indissoluble unity between the cosmos, man, and society. These ideas were, of course, intrinsic to ancient Indian thought and made sense to the common people, but they smacked of obscurantism to the Western-educated élite.

Gandhi invoked traditional concepts, but he imparted to them a new social content. The very word 'religion' received a refreshing definition from him; it was 'not the Hindu religion ... but the religion which transcends Hinduism, which changes one's very nature, which binds one indissolubly to the truth within and which ever purifies'. True spirituality, he averred, was not merely speculation on the Absolute, however profound or philosophical; nor was it a quest for personal salvation. He loved to sing: 'He alone is a true devotee of God who understands the pains and sufferings of others.' 'The divinity of man', he affirmed, 'manifests itself according to the extent he realizes his humanity, i.e., his oneness with his fellow-men.' Gandhi's religion sometimes looks indistinguishable from humanism. He gave a creative reinterpretation to several age-old Hindu concepts. As for maya, the world being an illusion, he argued that 'we cannot dismiss the suffering of our fellow creatures and therefore provide a moral alibi for ourselves'. Dharma was the performance of duty not only by the citizen, but by the ruler as well. Fasting had long been part of a spiritual regimen; Gandhi made it a part of the armoury of satyagraha. An ashram was considered a refuge from the hurly-burly of life for one's personal *sadhana* (spiritual discipline); Gandhi used his ashrams to train social and political workers.

He did not make a frontal attack on the caste system, but he did more to undermine it than anyone else. He rejected stratification of society based on birth and denounced untouchability. The caste system was no more than an occupational division, a sort of guild system, in which no particular caste could claim to be superior to another. The Mahatma's views on caste became progressively more radical; the climax was reached when he insisted that for a marriage to be celebrated in his ashram, one of the partners had to be an 'untouchable'.

Most of Gandhi's Indian critics did not understand the idiom that Gandhi used, and so could not see how radically he had modified it. Curiously, it was, and is, perfectly possible to be a brilliant product of the universities of Allahabad, Calcutta, Bombay, or, for that matter, Oxford or Cambridge, without a nodding acquaintance with India's cultural heritage. Our brilliant men may quote from Aldous Huxley, Karl Marx, Bertrand Russell and Jean Paul Sartre, but may not have a nodding acquaintance with the Upanishads, the Ramayana or the Mahabharata; so when Gandhi talked of 'Ram Rajya' metaphorically, he was taken literally, as if he wanted to resurrect the ancient Indian polity of thousands of years ago.

It must, however, be acknowledged that the difficulty was more fundamental than that of semantics. Gandhi's chief mission in life, as he saw it, was to work out non-violent techniques which could be applied to social and political problems. It was because he was the author, and practically the sole practitioner, of satyagraha that he came to occupy his central position in Indian politics. Most of his colleagues in the Congress organization accepted non-violence as a political tactic in the struggle against the British Raj, but did not subscribe to it as a way of life. When Gandhi filled the pages of *Young India* and *Harijan* with homilies on non-violence, they were often dismissed either as bees in his bonnet or as doctrines too lofty for ordinary mortals. During the years immediately preceding the Second World War, when the Congress was in office in eight provinces, his opposition to the use of police to quell riots seemed odd to Congress ministers. Then, during the Second World War, when he talked of defending India non-violently against external aggression, the Congress Working Committee confessed that it did not share his unlimited faith in non-violence; it was willing enough to support the war against the Axis Powers, provided nationalist India was conceded real power to do it. Gandhi wrote extensively and discursively, on the duties of citizens and the state, but he did not draw up a blueprint of the political structure of independent India. However, in 1946 when S.N. Aggarwal published *A Gandhian Constitution for Free India*, Gandhi wrote in his foreword to the book that nothing in it jarred on him or seemed inconsistent with what he stood for. The fundamental assumption of Aggarwal's constitution was that the essence of non-violence was decentralization, and that the aim should be the development of self-sufficient, self-governing village communities. The primary political unit was to be the village panchayat elected by the adults of the village; the panchayat was to assess and collect revenue, supervise cooperative farming, irrigation, village industries and manage the schools and the police. Above the village panchayats was to come a hierarchy of indirectly elected panchayats, at the *taluka*, district, provincial and all India levels. This constitution, which considered political parties unnecessary also assumed what Gandhi had often said: 'The State that governs best, governs least.' A country which adopted such a constitution was likely to remain primarily a rural society with its base in agriculture and with minimal industrialization.

These ideas do not seem to have made much of an impression on the framers of the Indian constitution. The Experts Committee formed by the Congress Working Committee in July 1946 recommended a federal and parliamentary form of government. A number of the committees of the Constituent Assembly deliberated on various aspects of the Constitution, but do not seem to have given much thought to the Gandhian approach. The Drafting Committee, which was in session for four months from October 1947 to February 1948, drew upon the American and British constitutions, and the Government of India Act of 1935, but did not even mention the word 'panchayat'. Not until November 1948, and almost as a second thought, was a clause added on 'panchayats'; it became Article 40 of the Constitution.

The question may be asked why the framers of our Constitution took so little note of the ideas of one whom they honoured as the father of the Indian nation. The truth is that the politically conscious class in India had always admired the British parliamentary system: Dadabhai Naoroji, Pherozeshah Mehta, B.G. Tilak, G.K. Gokhale, Lajpat Rai, Motilal Nehru, C.R. Das are some of the distinguished names that come to mind. There was scarcely a prominent Indian leader who had not at heart cherished the Westminster model. The Commonwealth of India Bill, drafted at the initiative of Mrs Annie Besant, the Nehru Report prepared under the direction of the Indian National Congress, and the Sapru Committee Report produced by a group of Liberal leaders took the parliamentary system of government for granted. To most Indian politicians, whether of the Right or the Left, the Gandhian model seemed neither practical politics nor practical economics. This was the more so in 1947, when the edifice of Indian society and state had been severely shaken by communal turmoil and the secession of the Pakistan provinces.

To Nehru, Patel, and other Congress leaders, the critical question in 1947–9 was how to repair the damage inflicted by Partition, and how to hold the country together in a dangerous world. They did not think Gandhi's village-based economy could generate enough resources to end poverty, and make up the backlog of lost centuries. They felt that a strong central government and a highly industrialized economy were essential to safeguard national independence and to rid the country of poverty and backwardness. They knew that Western political and economic models were not perfect, but they hoped to improve upon them. Bureaucratization was an admitted evil, but would not the substitution of a brown for a white bureaucracy be a redeeming feature? Again, might it not be possible to mitigate or even to eliminate the evils of industrialization through socialist planning?

III

After his death, Gandhi seemed to have had a somewhat better prospect of being understood when some of the barriers to understanding that existed during his lifetime disappeared. After the liquidation of colonialism, the life and thought of its principal antagonist could be seen in the West without imperialist blinkers. Besides, some of the complacency and even arrogance that unlimited vistas of progress inspired in the developed countries earlier during this century have begun to wear off. It is becoming increasingly clear that while science and technology have provided mankind tremendous service they are likely before long (to use the words of André Malraux) to present their bill, and the bill is going to be heavy. The looming threats of nuclear proliferation and ecological devastation have had a chastening effect. Grave social stresses, the by-products of a runaway technology and unbridled economic growth, have cast a shadow on the long-term viability, and even wisdom of the Western economic model. In several Third World countries, even when vast scientific, industrial, and financial infrastructures have been built up and GDPs significantly increased, the great majority of the population has not been lifted out of the mire of poverty, and still remains on the periphery of the processes of economic development.

Gandhi's views on industrialization came in for much criticism in his own time. He avowed opposition not to machinery as such, but to the 'craze for machinery'; but such qualifications do not alter the basic fact of his scepticism about the industrial civilization as it has evolved in Europe and America over the past two hundred years. Gandhi insisted that as the supreme consideration was man, 'the machine must not make atrophied the limbs of man ... The mad rush for wealth must cease and the labourer must be assured not only of a living wage, but a daily task that is not a mere drudgery.' When he referred to the possibilities of machinery 'mastering' or 'enslaving' man, Gandhi seemed to his contemporaries guilty of indulging in hyperboles. However, we now know how real the dangers of runaway technology are. In his *Technological Society,* Jacques Ellul launched a powerful onslaught on the domination of man by 'technique'. This onslaught was carried further by Herbert Marcuse in his *One Dimensional Man*, and by Jurgen Habermas in his *Towards A Rational Society*, who have shown how 'technique' instead of being the slave has become the master of man. Because of the search for the most efficient way of optimizing some abstract utility or goal of the organization, there is an increasing reliance on 'systems' and hierarchical bodies with their prescribed routines and features. The management of the industrial society thus becomes a 'system' that leaves little scope for choice and judgment of the individual, and often excludes judgements about values because these values cannot be verified by appeal to experimental data. It is this 'manipulation' of man in the industrialized society that alarms thinking men and women. As Ivan Illich points out in his *Tools for Conviviality*, the hypothesis of the makers of the industrial revolution was that machines can replace slaves, but 'the evidence shows that used for this purpose, machines enslave men'.

Gandhi had the prescience to see that in the relationship between man and machine, man was likely to lose; that what he really needed was tools to work with, rather than tools to work for him. 'Pandit Nehru wants industrialization', Gandhi told an American businessman in 1940, 'because he thinks that if it is socialized, it would be free from the evils of capitalism. My own view is that the evils are inherent in industrialism, and no amount of socialization can eradicate them.' The tremendous growth of technology since Gandhi's time has revealed that large-scale industrialization has an inevitable concomitant: the alienation of man, which is not essentially related to the nature of the political system. A recent writer has indeed suggested that Karl Marx may have been aiming at the wrong target; at capitalism rather than large-scale organization of industry.

The intractability of the socio–economic problems in the developing countries, and the emergence of new tensions and dangers in the affluent

West are inducing a mood of introspection and sending thoughtful men back to Gandhi. This process of reappraisal was perhaps best epitomized in the case of Aldous Huxley. In *Jesting Pilate*, Huxley wrote that to 'one fresh from India and Indian spirituality' Ford seemed a greater man than the Buddha. At about the same time, in a letter to his brother, Julian Huxley, he ridiculed Gandhi as one 'who plays the ascetic with his loin cloth'. *In Do What You Will* (1936) he criticized Gandhi's advocacy of a rural economy based on handicrafts and argued that it would amount to a 'massacre', as the rising population could be fed and clothed only by large-scale industrialization.

Ten years later, the wheel had come full circle. In *Science, Liberty and Peace* (1945) Huxley argued that the record of Gandhi's achievements was not irrelevant to the historical and psychological situation of the industrial West, and predicted that 'in the years ahead, it seems possible that Satyagraha may take root in the West'. He echoed Gandhian doubts on industrialism, which made life fundamentally unliveable for all and suggested that scientists should work on small-scale machinery, cooperatives, and natural sources of energy like the sun and wind. In one of his novels Huxley spoke through one of the characters: 'We killed him because he tried to bring us back to the concrete and cosmic facts of real people and the inner light.' Then finally, in the 'Gandhi Memorial Peace Number' of *Visva-Bharati Quarterly*, October 1949 Huxley wrote: 'Gandhi's social and economic ideas are based upon a realistic appraisal of man's nature and the nature of his position in the universe. He knew, on the one hand, that the cumulative triumphs of advancing organization and progressive technology cannot alter the basic fact that man is an animal of no great size, and in most cases of very modest abilities. On the other hand, he knew that these physical and intellectual limitations are compatible with a practically infinite capacity for spiritual progress. For this amphibious being on the borderline between the animal and the spiritual, what sort of social, political, and economic arrangements are the most appropriate? To this question Gandhi gave simple and eminently sensible answers. Men, he said, should do their actual living and working in communities of a size commensurate with their bodily and moral stature; communities small enough to permit of genuine self-government and the assumption of personal responsibilities, federated into large units in such a way that the temptation to abuse great power should not arise. The larger a democracy grows, the less real becomes the rule of the people and the smaller is the say of individuals and localized groups in deciding their destinies.

Index

Petra Kelly on, 253;
and Abdul Ghaffar Khan, 107–23;
J.B. Kripalani on, 255;
and J.C. Kumarappa, 183–90;
Linlithgow on, 77;
and Jawaharlal Nehru, 171–91;
Jawaharlal Nehru on, 75, 170;
and non-violence, 247–53;
and partition of India, 147–60;
and Pyarelal, 202–5;
and racialism, 31–51;
and Rajchandra, 13;
and relevance of, 244–53, 259–61;
General Smuts on, 222;
and trade unions, 197–201;
and Vivekananda, 65–72;
Wavell on, 59, 77;
and the West, 222–5;
Willingdon on, 77
——, Maganlal, 173, 207
——, Manilal, 42
——, Manu, 211
Gandhi: Pan-Islamism, Imperialism and Nationalism in India (B.R. Nanda), 6, 27
Gandhi, Rajmohan, 60
——, Ramdas, 45
Gandhi, The Saint and Statesman, (Syed Hossain, 1937), 61
Gandhi-Smuts agreement, 1914, 34
Gandhi 125 Years, 10
Gandhiji's Mirror, 202
Gandhi's Truth (Erik H. Erikson), 200
Gardner, Howard, 224
George VI, King, 59, 142, 222
George, Lloyd, 90, 100–1, 182
Ghose, Aurobindo, 14, 53, 163
Ghosh, Rash Behari, 58
Glancy, Bertrand, 133
Godse, Nathuram, 51
Gokhale, Gopal Krishna, 5–6, 25, 45, 49, 60, 70, 75, 143, 163, 197, 217, 230, 233, 235–6, 258;

farewell address at Fergusson College by, 70
Good Boatman, The (Rajmohan Gandhi), 60
Gore, Charles, 232
Gram Udyog Patrika, 188
Green Peace Movement, 253
Gregg, Richard, 22
Gujarat Vidyapith, 185
Gunther, Frances, 250
——, John, 250

Haig, Harry, 80
Halifax, Lord, 182
Hamdard, 88
Haq, Mazharul, 27, 105
Hardinge, Lord, 34, 235, 238
Harijan, 138–9, 142, 150, 174, 188, 202, 220–1, 257
Harijan Sevak Sangh, 205
Harrison, Agatha, 182, 212, 241
Hasan, Mahmud-al, 89, 108
Havel, Vaclav, 252
Hibbert Journal, The, 37
Hijrat, 94, 99, 101
Hind Swaraj (1909), 35, 59–60, 143, 255
Hinduism, 13, 15–17, 19, 23–4, 35, 55–7, 65, 67, 69, 256
Hitler, Adolf, 189, 220
Hoare, Samuel, 132–3, 142, 182
Holmes, John Haynes, 223, 254
Hossain, Syed, 61
Hoyland, John S., 222
Hume, A.O., 238
Hunter Committee, 173, 238
Hussain, Zakir, 196
——, Fazl-i-, 113
Hutheesing, Raja, 129
Huttenback, Robert A., 38
Huxley, Aldous, 257, 261
——, Julian, 261

Illich, Ivan, 225